Yuan-li Wu

U.S. Policy and Strategic Interests in the Western Pacific

Crane, Russak & Company, Inc.
NEW YORK

University of Queensland Press
ST. LUCIA

U. S. Policy and Strategic Interests
in the Western Pacific

Published in the United States by

Crane, Russak & Company, Inc.
347 Madison Avenue
New York, New York 10017

Library Edition ISBN 0-8448-0622-6
Paperbound Edition ISBN 0-8448-0714-1
LC 74-33204

Published in Australia and New Zealand by

University of Queensland Press
St. Lucia, Queensland

Library Edition ISBN 0-7022-1030-7
Paperbound Edition ISBN 0-7022-1031-5

Copyright © 1975 Crane, Russak & Company, Inc.

No part of this publication may be reproduced,
stored in a retrieval system, or transmitted
in any form or by any means, electronic,
mechanical photocopying, recording,
or otherwise, without the prior
written permission of the publisher.

Printed in the United States of America

WITHDRAWN

U.S. Policy and Strategic Interests in the Western Pacific

To Suzanne
and her Generation

May they continue to enjoy
security and freedom *and*
take neither for granted

Contents

Preface xi

Introduction xiii

CHAPTER I
America's Search for a New and Stable Equilibrium 1

CHAPTER II
Why the Nixon Doctrine?
Some Parameters of U.S. Strategy and an American Perception 19

CHAPTER III
Negotiation with an Adversary 57

CHAPTER IV
Perception and Response I:
Toward Realignment in Northeast Asia? 89
Appendix: A Diagrammatic Presentation of Alignment Patterns 130

CHAPTER V
Perception and Response II:
From Indochina to the Indian Ocean 135

CHAPTER VI
The Soviet Union in Pacific-Asia 171
Appendix: Foreign Trade Statistics of Selected Countries
in Pacific-Asia and South Asia 184

CHAPTER VII
Conditions for Security in Pacific-Asia
and U.S. Strategic Interests 191

Index 207

Tables

TABLE II.1
Comparative Statistics of U.S. and Soviet Strategic Nuclear Weapons 22

TABLE II.2
Comparative Strength between NATO and the Warsaw Pact 30

TABLE II.3
Federal Budget Outlay by Functions 37

TABLE II.4
U.S. Defense Outlay 38

TABLE II.5
Defense Outlays at Constant 1964 Prices, 1953–74 39

TABLE V.1
Comparative Statistics of Economic Growth and Defense Expenditure in Southeast Asia and Australia-New Zealand 139

TABLE V.2
Comparative Military Strength of Selected Non-Communist Countries in Southeast Asia and Oceania 140

TABLE V.3
Number of Persons on Government of Vietnam Payroll 147

TABLE V.4
U.S. Military Transfers to Southeast Pacific-Asia (Excluding Indochina) 153

TABLE VI.1
Countries in Pacific-Asia Ranked in Terms of the Percent Shares of Eastern Europe (Including the Soviet Union) and the Soviet Union in Their Total Exports and Imports in 1970 181

Preface

This book has three purposes. It attempts to interpret United States foreign and defense policy in the Western Pacific during the first term and the first year and a half of Mr. Nixon's unfinished second term. It tries to point out how slippery the process of adjustment can be for the United States to move from its preeminent position of a superpower in a bipolar balance to that of a "balancing superpower" in a multipolar world. Not the least of the difficulties is the assumption of true multipolarity. Finally, the book points to an obvious yet frequently overlooked fact, namely, that the impression a nation's policy gives to other interested parties, including its own public, may be greatly at variance with the original intent of the makers of policy, and that this divergence could create serious problems of a dynamic nature. As the Ford Administration reexamines U.S. foreign and defense policy, it is hoped that the issues raised in this book will not be forgotten.

The original basis for this book was a work which I began three years ago under the title *Are We in Asia to Stay?* That book was never published, but was rewritten in the light of subsequent events and is now published in this form and under the new title *U.S. Policy and Strategic Interests in the Western Pacific.*

Thanks are due to a number of persons and institutions whose encouragement, support, and assistance have made the preparation of this study possible.

An invitation from the Institute for Sino-Soviet Studies of George Washington University and its former director, Professor Franz Michael, to present a series of seminars on the Western Pacific several years ago gave me the initial impetus and focus. Research support from the Earhart Foundation for a related study, the results of which have already appeared in a separate monograph, *Strategic Significance of Singapore: A Study in Balance of Power* (December, 1972), was most opportune. Many knowledgeable and thoughtful persons in a number of the countries I visited in the course of my research have generously shared their ideas with me. The Hoover Institution on War, Revolution and Peace of Stanford University has provided me with the benefit of its vast collection of contemporary material. To all of them I wish to register my warm appreciation.

Above all, however, I wish to thank those persons in and out of Washington who have devoted their lives to keeping this country safe and free and a few of whom I have learned to know. Their example has been a mainspring of my own education.

YUAN-LI WU

University of San Francisco

Introduction

In a study of the security aspects of current U.S. foreign policy, one of the first problems to be faced squarely is the time lag involved. First, important events are taking place constantly while information becomes available only some time later. Nor does all relevant information become available at one time. Second, there is another unavoidable time lag between the analyst's assessment and its appearance in print. Finally, the inevitable information lag applies to policy-makers themselves, given the varying degrees of efficiency of the intelligence and research capabilities available in different countries and their own efficiency in making use of what is available. Hence, a study on current policy must take into account this substantive aspect of the time lag and distinguish between reality and its perception by different parties.

In spite of the above warning, we cannot stop assessing current policy, because it is important that we continue. Policy-makers cannot refrain from making decisions for lack of final and complete information; to postpone decision-making is sometimes tantamount to decision-making by default. Policy-makers are required to take risks, and there always is the possibility that sometimes wrong decisions are made. Since it is necessary in a society where individuals try to shape their own destiny that government policies be carefully scrutinized, it is no less important that we assess government policy on the basis of incomplete information. For policy-makers, the penalty of failure as a result of mistaken policies or their poor implementation can be minimized if a mechanism of error-perception and correction is built into the system. For objective analysts of government policy, the risk of faulty analysis can be minimized if alternative interpretations are borne in mind and single events are examined from the point of view of trends and of larger categories of policy determinants.

The present study of U.S. foreign and defense policy focuses on the period between 1969 and the first part of 1974. Consequently, the information base is more comprehensive for the first term of the Nixon Administration than for the 1973-74 period. Additional information on relevant later developments will doubtless be forthcoming in the future. It is possible, however, to deal with such incomplete information concerning later developments as is now available from the point of view of the trends they appear to indicate. This approach would provide the reader with a framework within which some of the same events might be reassessed in the future when more information is at hand. By the same token, new developments or past events that are as yet unknown to us because of the information lag can be interpreted by the reader on his own.

As will be discussed in Chapter I, the main body of ideas that constitute what was generally known as the Nixon Doctrine took shape in 1969-71. Allowing for some overlap, implementation of these ideas, including, for instance, the disengagement of U.S. ground forces from Vietnam, the new China policy, the reduction of American military presence elsewhere in Asia, the realignment of the basing structure, etc., could not begin to take place at the earliest until the latter part of 1969 or 1970. Some aspects, such as Mr. Nixon's Peking and Moscow visits, could not be implemented until 1972; others, such as the negotiation with Thailand on the basing structure, could only be implemented in the light of developments after the completion of U.S. force withdrawals from Vietnam in March, 1973. Given this time sequence, foreign perception of U.S. policy must lag somewhat further behind. During 1971-73 there were changes in government structure in Korea, Thailand, and the Philippines, all being related in varying degrees to perceptions of events following U.S. policy shifts. There were new approaches to Peking by a number of countries in terms of trade, exchanges of athletic teams, etc. Above all, there were the "normalization" of relations between Japan and the People's Republic of China (PRC) in 1972, the intensification of U.S.S.R.-Japanese discussions on economic cooperation for the development of Siberian resources, concessions by Japan to both Peking and Moscow following the 1973-74 energy crisis, and the establishment of diplomatic relations between the PRC and Malaysia in mid-1974. These are merely a few examples of (1) responses on the part of countries in the Western Pacific to

U.S. policy changes based on their perceptions of earlier developments and their anticipations of what might follow, as well as (2) responses not directly related to developments in the area, such as the Arab oil embargo of late 1973. However, even responses to developments outside the region and initiatives taken by Asian countries are frequently strongly affected by their perception of U.S. policy. Because of the time lag involved, a number of events that occurred in 1972–73 constituted perhaps only a part of the "responsive" changes U.S. policy shifts have helped bring about. (Some have been directly unleashed by U.S. policy and the manner of its implementation.) For some time to come, more such "responsive" changes should be anticipated. Together with the initiatives other nations, notably the U.S.S.R., may take, they will alter the international environment and modify the validity of the basic assumptions of U.S. policy-making.

Let us categorize some of the relevant events in 1973–74 as an indication of the types of future events to watch for, as well as the questions they raise.

First, one of the hopes entertained in U.S. policy, especially in negotiating with adversaries, was that the Soviet Union could be persuaded to observe restraint in regard to the balance of strategic arms agreed to in SALT I in 1972. New developments in Soviet strategic arms made public in 1973–74, some of which are discussed in Chapter II, and Soviet attitude in SALT II negotiations have raised very serious questions about Soviet intentions. How far can one safely negotiate with the Soviet Union on the strategic balance? At what point should one conclude that an error in policy has been committed and that correction is necessary? How much U.S. nuclear capability would constitute "sufficiency?" How much would represent "essential equivalence" to Soviet capability?

Second, a basic assumption of the policy approach discussed in this study is that given "parity" in strategic arms, the Washington-Peking rapprochement can have a restraining effect on Soviet behavior in the non-nuclear arena. Public information on the exact behavior of the Soviet Union during the Arab-Israeli war of October, 1973, is far from complete. Even if Soviet policy was less extreme than it could have been, there is as yet no convincing evidence that the new global power balance U.S. policy hoped to construct had the desired effect in the Middle East. Will the Soviet Union continue to try to embroil the United States in this geographical region? To what extent will Peking be able to take advantage of the unresolved Arab-Israeli and inter-Arab issues and try to embroil both the Soviet Union and the United States?

Third, one major plank of U.S. policy in negotiating with Peking was the hope that the PRC would be internally sufficiently united and stable as to be able to act as a dependable balancing force against the Soviet Union. Internal developments in mainland China during 1973–74 indicated, on the contrary, that the power struggle involving segments of the military, the bureaucracy, and different party factions remained largely unresolved. The PRC did not show itself as a reliable balancing force in 1973-74. Furthermore, Peking could become a destabilizing force regionally. Its occupation of the Paracels in early 1974, its attempt at the UN to lead Third World nations at the 1974 session on raw materials and the Law of the Sea Conference, and its vigorous albeit, up-to-now, isolated efforts to damage the Taiwan economy—for example, its insistence that Japan sign the 1974 civil aviation agreement at the cost of allowing the severance of similar arrangements with Taiwan and its apparent effort to disrupt the fishing activities of Taiwan—are straws in the wind. Will there soon be additional tests of the terms of the Shanghai communiqué of 1972?

Fourth, another basic assumption of U. S. policy is that PRC-Soviet hostility will continue at a controlled level—sufficiently high to have a restraining effect on both, but not too high as to lead to war. This condition has held up to now. However, the continued instability of the PRC and the greater overall strength of the Soviet Union could well lead to a different situation during the balance of the 1970s. Soviet behavior after the completion of a second trans-Siberian railway in a few years could be quite different.

Fifth, a major premise of U.S. policy in the Western Pacific was the continuation of a close U.S.-Japan alliance. Events since 1971 have, on the contrary, demonstrated the progressive erosion of this relationship. Japan's foreign policy performance during and after the energy crisis of 1973-74 demonstrated rather plainly the country's serious economic vulnerability and its implied undependability. (This is not to say that Japan alone is at fault.) Furthermore, the hostile reception of Prime Minister Tanaka's visit in Southeast Asia in 1973 suggested that conflicts born of economic nationalism may lessen Japan's suitability to serve as a balancing force in Asia, as U.S. policy originally envisaged. What additional economic and other conflicts involving Japan, the United States, and other Asian countries does the future hold in store? The balance of payments burden on many countries, including both Japan and the United States, not to mention Western Europe, created by the price hike on Arab oil, is almost bound to lead to economic conflicts involving Japan and others, barring some effective international agreements. The only question is when, where, and in what form.

Sixth, another essential component of U.S. policy since 1969 has been the hope that countries in Asia other than Japan would be able to develop sufficient resilience and stability so that one or more new regional groupings would emerge to complement the lowered U.S. military presence and the emerging role of Japan. Up to 1973, in spite of changes in government in several countries and new approaches to Peking, no wholesale realignment had occurred. Innate caution and nationalism, plus the fact that U.S. force withdrawals from Vietnam were not completed until March, 1973, may have forestalled some of the responses to the new U.S. policy. Other potentially adverse responses, however, may have only been delayed. If U.S. withdrawals from Thailand are continued or accelerated, the trend toward realignment may also accelerate.

Finally, one outcome of the 1973 war in the Middle East is the reopening of the Suez Canal, which probably will become a reality during 1974-75. To what extent the Soviet Union will be able to exploit the greater mobility its expanding navy will acquire in order to exert political influence globally, now that its strategic arms already enjoy acknowledged parity, if not superiority, remains to be seen. In Asia, the Soviet Union will at least enjoy a greater range of options if it wishes to pursue its hitherto somewhat nebulous concept of collective security. Here too lies uncertainty ahead of us.

In listing the above categories of recent developments that have affected some of the basic assumptions of U.S. policy since 1969, we have pointed to the essentially dynamic nature of international stability. If anyone had expected in 1969-72 the creation of a new set of international conditions and power relationships so that U.S. interests can be safeguarded and international stability preserved without further effort—even major effort—on the part of the United States, he would, of course, be woefully disappointed. If, however, we understand from the very beginning that the new equilibrium we seek is not a predetermined static position and that maintenance of stability requires the undertaking of timely counteractions by the United States, then all those developments that tend to undermine the assumptions of successful U.S. policy outlined above will not necessarily be disastrous. A disastrous outcome could follow only if errors are not recognized, countermeasures are not taken in time, and options have been gratuitously discarded.

Two prime examples of U.S. efforts either to maintain or to restore equilibrium during 1973-74 were Secretary of Defense Schlesinger's proposal to give the United States greater capability to make nuclear responses on a limited scale and the stepped-up program of military assistance included in the proposed defense budget for Fiscal Year 1975. In his reply to an inquiry by Senator Kennedy, Secretary of State Kissinger noted on March 25, 1974,[1] that the ceiling of U.S. military assistance to South Vietnam requested for FY 1975 would be $1.6 billion and the new obligational authority would be $1.45 billion. These figures compare with a ceiling of $1.126 billion and new obligational authority of $907.5 million for FY 1974 for both South Vietnam and Laos. The proposed increase in military assistance to South Vietnam is only one example of the kind of offsetting measures indispensable to the success of U.S. policy. In assessing future developments and in reassessing events previously known but about which new information may become available, the reader should pay attention not only to successes and mistakes of past policy-making, concerning underlying assumptions and projections, but also to the readiness of corrective measures designed to safeguard stability. The latter are an integral part of policy-making in a dynamic world.

NOTE
1. *Congressional Record,* Senate, April 1, 1974, S4885. Congressional reaction to both the Schlesinger and the Kissinger proposals was discouraging as of early May, 1974.

U.S. Policy and Strategic Interests in the Western Pacific

Chapter I

America's Search for a New and Stable Equilibrium

SOME SIGNIFICANT CHANGES IN AMERICA'S INTERNATIONAL POSTURE IN PACIFIC-ASIA SINCE 1969

The "Nixon Doctrine," a shorthand expression introduced by President Nixon in 1969, has governed the U.S. approach to foreign and defense policy since that time. Barring any radical change, under the Ford Administration or later, it may well be regarded by future historians as an apt description of U.S. external policy of most of the 1970s. However, as a "doctrine," it does not lend itself to precise definition. For it describes a necessarily incomplete vision of objectives for the 1970s that include a reduced U.S. role in the world, in comparison with the pre-Vietnam War period, a role more in keeping with what many believe is required by the times and the temper of the American people. These objectives and the U.S. role are, however, not fully defined with respect to specific geographical areas or even issues. At its inception, the Nixon Doctrine pointed to a process of downward readjustment of the U.S. defense posture. This was a normal expectation, because the Vietnam War had made U.S. posture in 1969, at least in Pacific-Asia, considerably higher than the American public seemed willing to sustain. However, what would constitute an optimum readjustment in this continuing process could not be spelled out in 1969 because some of the criteria of optimization were still wanting. As long as the emotional entanglement of Vietnam continued, it was impossible to arrive at a consensus on long-term U.S. national interests. Without such a consensus it was not possible to say how far the United States should draw back from its pre-Vietnam posture, or how far it would have to do so simply for lack of domestic support.

There are Americans who, in 1969, were essentially satisfied with the preeminent position the United States had occupied in the world until then. They were, and continue to be, interested only in finding less costly and, therefore, more easily sustainable ways of maintaining this general position. This group obviously would like to minimize the downgrading of America's relative position in the world. At the other extreme, others are anxious to see the United States maintain only the minimum effort required for national security—without, however, a definition of the specific attributes of security. In effect, therefore, they assume that it would be possible to devote virtually all resources to domestic welfare without risking rude interference by less altruistic nations. (It is not clear, however, how many Americans in the second category would wish to reconsider their position should they become convinced that their happy assumption cannot be obtained.) The Nixon Doctrine, therefore, is a reflection of our time and is characterized by an amorphous state of mind. It is, however, a conscious search for a new and stable equilibrium. Above all, the Nixon Doctrine affirms America's need for such a new equilibrium in international relations.

As long as the policy adjustments of the United States and their interaction with the initiatives and adjustments of other nations are incomplete, the new hypothetical equilibrium can be perceived at best only in broad outline. By the same token, whether the new equilibrium, if it can be found, will be stable also remains to be seen. Theoretically, the process of adjustment can never come to a full stop, since dynamic equilibrium is not synonymous with the absence of change. One can speak of arriving at a new, stable equilibrium only in the sense of coming to an end of a series of large, discrete changes.

A crucial question is whether such a new and stable equilibrium can be established so that the U.S. national interest on a broadly defined basis can be safeguarded. This will be possible if we assume that the relative preeminence for the United States, in lieu of supremacy, will be acceptable to the American people and sustained by them once the full consequences of this new position are known. A corollary to this question is the magnitude of the risk involved in U.S. policy under the Nixon Doctrine and in view of the manner of its implementation. Have U.S. policy and its execution been best designed, and are they best designed, to arrive at such an equilibrium and to guarantee stability of the equilibrium? An even more fundamental question, of course, is whether the American public knows its own mind or what choices it has available now and is likely to have in the future.

TOWARD A NEW U.S. POSTURE IN PACIFIC-ASIA

A priori, the Nixon Doctrine is applicable to U.S. policy in all parts of the world. In practice, during Nixon's first term (1969–72), it was identified primarily with changes in U.S. policy and defense posture in Asia and the Western Pacific, or Pacific-Asia for short. After the U.S. disengagement from Vietnam in 1973, while adjustments in Asia continued, the Middle East and Europe became the locale of new large, discrete shifts.

A number of very significant international events involving the United States took place in Pacific-Asia during 1969–72, reflecting major shifts in U.S. foreign policy and defense arrangements. One of the most significant early developments was the agreement between the United States and Japan in November, 1969, to negotiate the reversion of Okinawa to Japanese administration by 1972. The detailed agreement was concluded during 1971 without serious opposition from the Congress. The final reversion on May 15, 1972, a date set by President Nixon and Japan's Prime Minister Sato at their San Clemente meeting in January, 1972, was carried out on schedule. The reversion of Okinawa, a bastion of U.S. strategic presence in the Western Pacific hitherto under direct American administration, did not mean the elimination of U.S. bases on the island. However, while a reduced number of very important bases remained, the reversion of administrative rights to Japan was more than symbolic; it was preceded by U.S. force reductions, as well as the consolidation and reduction of U.S. bases in Japan. From the end of 1970 to July, 1971, according to the February 25, 1971, Presidential Report to the Congress,[1] U.S. military personnel was expected to be reduced by 12,000 in Japan and 5,000 in Okinawa. The actual reduction in authorized strength in Japan during 1971, though smaller, came, nevertheless, to 6,000 men. In Japan proper, a notable reduction, again symbolic of the declining U.S. military presence, was the decision, announced in January, 1973,[2] to return to Japan the large U.S. Air Force base at Tachikawa in the crowded Kanto plain and the consolidation of U.S. air facilities at Yokota.

In Korea, where U.S. forces had remained under U.N. command ever since the Korean Armistice in 1953, a reduction of 20,000 men, or about one-third of the U.S. troop complement, was carried out in 1970 and 1971. This reduction was accompanied by a pullback of U.S. troops guarding a section of the front line facing the demilitarized zone, as well as the redeployment of some U.S. aircraft from Japan to Korea and an expansion of American military assistance for the modernization of the South Korean armed forces.

In Vietnam, the policy of Vietnamization, a program designed to turn over the war effort gradually to South Vietnam, especially on the ground, enabled the United States to reduce both the size of its forces and their direct involvement in combat. However, in the course of gradual withdrawals, U.S. forces actively participated during 1970 in an incursion into the Cambodian sanctuary of North Vietnam. Later, U.S. forces lent support to a similar operation in Laos in order to interdict North Vietnam's supply lines and sanctuaries for operation in the South. Toward the end of 1971, American air operations against North Vietnamese forces were stepped up while withdrawals continued on the ground. In the summer of 1972, in response to the open invasion of South Vietnam by the North, the U.S. Navy and Air Force undertook the mining of North Vietnamese harbors and waterways and stepped up bombing in the North in order to curtail war supplies for the invading forces.

In the course of these divergent activities, the authorized American troop strength in Vietnam was reduced from a high of 549,000 at the beginning of 1969 to 344,000 on January 1, 1971, 284,000 on May 1, 1971, 69,000 on May 1, 1972, and 49,000 on July 1, 1972.[3] Actual troop strength even went below the authorized level of 335,000 at the beginning of January, 1971.[4] At that time, American troops in Vietnam were expected to be down to 184,000 by the end of the year. In fact, the number had dropped to 139,000[5] before Mr. Nixon presented his third foreign policy report, published on February 9, 1972.[6]

The decline continued steadily after that until there were no more than 24,000 men[7] at the time of the Vietnam cease-fire (January, 1973) less than a year later, and only 8,000 men on March 7, 1973. During March, two months after Mr. Nixon's inauguration for a second term, the U.S. Command in Vietnam was finally closed down.

This accelerated U.S. force reduction in Vietnam was accompanied by slower reductions elsewhere. According to Mr. Nixon's report on February 25, 1971, 16,000 U.S. troops were to be withdrawn from Thailand—and 9,000 from the Philippines—by July, 1971. The authorized strength, as reported by the State Department, was reduced by 6,000 during 1971 in both cases.[8] After the end of U.S. withdrawals from Vietnam, the U.S. air presence in Thailand was also reduced. A further reduction by a third, leaving 27,000 U.S. military in Thailand, was announced in March, 1974, a year after the full Vietnam withdrawal.[9]

On July 15, 1971, Nixon announced that he had accepted an invitation to visit Peking before May, 1972. Although this announcement had been heralded by a series of relaxations of U.S. travel and trade restrictions of long standing against Peking and by the resumption of ambassadorial talks between the two countries in Warsaw[10] in 1969, it took most of the world by surprise. Subsequently, it became known in Asia, especially Japan, as the first of the "Nixon shocks." Shortly after the President's July announcement, Secretary of State William P. Rogers officially expressed the readiness of the United States to vote for the admission of Peking's representative to the United Nations during the 1971 UN session while insisting on the continued and concurrent representation of the Republic of China (ROC) in the same body.[11] The United States also indicated that it would leave the question of Chinese representation on the Security Council up to the UN membership. On October 25, 1971, a U.S. resolution, designed to save a UN seat for the ROC and co-sponsored by Japan, Thailand, Australia, the Philippines, and others, that would make the expulsion of a member an "important question" requiring a two-thirds majority, was defeated in the General Assembly.[12] This setback was followed by the passage, on the same day, of an Albanian resolution to seat Peking and expel Taiwan. The Republic of China announced its withdrawal from the United Nations immediately before the Albanian resolution was voted. At the time of these UN maneuvers, Dr. Henry A. Kissinger, then President Nixon's Special Assistant for National Security Affairs, who had previously brought back Chou En-lai's invitation to the U.S. President, was visiting Peking for the second time, ostensibly to make arrangements for Mr. Nixon's Peking visit, scheduled for February, 1972. It would be difficult to find a more graphic illustration of America's new policies and attitudes than these seemingly contrary pursuits, as well as their timing.

This series of events culminated in Mr. Nixon's visit to Peking in February, 1972. In the Nixon-Chou En-lai Joint Communiqué issued at the end of their meetings, the United States declared (1) its intention ultimately to withdraw U.S. troops from Taiwan following the reduction of tension in the area, (2) its interest in the peaceful settlement of the Taiwan problem by the Chinese themselves, and (3) its essentially passive attitude toward the claim of both Chinas that Taiwan is a part of China.

Again, during the winter of 1971–72, the United States took a semi-neutral stance in the military confrontation between India and Pakistan over East Pakistan, although Pakistan was a U.S. ally in the Southeast Asia Treaty Organization while India was given substantial support by the Soviet Union. The United States chided India for being an aggressor and provided moral support and some arms shipments to Pakistan but could do little to stop the latter's ultimate defeat. Especially noteworthy was the dispatch during the short-lived conflict of a U.S. naval task force, headed by the aircraft carrier *Enterprise*, toward the Bay of Bengal, ostensibly for possible use in evacuating U.S. citizens from East Pakistan. However, the task force was recalled without coming close to South Asian shores while Soviet vessels maintained their presence in the Bay of Bengal.

In a larger context, the United States, in order to slow domestic inflation and ease its external monetary crisis, suspended the convertibility of the dollar into gold on August 15, 1971, froze both wages and prices, and imposed a ten percent temporary surcharge on all dutiable imports not already subject to quantitative restrictions. In Japan, this set of major economic measures was sometimes described as the second "Nixon shock." It led to the subsequent upward revaluation of many of the world's currencies, including the yen, and an eight percent devaluation of the dollar in terms of gold, which was passed by Congress in March, 1972.[13] A second devaluation of the dollar by another ten percent took place in February, 1973.

Lastly, and again in a larger context, the Nixon Administration began the 1969–72 period by negotiating with the Soviet Union on limiting strategic nuclear arms. Meeting alternately in Helsinki and Vienna, the delegations of the two countries engaged in a prolonged exploration of each other's intentions and capabilities. After the announcement of his planned visit to Peking, Mr. Nixon disclosed on October 12, 1971[14] that he would visit Moscow in May, 1972. Subsequent speculations that some initial limited agreement with the Soviet Union on strategic arms might be reached by that date were confirmed by the announcement at the Moscow meeting of a treaty limiting ABM deployment by both countries to 200 missile launchers each, together with a five-year executive agreement on offensive missiles.[15] In essence, the latter agreement put a ceiling on both land-based and seaborne ICBMs at the levels of their current deployment *and* construction but allowing both quality improvement and some limited substitution of seaborne for land-based missiles. Because of its larger ongoing construction programs and its already greater number of land-based missiles, the Soviet Union could, within the terms of the agreement as understood by the United States, possess a greater number of both land-based and seaborne missiles at the end of the stipulated five years. On the other hand, because of (1) the larger number of U.S. warheads, as distinct from that of missile launchers, (2) exclusion of long-range, nuclear-capable bombers of which the United States possessed a larger number, and (3) quality differences, this first agreement still left the United States in a superior position in certain areas of nuclear armament *as of 1972*. There were, in effect, combinations of superiority and equality on both sides. In political terms, however, there was an apparent public acknowledgment by the United States of virtual parity with the Soviet Union. Any claim to undisputed superiority in all essential aspects of strategic arms could no longer be made by the United States. Furthermore, as a result of progress made by the Soviet Union after the 1972 agreement in developing multiple, independently targetable warheads (MIRV) or "re-entry vehicles," reusable silos for land-based ICBMs, probably mobile land-based missiles, and long-range submarines and seaborne missiles, the U.S. position continued to worsen relatively in 1973–74.

THE NIXON DOCTRINE IN ITS INCEPTION

The cynic could argue that most of the actions taken by the Nixon Administration, some of which we have just enumerated, were pragmatic measures dictated by pressures of public opinion and budgetary exigencies. However, a policy born of necessity is not necessarily the worse for it. While some details show signs of temporizing—in particular, the timing of certain official announcements may have been partially governed by considerations of their public impact—one should not overlook the significance of the emergence out of these actions and pronouncements of a consistent new approach to foreign policy and defense problems.

On the other hand, the body of ideas underlying the basic approach of the Nixon Administration was not outlined in a crystallized and comprehensive form from the very beginning. At the outset, even the descriptive terminology varied. The first public enunciation was made by President Nixon at Guam—which gave rise to the expression, the "Guam Doctrine." Additional ideas were developed and explained later in various addresses and pronouncements by the President and some of his principal Cabinet members.

The first major attempt at a comprehensive discussion of the "Guam" or "Nixon" Doctrine was President Nixon's first (1970) report on U.S. foreign policy.[16] The U.S. force reductions in Asia noted earlier, in particular Vietnamization, and the initial moves in a shift in America's China policy were heralded in this report. Modifications of the Nixon Doctrine based on developments during 1970, were emphasized in the President's 1971 and 1972 foreign policy reports. The 1971 report, in particular, added new nuances, while the 1972 report provided considerable clarification, especially if it is read with the actual developments of 1971 in mind. It is important that America's foreign and defense policy changes in Nixon's first term (1969–72) be interpreted in the light of these official statements and the evolving ideas, perhaps even some afterthoughts, embodied in them.

The new approach to foreign and defense policy expressed in the 1970 foreign policy report consists of the following elements:

First, in keeping with its new policy, the United States looks to its allies to assume a greater share of the burden of, and responsibility for, their common defense.

Second, this desired shift in the relative shares of burden and responsibility is envisaged as a shift within a partnership. In the Asian and Pacific context, the United States regards Japan as its principal partner.

Third, one important substitute for the reduced American military presence will be provided by the regional cooperative efforts of independent nations. In Pacific-Asia, SEATO, ANZUS, and the five-power defense arrangements of Australia, New Zealand, the United Kingdom, Malaysia, and Singapore are already in existence. Other regional groupings, including those created for non-defense purposes, could conceivably also contribute to the promotion of international security.

Fourth, in revamping the American role in international security, the Nixon Doctrine stresses that the United States will remain involved in Asia, albeit in a role yet to be fully redefined.

Fifth, under the basic principle of continued involvement, the United States will honor its existing commitments. However, the 1970 report stressed that national interests, which are the basis of commitments, may change under changing conditions; therefore, some present U.S. commitments may have to be modified.

Sixth, the new approach will attempt to safeguard the interests of small nations. Terms of settlement will not be dictated by a few superpowers.

Seventh, the defense role of the United States under the principle of continued involvement is outlined in the following terms:[17]

(a) We shall provide a shield if a nuclear power threatens the freedom of a nation allied with us, or of a nation whose survival we consider vital to our security and the security of the region as a whole.

(b) In cases involving other types of aggression, we shall furnish military and economic assistance when requested and as appropriate. But we shall look to the nation directly threatened to assume the primary responsibility of providing the manpower for its defense.[18]

Eighth, the United States will seek to use the total "common resources" of the United States and its allies more effectively. This objective and approach are already implied in Point Seven.

Ninth, the Nixon Doctrine envisages negotiations with adversaries. These negotiations, however, will not be based on illusions on our part of the goodwill of the adversaries or of the prospects for sudden about-face shifts in their policies. On the contrary, negotiations will be conducted while adequate strength and mutual consultation are maintained by the United States and its allies.

Tenth, under the Nixon Doctrine, concrete solutions will be found for each problem on the basis of specific considerations of the case. The choice of solutions will be flexible; no uniform rule is prescribed for all cases.[19] This point is stressed, especially with reference to Asia.

Finally, the net objective is a defense posture and foreign policy which will be sustainable over a long period of time, based presumably on a national consensus yet to be developed.

In short, Mr. Nixon's first foreign policy report proposes that the United States should reduce its role in safeguarding international security, reexamine its existing commitments, and remain flexible in the choice of methods to honor its existing commitments and fulfill its responsibilities. The same statement of policy also asks that America's allies assume a greater share of the defense burden while they build up their defense capability with American assistance. At the same time, the total defense effort required will be reduced through negotiation with adversaries. The 1970 report, however, has little to say about how existing commitments are to be reduced or how selection of individual commitments for readjustment is to be made. It assumes that U.S. assistance to allies will be forthcoming and that allies that can will be willing, or can be readily persuaded, to shoulder a larger share of the defense burden as members of a partnership with the United States. It assumes further that allied confidence in American intentions and capability to fulfill its commitments or to play its self-assigned role will be unaffected by U.S. flexibility in dealing with specific situations, the avowed U.S. intention to make adjustments in its commitments, and U.S. negotiations with adversaries. The implicit assumption, though never articulated by official spokesmen, seems to be that the disadvantages to America's adversaries as a result of their uncertainty about U.S. policy will more than outweigh the advantages they may enjoy as a result of the uncertainty experienced by America's allies or by the American people themselves. Why these assumptions could be safely made or what would be done if they turned out to be mistaken was not made clear.

FURTHER EVOLUTION OF THE NIXON DOCTRINE DURING 1970

The 1971 Presidential report on foreign policy, whose authors had the benefit of the experience of the preceding year, repeats most of the ideas already expressed a year earlier. However, certain points were expanded and others reemphasized.

First, the 1971 report reiterates America's intention to remain involved in Asia but in a redefined role. Given a state of mutual deterrence in terms of strategic nuclear weapons, the importance of conventional forces seems to have gained greater recognition than before. Since U.S. forces have been reduced primarily in Asia, the following passage in the 1971 report deserves special attention:

> Our general purpose forces are more and more keyed to our partners' capabilities, to provide truly *flexible response* when our commitments are

involved. And our *security assistance* program will provide indispensable support to our friends, *especially where there are reductions in U.S. manpower.*[20] (Italics added.)

Even more explicitly, while speaking of the guidelines for general purpose forces during 1971, the President pointed out in the 1971 report:

> Our capabilities thus must rest on *our allies' strength, strong U.S. overseas forces and the availability of credible reinforcements.* We could not hide deficiencies from a potential enemy; weakness in conventional forces invites conventional attack.... We must not be in a position of being able to employ only strategic weapons to meet challenges to our interests. On the other hand, *having a full range of options does not mean that we will necessarily limit our response to the level or intensity chosen by our enemy....*[21]

It would seem that this elaboration revolves around a capability for flexible response and should provide concrete guidance in both foreign policy and defense planning. It should be mentioned further that the preceding statement is made with reference to both the U.S.S.R. and the Chinese Communists in Asia; these two countries are credited with "substantial forces that can be rapidly reinforced."[22]

Second, in reemphasizing U.S. intention to fulfill its commitments, the 1971 report again calls for a shift of the relative burden of international security borne by the United States and its allies. It now speaks of the "liquidation" of some of the relationships and practices that are vestiges of the past.[23] However, the report takes pains to stress the need for orderly transition and the paramount importance of not undermining U.S. credibility. Past commitments are to be fulfilled "both because of their intrinsic merit, and because of the impact of sudden shifts on regional or world stability."[24] "The Nixon Doctrine recognizes that we cannot abandon friends, and must not transfer burdens too swiftly. We must strike a balance between doing too much and thus preventing self-reliance, and doing too little and thus undermining self-confidence."[25]

Third, the 1971 report emphasizes time and again that "partnership involves close consultations with our allies both to protect their interests and solicit their views."[26] While this comment on the negotiating posture is made in connection with bilateral negotiations with the U.S.S.R., it is presumably intended to be no less applicable to the Pacific Basin.

Fourth, in redefining America's role in the maintenance of international security, the 1971 report stresses the polycentrism of Communist nations as one of the major factors in the world's changing scene.

Finally, in an uncharacteristically negative tone, the report speaks of

America's weariness in playing a dominant and lonely role in maintaining the free world's security. "To continue our predominant contribution might not have been beyond our physical resources ... but it certainly would have exceeded our psychological resources."[27]

In summary, the 1971 report offers little that is really new. It is, however, more directly stated and has brought out additional implications. It would liquidate some old commitments, although it stresses consultation with allies and warns against sudden shifts that may undermine the self-confidence of America's friends, as well as U.S. credibility. These points of emphasis are particularly interesting. Their appearance in the February, 1971, statement anticipated events that took place later in the year—notably the shift in United States policy on Chinese representation in the United Nations. On another level, the emphasis on consultation with allies stood in sharp contrast to the absence of prior consultation with Japan before the announcement, on July 15, 1971, of Mr. Nixon's planned visit to Peking the following year.

NEGOTIATIONS WITH PEKING AND MOSCOW UNDER THE NIXON DOCTRINE

True to its title, "The Emerging Structure of Peace," Mr. Nixon's 1972 Report on *U.S. Foreign Policy for the 1970's* offers a far greater degree of clarification than the two previous reports. Developments during 1970–71 helped in making the clarification possible, not only for those who seek understanding of U.S. policy but possibly also for the policy-makers themselves, who could now begin to see where events were taking them. In addition to some restatement of the same general philosophy developed since 1969, the 1972 report presents the following salient points, which may be interpreted as the underpinnings of U.S. policy as we approach the mid-1970s:

First, the bipolar world that emerged after World War II is now history, but this development is not necessarily to be deplored. "The end of the bipolar postwar world," writes President Nixon, "opens to this generation a unique opportunity to create a new and lasting structure of peace."[28]

Second, the disappearance of bipolarism has specific implications for both the Communist countries and for the West. According to the report, "The breakup of a single Communist entity ... relaxed some of the ideological inhibitions against dealing with the U.S. and forced the Soviet Union to reevaluate its security concerns."[29] The same development, as we shall see in Chapter III, contributed to Communist China's readiness to negotiate with the United States.

As for the West, multilateral cooperation in defense, with shared risks and responsibilities, must nevertheless continue in order to maintain stability. "Our alliances are no longer addressed *primarily* to the containment of the

Soviet Union and China behind an American shield. They are, instead, addressed to the creation with those powers of a stable world peace. *That task absolutely requires the maintenance of the allied strength of the non-Communist world.*"[30] (Italics added.)

Third, realignments will be expected and are perhaps inevitable. Erstwhile enemies hopefully will no longer be enemies, for "Our enmities are not immutable."[31] Conversely, the form of U.S. alliances may also be modified. In the words of the report, "Our friendships are constant, but the means by which they are mutually expressed must be adjusted as world conditions change."[32] What these words may mean in practice was illustrated by the phased modification of America's China policy during 1969–72. Events in 1971, some already described, also provided examples of the style of implementation of the Nixon Doctrine.

Lastly, negotiations with adversaries and further readjustments of international arrangements will continue. President Nixon's visit to Peking is described by the report as "the launching of a new process."[33] Discussions with Moscow are necessarily a continuing dynamic process as well. In pursuing its part of this process, Moscow is urged "to exercise restraint and to recognize and accept the legitimate interests [of other nations.]"[34] As one of the tasks requiring examination at the May, 1972, visit of Nixon to Moscow, the report includes "an exploration of our policies in other areas of the world and the extent to which we share an interest in stability."[35] Asia and China loom large among these "other areas."

By the end of 1972 *the Nixon Doctrine had emerged as a full-fledged attempt to seek world stability and equilibrium through the establishment of a new balance of power in which the participants would understand and accept the rules.* The rules are to be based on enlightened nationalism, motivated by self-interest but tempered with restraint, mainly because unrestrained action will meet resistance and frustration.

SOME DEVELOPING CRITERIA IN U.S. DEFENSE PLANNING

Some principles of defense planning were developed *pari passu* with the general ideas on foreign policy. The Nixon Doctrine's emphasis on partnership and burden sharing with allies gave rise to the concept of "total force" in defense planning during the tenure of Melvin R. Laird in the Pentagon. The free world's security needs should be met through the optimum use of all military and related resources available, which, in Laird's words, constitute the *"total force"* and should *"include both active and reserve components of the United States, those of its allies, and the additional military capabilities of our allies and friends that will be made available through local efforts, or through provision of appropriate security assistance programs."*[36] (Italics added.) This emphasis on expanded allied capability caused greater importance to be given to military assistance and resulted in the creation within the U.S. Defense Department of a Defense Security Assistance Agency[37] to oversee the coordination of defense planning with allies. This approach was applied to Vietnamization, to Laos and Cambodia, to Thailand, and to Japan and Korea.[38]

The movement toward a lowered U.S. defense posture, first symbolized in the early abandonment of the erstwhile planning objective that the United States should be prepared for "2-1/2 wars" in peacetime, was translated into a concept of "realistic" and "credible deterrence." Being "realistic" in this context has two meanings. First, one should aim at a defense effort that is sustainable in spite of anticipated budgetary, balance of payments, and manpower constraints. Planned levels must obviously correspond to the burden the U.S. Congress and public are willing to bear. Second, a realistic deterrent must work; it must have the intended effect on the potential adversaries and in maintaining cohesion of alliance. Consequently, it must be credible to adversaries and allies alike.

In regard to America's deterrence posture, the guideline for defense planning was contained in the following statement by Mr. Laird: "Our goal is to prevent wars, to maintain a realistic and *ready* military force aimed at deterring aggression—adequate to handle aggression should deterrence fail." [39] (Italics added.) The emphasis on a force-in-being which can deter aggression and is capable of fighting a war if it occurs should be especially noted. In the case of general purpose forces, this approach led to a new emphasis on the National Guard and the Reserves and their modernization; at the same time, U.S. manpower reductions in an all-volunteer force were envisaged.

In the Asian context, as elsewhere, U.S. defense capability should be sufficient to deter (1) strategic nuclear war, (2) theater nuclear war, (3) theater conventional war, and (4) subtheater, theater or localized warfare. The United States, according to Laird's defense planning criteria, will be primarily responsible for preventing the first two types of conflict; both U.S. and allied forces are to share deterrent responsibility for the third, and the country or area which is threatened is to bear the primary burden in the last case. Furthermore, in the case of subtheater or local warfare, the country or area in question should be primarily responsible for providing manpower, while the United States "must be prepared to provide help as appropriate through military and economic assistance" if the recipients in question are "willing to assume and share all responsibility for their own defense." This is a clear statement of U.S. willingness to provide assistance to those who will defend themselves. Lest the emphasis on the primary responsibility of the other countries to provide manpower be misconstrued, it was pointed out in Secretary Laird's 1971 statement that the participation of U.S. manpower was by no means ruled out; this statement has not been rescinded as of this writing. In his words, "When required and appropriate, this help would consist essentially of backup logistical support and sea and air combat support. In some special cases, it could include ground combat support as well."[40] Resumption of U.S. bombing of North Vietnam with B-52s immediately before the Vietnam cease-fire and air support to government forces in Cambodia and Laos in early 1973 as a countermeasure against Communist attacks, accompanied by North Vietnamese violations of the cease-fire agreement, provided a graphic illustration of U.S. emphasis on the air arm.

In deterring Soviet and Chinese adventures below the level of general nuclear war, the forces involved are required to possess "adequate warfighting capability, both in *limited nuclear and conventional options*."[41] (Italics added.) Inclusion of the Chinese in this reference underlines the desire to retain these options also in Asia. Defense Secretary Schlesinger's proposal in 1974 on "retargeting" for U.S. strategic weapons in order to deter possible Soviet use of nuclear weapons on selected military targets and to give the United States an extra option short of nuclear retaliation against enemy urban centers was a logical development of the same idea.[42]

The Nixon Doctrine's emphasis on cooperative efforts by others was translated into an exhortation to promote regional defense arrangements. The objective was and still is, apparently, to deter localized conflict short of a large-scale Soviet or Chinese attack.[43]

Finally, perhaps the most important of all these ideas is that U.S. defense will be based on maintaining technological *superiority*[44] and alertness through constant assessment of all advantages and disadvantages facing U.S. defense. Put in another way, a normally lower posture will be accompanied by an undiminished capability to respond in time to new threats.

SOME CRUCIAL QUESTIONS

A self-assessment of the outcome of U.S. policy under the Nixon Doctrine was made after the Vietnam cease-fire in January, 1973, in the President's 1973 foreign policy report which appeared in May of that year, two months after the completion of U.S. force withdrawals from Vietnam and the return of all American prisoners of war accounted for by the North Vietnamese. Speaking of the foreign policy record of his first term, Mr. Nixon wrote, "We have cleared away vestiges of the past. We have erased or moderated hostilities. And we are strengthening partnerships."[45] The first sentence clearly refers to the completion of the withdrawal of U.S. ground forces from Vietnam and the establishment of direct governmental, if not yet full diplomatic, relations with Communist China, now more than a little pointedly referred to as the People's Republic of China by the U.S. government. The second sentence reflects the results of American negotiations at Peking and Moscow. The third sentence points to a major portion of the problems of Mr. Nixon's second term and of the Ford Administration. The Japanese alliance and negotiations with Western Europe are viewed as two principal areas of serious concern in Mr. Nixon's report. In addition, in Mr. Nixon's judgment, "The process [of normalization of U.S.-PRC relations] is not inexorable...."[46] (Italics added.) In regard to the Kremlin, "areas of tension and potential conflict remain, and certain patterns of Soviet behavior continue to cause concern." Finally, peace in Indochina is still more than a little fragile.

So far, so good; but what will come next? Such was the situation in early 1973. The October, 1973, war in the Mideast, the Arab oil embargo, and the reactions of both Japan and individual countries in Western Europe were sufficient to justify the worst forebodings both about Soviet intentions and about the fragility of U.S.-allied partnerships. The PRC occupation of the Paracels in January, 1974, and internal rumblings in mainland China suggesting renewed ideological and political struggles raised serious questions about the future policies of Peking. By 1974, the first part of our statement—"so far, so good"—seemed somewhat less relevant than the question "what will come next?" Enough has been said and even more has happened to convince the world, including both enemies and friends of the United States, that America desires to reduce its military presence and its defense role in Asia. An unanswered question is how far this reduction of U.S. presence should and will go. It is plain that the United States would like to see its allies play a larger defense role. This is evident from U.S. force reductions alone. Some U.S. allies, such as Vietnam, have already begun to do so. It is not as clear whether all U.S. allies can and are willing to play larger roles or how large their respective roles should be. From an operational viewpoint, an obvious need will be an efficient dovetailing of the defense functions of the U.S. and its allies, a prerequisite of which is U.S. and allied agreement on this point. It is understood that the United States looks upon the process of policy adjustment it initiated as a dynamic movement involving partners. What is not as well understood is who, in the American view, will remain as "partners" or, from the point of view of other nations, who will remain willing partners, if the United States is to liquidate some of its outmoded relationships, and if other nations "must define the nature of their own security and determine the path of their own progress?" Can "partnership" remain unaffected both by the adjustment process and by the changing world conditions which made the adjustments necessary in the first place? It should not be inferred that these questions have been ignored in official statements on the Nixon Doctrine. The general problems are acknowledged by the Administration in Mr. Nixon's successive foreign policy reports. In particular, the 1971 report has addressed some uncertainties which emerged following the first report. The 1972 report covers much of the same ground, especially the assurance of prior consultation with allies, although, as already noted, 1971 had seen at least one notable lapse. The proof of a pudding is in the eating, and the success of the Nixon Doctrine will depend on its actual performance.

The Nixon Doctrine envisages a gradual adjustment of U.S. commitments and the respective roles of the United States and its allies. However, how gradual is "gradual"? Timing is one of several questions which may lead to differences of opinion between the United States and other countries—not necessarily allies alone. Since American policy cannot be implemented in a vacuum, the responses of other nations to U.S. policy must be taken into account. Will U.S. allies accept U.S. interpretations of its policy? Given their own perceptions of U.S. policy, will they act in a manner foreseen by the United States? Will their actions, together with the responses and initiatives of America's potential adversaries, result in a new and stable equilibrium? Official policy statements do not, nor can they be expected to, supply the answers.

Nevertheless, it is unfortunate that U.S. policy statements have not made clear at least one special point; namely, what are the long-term U.S. national interests in Asia? How do U.S. planners envisage the specific security arrangements and military and political alignments that can serve these interests best? If optimal arrangements for a given definition of U.S. national interests are not feasible, will we be forced to redefine our national interests simply because we believe that we cannot do better? Lastly, what are the parameters that define the feasible? Are they really inviolable and to be accepted as given, or can they too be changed? For instance, should the U.S. government take public opinion on America's proper role in Asia as given and mold policy accordingly? Is there a role for aggressive government leadership? How does one determine what Americans really want? What if there is a wide gap between what they really would want, given full knowledge of the relevant facts, and what they think they want, given the little they know, compounded by deliberate, as well as unintentional efforts that confuse them? Public opinion polls, at best, can only determine the latter, not the former.

NOTES

1. *U.S. Foreign Policy for the 1970's*, II: *Building for Peace*, A Report to the Congress by Richard Nixon, President of the United States, U.S. Government Printing Office, Washington, D.C., February 25, 1971, p. 18. See also *United States Foreign Policy, 1971, A Report of the Secretary of State*, Department of State Publication 8634, Washington, D.C., March 1972, p. 50.
2. Associated Press report, Tokyo, January 23, 1973.

3. *Ibid.*, p. 59, and *U.S. Foreign Policy for the 1970's*, III: *The Emerging Structure of Peace*, Washington, D.C., February 9, 1972, p. 11.
4. Statement by Secretary of Defense Melvin R. Laird at a Paris news conference, January 6, 1971.
5. President Nixon's question and answer session at the Convention of the American Society of Newspaper Editors, April 16, 1971.
6. *U.S. Foreign Policy for the 1970's*, III, February 1972, p. 11.
7. Associated Press, March 7, 1973.
8. *United States Foreign Policy, 1971*, March 1972, p. 50.
9. UPI report, Bangkok, March 29, 1974.
10. The Warsaw talks were again interrupted in 1970 at the time of the U.S. incursion into Cambodia. For a detailed description of the various steps signaling U.S. intention to Peking, see *U.S. Foreign Policy in the 1970's*, III, February 1972, pp. 29–33.
11. Secretary of State William P. Rogers stated on August 2, 1971,

    "Representation in an international organization need not prejudice the claim or views of either government (i.e., Peking and Taipei). Participation of both in the United Nations need not require that result. . . .

    "The United States accordingly will support action at the General Assembly this fall calling for seating the People's Republic of China. At the same time the United States will oppose any action to expel the Republic of China or otherwise deprive it of representation in the United Nations.

    "Our consultations, which began several months ago, have indicated that the question of China's seat in the Security Council is a matter which many nations will wish to address. In the final analysis, of course, under the Charter provisions, the Security Council will make this decision. We, for our part, are prepared to have this question resolved on the basis of a decision of members of the United Nations. . . ." *U.S. News and World Report*, August 16, 1971, p. 21.
12. The "important question" resolution was defeated by a narrow margin of 59 to 55 with 15 abstentions and two absences. A number of last-minute vote switchings apparently tipped the balance. The Albanian resolution was then passed by a majority of 76 to 35 with 17 abstentions and 3 absences. See the *New York Times*, October 27, 1971.
13. The official price of gold was raised from $35 to $38 an ounce in March, 1972.
14. *U.S. Foreign Policy for the 1970's*, III, February 1972, p. 24.
15. For the text of the Treaty to Limit ABMs and the Interim Agreement on Offensive Missiles, see the *New York Times*, May 27, 1972.
16. *U.S. Foreign Policy for the 1970's*, I, February 1970.
17. *U.S. Foreign Policy for the 1970's*, I, February 1970, pp. 55–56.
18. *Ibid.*, p. 56.
19. *Ibid.*, p. 60.
20. *U.S. Foreign Policy in the 1970's*, II, p. 19.

21. *Ibid.*, pp. 178–79.
22. *Ibid.*, p. 178.
23. *Ibid.*, p. 15.
24. *Ibid.*, pp. 12–13.
25. *Ibid.*, p. 16.
26. *Ibid.*, p. 20.
27. *Ibid.*, p. 11.
28. *U.S. Foreign Policy for the 1970's*, III, February 1972, p. 3.
29. *Ibid.*, p. 19.
30. *Ibid.*, p. 6.
31. *Ibid.*, p. 4.
32. *Ibid.*, p. 3.
33. *Ibid.*, p. 28.
34. *Ibid.*, p. 17.
35. *Ibid.*, p. 24.
36. Statement of Secretary of Defense Melvin R. Laird on the Fiscal Years 1972–76 Defense Program and the 1972 Defense Budget (Annual Defense Department Report for FY 1972) before the House Armed Services Committee, March 9, 1971, p. 21.
37. *National Security Strategy of Realistic Deterrence*, Secretary of Defense Melvin R. Laird's Annual Defense Department Report for FY 1973, February 1972.
38. *Ibid.*, pp. 124–25 and 139–40.
39. Annual Defense Department Report for FY 1972, p. 11.
40. *Ibid.*, p. 22.
41. *Ibid.*, p. 18.
42. *Report of the Secretary of Defense James R. Schlesinger to the Congress on the FY 1975 Defense Budget and FY 1975–79 Defense Program*, March 4, 1974, pp. 4–5.
43. *Ibid.*, p. 18.
44. See Annual Defense Department Report for FY 1973, p. 73. The Report states unequivocally that "second place in that technological race is simply not good enough."
45. *United States Foreign Policy for the 1970's: Shaping a Durable Peace*, President Nixon's Report to the Congress, May 1973, p. 230.
46. *Ibid.*, p. 10.

Chapter II

Why the Nixon Doctrine? Some Parameters of U.S. Strategy and an American Perception

An analysis of the basic concepts and attitudes implicit in the Nixon Doctrine, particularly as they relate to Pacific-Asia, calls for a detailed consideration of a number of related questions. Some of them are:

1. Why has the United States felt the need to inaugurate this new approach to international security, especially in Asia?

2. What circumstances, international and domestic, have made the new approach seem feasible to U.S. policy-makers?

3. How is this policy perceived, in the Asian context, by U.S. allies and other countries? What have been, thus far, their initiatives and responses to U.S. policy in the light of their own security problems? What additional developments are likely to occur in the future, or, at any rate, by the end of the 1970s?

4. Is the new approach, both in general terms and in its specific application to Pacific-Asia, the only alternative open to the United States, at least in theory? Why has it been adopted in preference to other alternatives? What are the chances of its success?

Although the Nixon Doctrine was first expounded in mid-1969, it reflects long-term external and domestic developments that came to a head in the 1960s. The international developments in question extend far beyond the borders of Pacific-Asia even though Mr. Nixon first spoke of these ideas at Guam within a specific Asian context.

AMERICA'S DETERIORATING STRATEGIC BALANCE VIS-À-VIS THE SOVIET UNION

First of all, one cannot divorce the principles of the Nixon Doctrine and its application to Pacific-Asia from the deteriorating overall strategic balance between the United States and the Soviet Union that became clearly discernible in 1969 to the new Administration. In this respect, a most significant factor is the shift in relative strategic power in favor of the Soviet Union during the last part of the 1960s, especially in the sphere of strategic nuclear forces in which the United States had enjoyed unquestioned superiority until then. One cannot, therefore, view the Nixon-Chou En-lai meeting in Peking in February, 1972, in isolation from the Strategic Arms Limitation Talks (SALT) between the Soviet Union and the United States, which began in 1969, or, for that matter, from other U.S.-Soviet negotiations and the balance of forces between NATO and Warsaw Pact countries, that were to approach a critical stage only in 1973, which Mr. Kissinger wistfully called the "year of Europe," and 1974.[1]

One of the most important aspects of the opening of SALT was public recognition by both the United States and other nations, including but by no means limited to America's friends, that the Soviet Union had attained strategic "parity" with the United States. In fact, by the time of Mr. Nixon's Moscow visit in May, 1972, the Soviet Union was already superior to the United States in varying degrees in several categories of nuclear weapons. It can also be pointed out that some aspects of Soviet superiority—for instance, in the number of land-based ICBMs in general and, in particular, the large SS9s, which could each mount a 25-megaton warhead or a number of warheads each larger than the one-megaton U.S. Minuteman—were attained and became known during SALT I. (See Figure II.1 and Table II.1.) There are those who argue that SALT made this Soviet superiority possible. Others maintain that, because of anti-Vietnam War sentiments and Congressional opposition to defense appropriations, the United States could not have prevented this adverse development in any case, and that SALT may even have slowed the Soviet advance, making it less than it might otherwise have been.[2] Neither contention, of course, can be conclusively proven objectively.

In this same connection, attention must be given to the term "parity." Parity is an elusive concept that can be interpreted in many different ways. It is no less ambiguous than "equal security," a term the Soviet Union prefers,

Why the Nixon Doctrine?

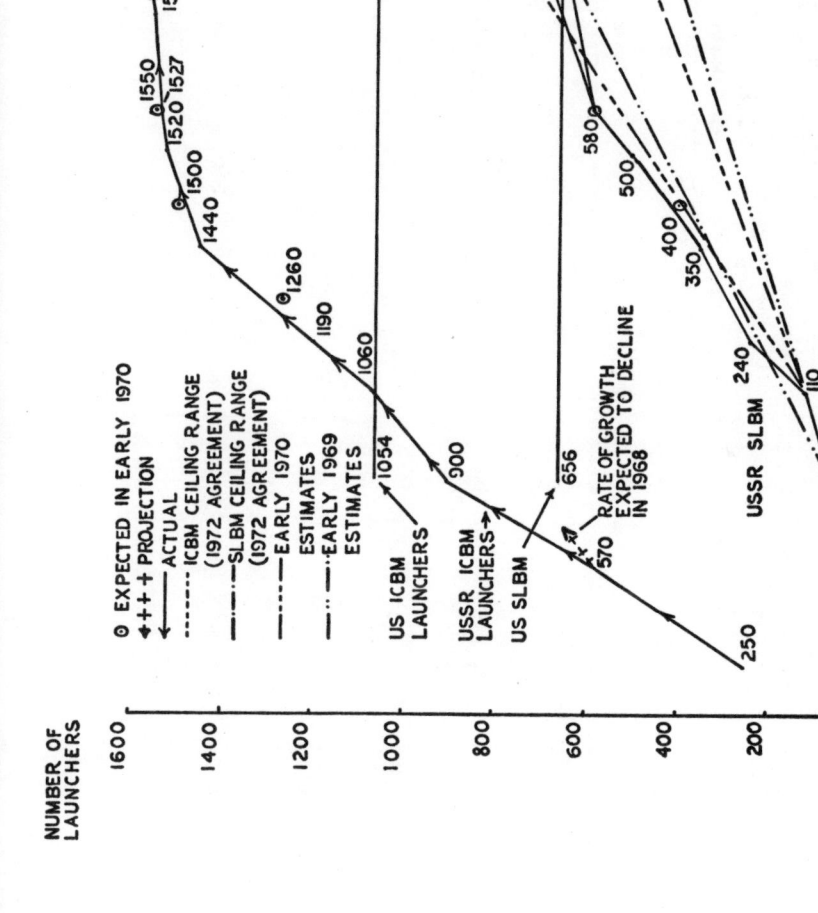

Figure II.1. A Numerical Comparison of U.S.-USSR ICBM and SLBM Launchers. SOURCE: See Table II.1.

Table II.1 Comparative Statistics of U.S. and Soviet Strategic Nuclear Weapons

Year	Date	Land-based Intercontinental Ballistic Missiles (ICBMs) U.S.	Soviet	Submarine Launched Ballistic Missiles (SLBMs) U.S.	Soviet	Long-range Bombers U.S.	Soviet	Number of Nuclear Warheads U.S.	Soviet
		(Numbers of launchers)							
Before the "SALT I" Agreement of 1972									
1968	Sept. 1	1,054[1]	900[1]	656[1]	45[1]	646[1]	150[1]	4,200[1]	1,200[1]
1969	Sept. 1	1,054[2]	1,060[2]*	656[2]	110[2]	581[2]	140–145[2]	4,200[2]	1,350[2]
	Year-end	1,054[3]	1,190[3]	656[3]	240[3]				
1970	Midyear		1,260+[2]**						
	Year-end	1,054[4]	1,440[4]	656[4]	350[4]	517[4]	195[4]	4,000[4]	1,800[4]
1971	Midyear	1,054[4]	1,500[4]	656[4]	400[4]	569[4]	175–195[4]	4,600[4]	2,000[4]
	Year-end	1,054[3]	1,520[3]	656[3]	500[3]	565[5]*	140[5]	4,700[5]*	2,100[5]
At the time of the "SALT I" Agreement									
1972	Midyear	1,054[5]	1,550[5]	656[5]	580[5]	531[5]	190[5]	5,700[5]	2,500[5]
			1,527[8]						
After the "SALT I" Agreement									
1973	Midyear	no change	1,547[7]	no change	...	...	...	...	...
1974	Midyear	no change	1,587[7]	no change	666[7]*	...[8]	...	...[8]	...

Why the Nixon Doctrine? 23

1977 Potential
number   (a) 1,054   (i) 1,618*   (a) 656   (i) 740
permissible   (b) 1,000   (ii) 1,409*   (b) 710   (ii) 950
under the
May, 1972,   —   **   —   **
interim SALT
Agreement(6)

SOURCES: 1. *The 1970 Defense Budget and Defense Program for Fiscal Years 1970–74*, Statement of Secretary of Defense Clark M. Clifford, January 1969, p. 42. This is the Annual Defense Department Report for FY 1970. The same source gives estimates of Soviet ICBMs as 250 in mid-1966 and 570 in mid-1967.
2. *Fiscal Year 1971 Defense Program and Budget*, A statement by Secretary of Defense Melvin R. Laird before a joint session of the Senate Armed Services and Appropriations Committee, February 20, 1970, pp. 102–103. This is the Annual Defense Department Report for FY 1971 referred to later in the text. *275 of these were the large SS9s. **Estimated in the FY 1971 Report at over 200 more than in September, 1969 (*ibid*., p. 103).
3. *U.S. Foreign Policy for the 1970's*, III, Report to the Congress by President Richard M. Nixon, February 9, 1972, p. 160.
4. *Toward a National Security Strategy of Realistic Deterrence, Statement of Secretary of Defense Melvin R. Laird on the Fiscal Year 1972–76 Defense Program and the 1972 Defense Budget*, (before the House Armed Services Committee), March 9, 1971, p. 165. Including 50 tankers. This Report is later referred to as the Annual Defense Department Report for FY 1972.
5. *National Security Strategy of Realistic Deterrence, Secretary of Defense Melvin R. Laird's Annual Defense Department Report FY 1973*, (statement before the Senate Armed Services Committee), February 15, 1972, p. 40. Excluding 50 tankers and some reconnaissance planes. *Dated November 1, 1971.
6. Text of the Interim Agreement on Offensive Missiles, *New York Times*, May 27, 1972. For the U.S., the difference between 1,054 and 1,000 land-based ICBMs consists of the 54 Titans that the Agreement allows to be converted to SLBMs. For the Soviet Union, the difference between 950 and 740 SLBMs consists of the number of additional SLBMs that may be used to replace older (pre-1964) Soviet land-based ICBMs. This would reduce the number of land-based ICBMs for the Soviet Union to 1,409 from the U.S. estimate of 1,618. Note that the basic figure of land-based ICBMs for the Soviet Union, 1,618 launchers, including those under construction, is not given in the Agreement. Cf. also Admiral Moorer's report to the House Armed Services Committee on April 10, 1973. *Including 313 SS9s. **Possible numbers estimated at 5,700 for the United States and more than 6,000 for the Soviet Union, depending upon the rate at which the latter will install multiple warheads.
7. *U.S. Military Posture for FY 1975*, statement by Admiral Thomas H. Moorer, Chairman of the Joint Chiefs of Staff before the Armed Services Subcommittee of the House Appropriations Committee, February 26, 1974. *Plus 60 on G-class submarines reclassified after the 1972 Interim Agreement as a part of Soviet "theater forces" instead of "strategic forces."
8. For a discussion of the new Soviet long-range bomber ("Backfire"), estimated deployment date 1974, see Admiral Moorer's 1974 report. The U.S. lead in number of nuclear warheads could be substantially reduced in 5 to 6 years, according to Moorer.

since security requirements for different countries are not the same. There are geographical differences between the Soviet Union and the United States, differences in the distribution of industry and population, which constitutes targets for enemy missiles, and differences in external commitments. Differences in value systems determine how heavy human and material losses any nation can and will endure, if it is attacked, without having to retaliate or to give up the contest. There are also qualitative and technological differences in each nation's nuclear forces. These forces can be employed in different ways, resulting in varying degrees of effectiveness in carrying out different "missions." Thus, it is impossible to define precisely when two countries can feel equally secure or when they are really at par in nuclear terms, not to mention in terms of overall strategic balance, allowing for other forms of threat and defense. "Parity" must therefore be judged by each of the superpowers according to its own light, and by third parties as they see the superpowers' strategic balance and as they understand it. Parity according to one set of criteria could well mean inferiority or superiority according to another.

In a very narrow sense, if we measure nuclear capability in terms of the level of damage the United States and the Soviet Union could inflict upon each other in retaliation to an all-out attack, both countries had possessed this capability of "assured destruction" in a "second strike," according to the U.S. definition, for quite some time before 1969. That is to say, even before the initiation of SALT, the level of damage each could inflict upon the other after having suffered the effects of an all-out nuclear attack exceeded what U.S. planners regarded as tolerable either for ourselves or for the Soviet Union.[3] On the other hand, it is not at all clear that the United States and the Soviet Union possessed at the end of 1969, when SALT began, the same nuclear capability in other terms, such as in a limited nuclear exchange or in safeguarding the survivability of each nation's retaliatory forces or in affording protection to vital centers of national life.

When one speaks of the attainment of strategic parity by the Soviet Union at the inception of SALT, the only new threshold of parity reached at the time was near equality in the number of land-based ICBM launchers. At the beginning of September, 1969, the Soviet Union was credited by the United States with 1,060 land-based ICBM launchers;[4] the United States, on the other hand, had possessed 1,054 land-based ICBMs since 1967.[5] In view of the inherent difficulty in defining real parity in the strategic balance, numerical equality in only one of the major nuclear weapons systems was significant primarily because of its psychological and political impact.

Although the number of Soviet land-based ICBM launchers had risen rapidly since 1966,[6] the United States had made no effort to offset this progressive shortening of its own numerical lead. One principal consideration underlying this U.S. inaction appeared to be an American assumption that the

Soviet Union would not be willing to enter into nuclear arms control negotiations from a position of numerical inferiority.[7] Since it wished to engage Moscow in such a dialogue, the United States was prepared to wait for the Soviet Union to catch up. This remarkable American restraint—it might yet turn out to be foolhardiness, but the historian will have to be the judge—was a deliberate choice made long before 1969. However, as Defense Secretary Laird told the Associated Press on April 20, 1970, "For the past five years the United States has been in neutral gear in the development of strategic offensive forces while the Soviet Union has moved into high gear in both deployment and development of strategic nuclear weapons." This change in relative position between the two countries was permitted to occur "because the United States deliberately chose to assume that the Soviet buildup at most was aimed at achieving a deterrent posture comparable to that of the U.S.... [and we] have not responded this year [1969–70] because we hope that SALT can render response unnecessary."[8] In short, political judgment both in 1969–70 and before was that the risk of holding back any U.S. response was worth taking.

When the point of U.S.-Soviet numerical equality was reached in land-based ICBMs at the inception of SALT, the ill-defined concept of Soviet parity with the United States gained wide currency. Such public acknowledgment of the significance of numerical parity, even though confined to a single key nuclear component at the time, could not but raise a gnawing question in some quarters regarding the continued usefulness of America's nuclear forces as a means of compensation in the future for an imbalance in conventional forces. The defense of NATO had for years rested on two factors: direct U.S. involvement, ensured by the presence of U.S. forces in Europe; potential escalation of any serious conflict to nuclear exchange reinforced by the U.S. nuclear presence on the spot. The deterrent effect was provided by the preceding two factors. As a matter of fact, if the deterrence concept is applied to cover all types of forces, the European members of NATO cannot enjoy the same degree of security as the Warsaw Pact countries without a noticeable nuclear superiority on the NATO side. Given the relatively small size of Western Europe and difficulty to carry out defense in depth, the exposed allied position, and the superior conventional forces of the Warsaw Pact countries, a compensatory advantage would be a logical requirement in NATO's defense plans. A principal source of concern to the United States which might result from an increase in Soviet nuclear arms and general public acknowledgment of parity would be the possible erosion of the cohesiveness of the NATO alliance and loss of confidence in the effectiveness of the U.S. nuclear shield in Europe.

One difference between U.S. and Soviet strategic concepts became clear early in SALT I. According to Mr. Nixon, the Soviet Union defines "strategic" offensive weapons as "those that can reach the other side's territory. These terms include our theater nuclear delivery system ... [including those on forward bases that] are essential components of integrated theater defense created under alliance commitments.... On the other hand, the Soviet approach would not include limitations on *its* own theater nuclear forces, including ... medium or intermediate range missiles.[9] This Soviet approach would seem to have an inherently divisive effect since it reflects basic differences between the two sides, both in terms of geography and in the nature of their respective alliances. The political overtones in the Soviet approach to bilateral discussions with the United States, therefore, reinforced America's need to enhance its credibility in the alliance.

If the preceding points were already relevant at the inception of SALT and with the mere attainment by the Soviet Union of numerical equality in land-based ICBMs—admittedly the Soviet position was reinforced by the large SS9s—their significance would rise if the Soviet Union could further increase and broaden its edge. Unfortunately this turned out to be precisely the case.

According to U.S. estimates, the number of Soviet land-based ICBMs rose from 1,060 in September, 1969, to 1,440 at the end of 1970, and 1,520 at the end of 1971. It was expected at the end of 1971 to reach 1,550 by mid-1972.[10] In contrast, the U.S. land-based ICBMs remained stationary at 1,054 after 1969 and during SALT, although there was some increase in the number of warheads mounted on U.S. missiles.

In the case of seaborne ballistic missiles (SLBMs), again according to published U.S. sources, Soviet strength rose from 45 in September 1968 to 110 in 1969, 350 at the end of 1970, and 500 at the end of 1971. The number was expected to reach 580 in mid-1972.[11] At the then estimated rate of Soviet nuclear-powered ballistic submarine construction, during 1973 (see Figure II.1), the number of Soviet SLBMs could surpass 656, the constant U.S. level since 1967. This estimate is in general accord with Laird's reports to the Congress for fiscal years 1972 and 1973, which put the date of U.S.-Soviet numerical parity in SLBM force at sometime in 1973–74[12] and the total number of the Soviet force at a high of 800 eventually.[13]

Table II.1 presents the permissible ceilings under the five-year U.S.-Soviet Interim Agreement on offensive missiles signed in Moscow in May, 1972. These ceilings, set at levels considerably higher for the Soviet Union than for the United States in both land-based ICBMs and SLBMs, effectively assured potential Soviet numerical superiority in both areas. This was apparently accepted by the United States in part as a result of America's lead in introducing independently targetable multiple warheads to a single delivery vehicle. The United States also enjoyed a large numerical advantage in long-range bombers. (The long-range bomber is in a sense a delivery vehicle with multiple warheads.) U.S. planners also claim that American weapons have other qualitative advantages, such as greater accuracy, which could compensate for the Soviet Union's numerical superiority and greater "throw-weight," i.e., heavier warheads.

In addition, the Agreement and the ABM Treaty implied:

1. U.S. acceptance, at least for the time being, of (a) the hypothesis that mutual vulnerability would continue to provide sufficient deterrence and (b) the asymmetric posture of a potentially large Soviet numerical superiority, which would give the Soviet Union a capability of limited nuclear attacks and might even lead to a first-strike—i.e., disarming—capability versus a U.S. second-strike capability; and

2. U.S. abandonment without the least fanfare of its historical position on on-site inspection, thus placing its faith in Soviet restraint, its own technical competence in intelligence gathering, and the good sense and ability of its future government and its own people to be adequately informed and to react quickly if need be.

As mentioned earlier, numbers alone are not totally indicative of the relative capability of the two countries to meet their respective requirements for nuclear forces. Assessment in terms of the number of warheads, with allowance for differences in quality, such as accuracy, ability to penetrate enemy defenses, and "size" or "throw-weight" also make simple numerical comparison not particularly meaningful. However, trends do indicate the actual *numerical* superiority or near parity the Soviet Union enjoyed in 1972, when the SALT I agreements were signed, in two principal components of strategic "offensive" nuclear forces.

From the point of view of quality differences, Soviet SS9 missiles can carry such large multiple warheads that sufficient numbers of them could conceivably cripple U.S. land-based ICBMs even in hardened silos. As of 1972, although the Soviet long-range bomber force remained numerically inferior to the aging U.S. bomber force, reduced somewhat during 1972 in bombing missions over North Vietnam, the U.S. bombers, if on the ground, would be susceptible to destruction from "sneak attacks" by Soviet "cruise missiles" which could come in at a low altitude and escape detection. Besides, the new Soviet long-range bomber "Backfire" had been under development for some time. The Soviet Union had also tested "fractional orbital bombardment systems" (FOBs) and/or ICBMs with depressed trajectories, using SS9s,[14] thus producing a means of attack with virtually no warning. Press reports of certain Soviet satellite tests suggest the development of a Soviet "satellite-destroying" system that could cripple the U.S. retaliatory force.

In terms of defensive weapons, the Soviet Union was, and still is, numerically vastly superior. In November, 1971, it had 10,000 surface-to-air missiles (SAMs) versus 895 on the part of the United States. Perhaps even more noteworthy was its possession of 64 anti-ballistic-missile (ABM) launchers at the end of 1971, while the United States had none by mid-1972.[15] The 1972 Treaty limiting ABMs, however, gives the United States and the USSR 200 launchers each as ceilings, not counting those at test sites. (The ceiling was lowered, in 1974, to 100 launchers each.)

In summary, the relative position of the United States vis-à-vis the Soviet Union in terms of strategic nuclear forces[16] had worsened before the Nixon Administration had gone into office, and the trend was allowed to continue thereafter. Two potential situations may, therefore, become a reality in the not too distant future unless contrary developments occur. First, the survival and retaliatory capability of U.S. land-based ICBMs and the U.S. bomber force may be seriously eroded, thus undermining the concept of retaining three separate strategic systems (the "triad"), each of which alone could possess an "assured destruction" second-strike capability. Such a development would place the burden of preserving this capability primarily on the U.S. Navy and the survivability of its nuclear missile force. A Soviet first-strike capability could then emerge in the event of a Soviet breakthrough in anti-submarine warfare. Secondly, once a significant overall numerical disparity in strategic forces has developed in favor of the Soviet Union, a Soviet disarming attack, partial if not total, during a crisis would no longer be inconceivable. Even if the United States should still possess a second-strike capability, it may be of very little political usefulness. The possessor of the superior force could conceivably employ a part of it in a very limited fashion, or threaten to do so, without undercutting its own second-strike, or even its first-strike, capability. The possessor of the inferior force would be faced with a very difficult dilemma and suffer a serious loss of flexibility in response. As Mr. Nixon noted in his 1972 foreign policy report to Congress, "no President should be left with only one strategic course of action, particularly that of ordering the mass destruction of enemy civilians and facilities. Given the range of possible political-military situations which could conceivably confront us, our strategic policy should not be based solely on a capability of inflicting urban and industrial damage presumed to be beyond the level an adversary would accept."[17]

Experts in nuclear strategy might argue that the United States has always lagged in its capability of flexible employment of nuclear forces, including the ability to limit damage from enemy attacks. It is clear, however, that continuation of the trends noted above would further reduce such flexibility as the United States may still possess. It is also clear that even the capability of dealing "assured destruction" to an adversary may be threatened if the effectiveness of the U.S. SLBM fleet or its survivability is questioned. The continuation of qualitative improvements and potential technological breakthroughs in ASW (anti-submarine warfare), etc., on the Soviet side may further reduce America's remaining margin of safety.

Compounding the uncertainty about the relative positions of the United States and the Soviet Union is our lack of complete information on Soviet capabilities. An example is the reported identification in 1973 of 100 new

ICBM silos under construction in the Soviet Union and the different interpretations of their possible intent.[18] The speed with which the Soviet Union will deploy its new supersonic bomber presents another question. The possible development of a satellite inspection and destruction space system and other systems that could negate present U.S. retaliatory capability very dramatically offers additional causes of serious concern.[19] Since the past record of U.S. reading of Soviet intentions has often left much to be desired, those who counsel caution have a strong case.[20]

Uncertainty is increased further as a result of the lead time required for an effective American response to Soviet advances. The lead time is technological, political, and economic. Not only must appropriate technological countermeasures be on hand, but there must also be sufficient political will in both the Administration and Congress, as well as the necessary production facilities, management, and technical labor to put such measures into effect. This consideration implies the need for watchfulness in terms of intelligence and R&D activities, congressional and public understanding of the issues, and advance production planning.

In conclusion, the deterioration in America's relative position in the nuclear strategic balance has reached a point where both the maintenance of security and of future freedom of action for the United States itself and the political and psychological requirements of the NATO and Asian alliances demand a greater U.S. effort in the nuclear field. In 1969, the need for this extra effort could well be anticipated. By 1972, it could no longer be delayed even with a limited SALT agreement. Some might even argue that the need has become more urgent because the strategic balance has deteriorated so much during SALT as a result of U.S. reluctance to be accused of obstructing negotiations.[21]

The cost of policing a SALT agreement must also be borne in mind. The effort to prevent technological surprises and to maintain permissible quantitative and qualitative adjustments in order to keep the agreed strategic balance stable cannot be relaxed. Since the United States leads the West in nuclear armament and technology, the additional effort required will, prima facie, have to be American. U.S. plans to develop a larger and longer-range undersea missile system (e.g., the Trident) and to stress R&D are all a part of the precautionary effort "to keep options open."

THE INCREASING SIGNIFICANCE OF SOVIET CONVENTIONAL POWER

Although strategic parity cannot be precisely defined, the present strategic balance between the Soviet Union and the United States is still such that neither side would wish to take the first step in risking a strategic nuclear exchange. Consequently, the usefulness of the strategic nuclear deterrent in preventing lower levels of conflict involving nuclear powers rests primarily on fear that such conflicts might explode into a nuclear exchange. However, not all conflicts of lesser intensity will carry the same risk. Consequently, the military capability of the two countries outside the arena of strategic nuclear weapons systems assumes increasing importance.

In this respect, it is well to note (1) the general superiority of the conventional forces of the Soviet Union and other Warsaw Pact countries versus those of NATO and (2) the unmistakable trend of the Soviet Union's increasing ability to project its power by sea. In regard to NATO, the following data present a clear picture in favor of the Warsaw Pact countries as of late 1971, that is, prior to the SALT I agreement:

Table II.2 Comparative Strength between NATO and the Warsaw Pact

	Northern and Central Europe		Southern Europe	
	NATO	Warsaw Pact*	NATO	Warsaw Pact*
Ground forces available in peacetime (number of division equivalents)				
Armored	8	28	7	9
Infantry (mechanized and airborne)	16	37	30	21
Tactical aircraft in operational service				
Light bombers	150	280	—	30
Fighter/ground attack	1,150	1,400	450	150
Interceptors	300	2,100	275	900
Reconnaissance	400	400	125	100

SOURCE: The International Institute for Strategic Studies, *The Military Balance, 1971–72,* London, 1971, pp. 76–79.
*Including the U.S.S.R.

If a comparison is made in terms of combat and direct support troops available, NATO had 580,000 men in Northern and Central Europe, excluding the manpower of France, versus 960,000 men for the Warsaw Pact countries. According to the International Institute for Strategic Studies of London, the Warsaw Pact figure included "the command for which the Pact High Commander has responsibility," but excluded "the armed forces of Bulgaria and Rumania." "Soviet units normally stationed in the Western U.S.S.R. and such troops as might be committed to the Baltic theater of operations" were, however, "included on the Warsaw Pact side."[22] In Southern Europe, on the NATO side, "the Italian, Greek, and Turkish land forces and such American and British units as would be committed to the Mediterranean theater of operations" totaled 525,000, while "the land forces of Bulgaria, Hungary, and Rumania and such Soviet units normally stationed in Hungary and Southern U.S.S.R. as might be committed to the Mediterranean theater" numbered 385,000 men. If the Northern, Central, and Southern fronts are taken together, excluding the French, the total manpower of NATO would number 1,105,000, versus a Warsaw Pact total of 1,345,000. Not to be forgotten is the comparative tank strength of the two sides. While NATO boasted of 5,500 medium and heavy tanks on the Northern and Central fronts in peacetime, the corresponding figure for the Warsaw Pact forces was 16,000. In Southern Europe, the NATO and Warsaw Pact figures were respectively 2,250 and 5,700. Although the NATO alliance might appear to have more men in Southern Europe, the Warsaw Pact's overall numerical superiority was overwhelming.

A later comparison of the relative situation on the Central Front in West Germany presented by Secretary Schlesinger consists of the following:[23]

Warsaw Pact	NATO
Soviet divisions in East Germany, Poland, and Czechoslovakia 27	4-1/3 U.S. divisions plus one Berlin brigade and two armored cavalry regiments
Divisions of East Germany, Poland, and Czechoslovakia 31	5 French divisions
Soviet tank and motorized rifle divisions in Hungary 4	20 German and other divisions
Total Warsaw Pact (including the U.S.S.R.) deployed manpower 925,000	Total NATO deployed manpower 890,000

Continued on page 32

Warsaw Pact	NATO
Tanks (Warsaw Pact) 15,500	Tanks 6,000
Aircraft (majority being air-to-air fighters) 2,800	Aircraft (around one-half being fighter-bombers) 2,700

These figures tell essentially the same preponderant conventional threat posed by deployed Warsaw Pact forces that the earlier data portrayed. How meaningful it is to include the French forces in view of the French tendency toward independent action, or of Greek and Turkish forces in view of the 1974 Cyprus dispute, is another question.

According to Rear Admiral Günter Poser of NATO, as of mid-1973 the Soviet Union and its European allies had 4,650,000 men under arms with 75 percent of the ground forces and 70 percent of the air forces aimed at Western Europe. There were 160 Warsaw Pact divisions facing NATO, plus 30 divisions in strategic reserve, and 50 percent more tactical aircraft than in 1968. Soviet strength has grown faster, it seems, than the allies have expected.[24]

A most important fact is the much greater speed and flexibility with which the Warsaw Pact forces can be reinforced. Secretary Schlesinger believes that the "mobilized threat" in the Central Region should be placed at 80–90 divisions, according to his 1974 report. Even if advance information should indicate a Warsaw Pact mobilization, one must still face the political difficulty of interpreting such information and of having it taken seriously by allied governments. Viewed in this light, the general numerical superiority in most categories of ground and air forces on the part of the Warsaw Pact countries poses a most serious problem for NATO defense planners. From the point of view of the United States, as the mainstay of the NATO alliance, the crucial question is how to correct this imbalance. This question assumes even more serious proportions if one considers the oft-repeated clamor for the reduction of U.S. troops in Europe for economic and other reasons and the improvement in the Soviet Union's strategic nuclear position discussed in the last section.

During 1969–72 the European NATO countries, including France and Canada, exhibited a far from consistent attitude toward defense. Total defense expenditures for thirteen countries increased by $1,959 million between 1969 ($23,293 million) and 1970 ($25,252 million), but declined by $49 million from 1970 to 1971 ($25,203 million).[25] If we focus attention on the six countries with significantly larger defense expenditures than the rest, viz., Great Britain, France, West Germany, Italy, Canada, and the Netherlands, the year-to-year fluctuations were greater in both directions. Aggregate defense expenditures of the six countries rose by $2,883 million in 1969-70; they then fell by $763 million in 1970-71.

Because of the devaluation of the U.S. dollar, NATO's total defense budget rose in 1972 to $30,638 million for the thirteen countries and $27,452 million for the six.[26] However, if allowance is made for price increases,[27] defense spending by the three principal European members of the alliance all registered declines during 1969-72. If 1968 is taken as the base year (= 100), the index numbers of defense spending for 1969 and 1972 at constant prices, were:

	1969	1972
Great Britain	88.6	77.9
France	88.0	83.8
West Germany	105.1	93.6

These declines between 1968 and 1972 were less than that of U.S. defense spending in the same period when the latter is measured at 1964 prices (Table II.5 below); they were, however, greater than the decline of U.S. defense spending measured at 1973 prices (Table II.4).

Partly in response to American prodding,[28] a European Defense Improvement Program was announced by ten European NATO members in December, 1970. The Program envisaged an increase of $1 billion in defense outlay by European members of the alliance over a five-year period. This action was followed in December, 1971, by another announcement by the same ten NATO countries that their 1972 defense budgets would be raised by $1 billion in the aggregate. All these efforts were aimed at redressing the NATO-Warsaw Pact imbalance and, from the American point of view, at transferring a larger share of the burden of NATO's much-needed defense buildup to some of the European nations. However, as the defense spending figures (at constant prices) show, U.S. hopes during Mr. Nixon's first term that Western Europe would increase its real defense effort were not realized.

It is equally clear that short of a much larger increase in Western Europe's defense effort, and/or American contributions, NATO cannot expect to match the Warsaw Pact in the strength of conventional forces. The need for a buildup of NATO strength is complicated by that of changing the member countries' relative shares of the total cost. Even the progress made in burden-sharing has not been sufficient to resolve the distribution issue, at least from the U.S. point of view. The problem is manifested, in particular, in its effect on the U.S. balance of payments. Referring to a new $2 billion offset agreement between the United States and West Germany, Mr. Nixon stated in his third (1972) foreign policy report, "These agreements are testimony to cooperation. They are not a long term solution, however, and they strain alliance relations each time they come up for renewal."[29] The balance of payments problem posed by the cost of U.S. forces in Europe has not yet been solved and will doubtless come up again as an increasingly serious issue in view of the successive devaluations of the U.S. dollar since 1971, and the new and disparate burdens imposed by higher oil prices, after the October, 1973, Middle East War, in Western Europe and the United States respectively.

It is also true that there is a general disinclination in Europe to sustain large defense efforts. From the European point of view, the political payoff in sharing more of NATO's defense costs consists only of additional ties to the United States. But might the United States reduce its forces so much faster if European manpower contingents were increased? Such a U.S. response would not be helpful to Europe if U.S. manpower involvement in Europe is desired. Furthermore, there is the lure of détente. This issue came to a head especially with the Soviet proposal to convene a European Security Conference and a NATO Proposal to discuss Mutual and Balanced Force Reductions (MBFR), initiated at the June, 1968, NATO Ministerial Meeting at Reykjavík. When the first Nixon Administration reached its halfway point, it was already quite clear that these discussions with the Soviet Union and their effect on the viability of NATO would become a central issue several years later.

EXPANSION OF THE SOVIET NAVY

On the Southern European front, the U.S. Sixth Fleet still maintains its pivotal position in NATO defense, but partly at the expense of the Atlantic Fleet. Furthermore, the unquestioned ability of the Allied Fleet to fight a war has not forestalled the erosion of its ability to deter lower-level conflict or to restrain the Soviet Union from using sea power to exert political influence. In contrast, the expansion of the Soviet Fleet in the Mediterranean has undoubtedly reduced the freedom of action of the United States short of war in the Eastern Mediterranean and adjacent areas.

What is true of the Mediterranean is no less true elsewhere. Symbolic of this development at the beginning of the 1970s is the appearance of the Soviet Fleet maneuvering off the Gulf of Mexico, in the Caribbean, and in the South China Sea. Press reports in November, 1970, about possible Soviet intentions to build a submarine base at the Cuban port of Cienfuegos and the visit of a Soviet ballistic missile submarine to Nipe Bay north of Santiago de Cuba in May, 1972, are other typical examples.[30] The presence of the Soviet Fleet in the Bay of Bengal at the time of the India-Pakistan War in late 1971 illustrated how the Soviet Union was gaining more experience in a new dimension of power. Soviet vessels frequently sail along the coast of mainland

China, including the Taiwan Strait, as a reminder of their presence to both Chinas.

The Soviet Union's expanding naval power was graphically brought to public attention when a Soviet cruiser and a destroyer, accompanied by support ships, sailed through the Malacca Straits in January, 1971, when the Commonwealth Prime Ministers' Conference was in session in Singapore.[31] The number of Soviet warships visiting the Indian Ocean increased steadily from 1967 to 1972.[32] In October, 1970, for example, there were five Soviet guided missile destroyers or cruisers in the Indian Ocean, accompanied by three submarines, six supply ships, and some other vessels.[33] "The U.S.S.R.," wrote Admiral Moorer in 1974,[34] "reached an average of 4,300 naval ship days per year for 1969–70 [in the Indian Ocean]. By 1973, it had more than doubled that presence; ... the Soviet Union now operates nine combatants/ submarines and twenty-one naval auxiliaries in the area...." Their increasing presence in this area is a reminder of the power vacuum left behind by the departed British Fleet which no other power has had the capability or expressed intention to fill. Most of the Soviet marine visitors to the Indian Ocean apparently came from their Pacific base in the Soviet Far East. A much larger increase in Soviet naval presence could result if and when the Suez Canal is reopened. The likelihood of this development has increased sharply as a result of the disengagement of Egyptian and Israeli forces after the October, 1973, war. The reopening of the Suez Canal to Soviet naval forces would lead to the linking of the Soviet Union's Black Sea and Far Eastern naval contingents. As a result, one can well imagine the forging of a Soviet naval chain arching around the Indian and Pacific Oceans. While this development is not imminent, its very possibility imparts special significance to Brezhnev's proposal for Soviet-sponsored Asian collective security arrangements[35] and the Soviet Union's well-known desire for a Mediterranean devoid of U.S. nuclear presence.

The Soviet Union's record of naval expansion suggests that such a state of affairs could come about much sooner than one might expect. The record rate of growth of Soviet land-based ICBMs in the 1960s offers little reason for complacency. In particular, the appearance of new warships with special characteristics seems to have become a habit with the expanding Soviet Navy. As *Jane's Fighting Ships* noted a few years ago,[36] "The U.S.S.R. is no longer copying and emulating. She is initiating and inventing. Regularly there appears a new class of warship peculiar to Soviet requirements. Each year for the last few years a new type of rocket cruiser or missile destroyer has appeared. Each year a new class of submarine has been observed, either nuclear or conventionally powered. And for years new improvements have progressively been made in a series of deadly little missile boats running into hundreds of units. ... The Soviet Union is not neglecting any aspect of naval warfare, and all classes of warships, from the largest to the smallest, are being built. Even the supposedly outmoded cruisers are being employed." The present Soviet helicopter carriers may soon be followed by larger carriers.

Soviet naval expansion has been accompanied by a large increase in the Soviet merchant fleet. The latter grew from 1,000 ships, totaling 2.3 million gross tons, in 1955, to 7,000 ships, totaling 16 million gross tons, in 1970. Soviet merchant vessels have called at Asian ports, and Eastern European shipping agencies have been established in Singapore and other trading centers.

In the face of these developments, the U.S. Navy has been encumbered by encroaching obsolescence, high replacement costs, and the need to maintain and upgrade the naval component of America's strategic deterrent force. While the American Navy is still much stronger than its Soviet counterpart, one should bear in mind the rising Soviet trend. This shift in relative balance offers the Soviet Union an increasing number of possibilities. More readily than before, the Soviet Union can attain local or regional naval superiority, inhibit the freedom of action of other navies and support Soviet policy by projecting power from the sea, especially in the case of peninsula and island nations. There are many such nations in the Western Pacific, from Korea to Singapore. The Soviet Navy can increasingly foster the image of an ascending power beyond the scale its present fighting potential might warrant. As an instrument of political influence, its range of operations is rapidly becoming worldwide.

THE U.S. DEFENSE BUDGET AND AMERICA'S "REORDERING OF PRIORITIES"

Our analysis of the deteriorating strategic balance of the United States in relation to the Soviet Union in both nuclear and conventional terms points to a need to enlarge the U.S. and allied defense effort in real terms in some areas, not just in terms of inflated dollars. This need becomes even more imperative if we bear in mind that, with the decline of relative strength, the cohesiveness of the American-led alliance system, painfully structured and assiduously maintained since World War II, especially in the case of NATO, threatens to erode. The process of erosion, if not offset, would, of course, further worsen the position of both the United States and its allies. There will then be the additional risk that processes of erosion often tend to accelerate. In spite of this obvious consideration the additional defense effort of U.S. allies in Europe has been limited to some "burden sharing," notably on the part of such NATO members as the United Kingdom, West Germany, and Italy. The entirely natural desire for détente has been reinforced by the very success of the deterrence policy of the last quarter century. An entire generation has grown up in security and increasing prosperity so that the public does not comprehend why collective security must still be maintained at heavy cost. Even more difficult for this public to understand is that the cost may have to become heavier in the near future.

The growing need to find an effective means to maintain America's relative strategic position has coincided during the period under study with certain important changes in American attitudes. The managers of America's defense effort are faced with the following domestic developments, all of which tend to intensify the difficulty of restoring the balance by U.S. efforts alone: (1) the smaller share of real resources being allocated to national defense, (2) increases in manpower cost as a proportion of defense outlay, and (3) increasing reluctance to provide assistance, especially military assistance, to foreign countries.

The declining share of "national defense" in federal outlay can be readily seen from the figures in Table II.3. Its proportion fell from 45 percent in

Table II.3 Federal Budget Outlay by Functions

	Fiscal Years							
	1964	1968	1969	1970	1971	1972	1973	1974*
	(in billions of dollars at current prices)							
Total Federal Budget Outlay	118.6	178.8	184.5	196.6	211.4	231.9	246.5	274.7
National Defense	53.6	80.5	81.2	80.3	77.7	78.3	76.0	80.6
"Human Resources Outlay"[1]	34.2	57.3	60.5	72.7	88.6	102.5	113.7	132.4
	BY PERCENTAGES							
Total Federal Budget Outlay	100.0	100.0	100.0	100.0	100.0	100.0	100.0	100.0
National Defense	45.2	45.0	44.0	40.8	36.8	33.7	31.2	29.3
"Human Resources Outlay"[1]	28.9	32.0	32.8	37.0	41.9	44.2	46.1	48.2

SOURCES: Table B-64, "Federal budget receipts, outlays, financing and debt, 1962–73," *Economic Report of the President,* January 1972, pp. 270–71. Also corresponding tables in the 1973 and 1974 reports.

[1] Including (a) education and manpower, (b) health, (c) income security, and (d) veterans benefits and services.
*Estimates.

1968 to 33.7 percent in 1972. (To put this reduction of the defense function in perspective, the authorized U.S. troop strength in Vietnam stood at a peak of 549,500 at the inception of the Nixon Administration; by May, 1972, it had been reduced to 69,000; by July 1, 1972, it had fallen to 49,000.)[37] In contrast, the share of "health and education," together with income transfers, increased from 32 percent in 1968 to 44.2 percent in 1972. In 1964, the last "pre-Vietnam" year, the share of "human resources outlay" was only 28.9 percent. While only estimates are available for the 1974 fiscal year, the trend set in the first term of the Nixon Administration has been continued.

The same change in priorities can be discerned if we look at spending through defense budget authorization only, which is usually some $2–3 billion below that attributed to "national defense." Table II.4 indicates "defense spending" in fiscal years 1964, 1968, and 1972–74, together with its relative importance in terms of certain economic aggregates.

If we allow for price inflation during the period, U.S. defense outlay in real terms has declined steadily from a peak of $68.4 billion (at 1964 prices) in 1968.[38] The 1968 outlay was the maximum reached during the 1960s.

More specifically, under the Nixon Administration, defense outlay in real terms fell from $65.4 billion in FY 1969 to $59.4 billion in 1970, $53.2 billion in 1971, and a projected $50.8 billion in 1972. Thus, the 1972 projected budget figure of $50.8 billion at 1964 prices is exactly the same as that in 1964 and comparable to outlays in the pre-Vietnam War years. It is

Table II.4 U.S. Defense Outlay

	Fiscal Years				
	1964	1968	1972	1973	1974
Defense spending in $ billion at FY 1973 prices	50.8	78.0	75.8	74.8	79.0
Defense spending as percent of GNP	8.3	9.4	6.9	6.2	6.0
Defense spending as percent of federal budget	41.8	42.5	31.7	29.0	28.4

SOURCES: *Annual Defense Department Report,* FY 1974, March 1973. *National Security Strategy of Realistic Deterrence,* (*Annual Defense Department Report* for FY 1973), February 1972, p. 203. Cf. also Department of Defense, *The Economics of Defense Spending—A Look at the Realities,* 1972, for a more detailed analysis of the defense sector.

Table II.5 Defense Outlays at Constant 1964 Prices, 1953-74

Fiscal Year	(Billions of dollars)
1953	60.7
1954	56.3
1955	46.6
1956	44.7
1957	45.5
1958	45.8
1959	46.7
1960	46.1
1961	46.5
1962	50.8
1963	51.0
1964	50.8 (1)
1965	45.3
1966	51.2
1967	61.7
1968	68.4 (1)
1969	65.4
1970	59.4
1971	53.2
1972	50.8
1973	(1)
1974	(1)

SOURCES: *Statement of Secretary of Defense Melvin R. Laird on the Fiscal Year 1972-76 Defense Program and the 1972 Defense Budget* before the House Armed Services Committee, March 9, 1971, pp. 156-57 and 161. It should be noted that slightly higher figures were estimated in the Secretary of Defense's 1970 statement for 1969-1971. These were $65.6 billion in 1969, $60.0 billion in 1970, and $54.6 billion in 1971, also at 1964 prices. See *Defense Department Report for FY 1970*, a statement before a joint session of the Senate Armed Services and Appropriations Committee, February 20, 1970, pp. 24 and 26.

(1) At FY 1974 prices, the figures for the following years are given in the FY 1974 *Annual Defense Report* to the Senate Armed Services Committee:

1964	87.8
1968	113.4
1973	79.2
1974	79.0

about $5 billion higher than the post-Korean War period under Eisenhower and well below that of 1953 ($60.7 billion) when the Armistice was signed.

At FY 1973 prices, the projected FY 1972 defense outlay would be $81.3 billion, considerably higher than at 1964 or 1972 prices. On the same 1973 price base, defense outlay in the FY 1973 budget would be $76.5 billion, or another *six* percent below that of FY 1972.[39] All of this reflects a sizable "reordering of national priorities" in government spending in the United States. The decline in defense spending was partly responsible for the increase in unemployment, especially in defense-related industries, and consequently for the increased volume of income "transfer payments" noted above.

The expected decline in employment from June, 1968, to June, 1973, attributable to a shrinkage in the defense sector has been estimated at (a) 1,440,000 persons on the federal payroll plus (b) 1,316,000 in defense-related industries, i.e., a total of 2,756,000 persons.[40] All but 345,000 of the estimated 2,756,000 jobs were lost between July, 1968, and December, 1971. According to the *Annual Defense Report* for FY 1973, the 1,440,000-person cutback in federal employment between FY 1968 and 1973 (fiscal year year-end figures) was estimated to be composed of 251,000 civilian employees and 1,189,000 persons on active military duty. The reduction in active duty personnel was expected to reach 1,314,000 by the end of FY 1974. The 1974 annual report on the defense budget for FY 1975 actually showed a reduction of 1,295,000 military personnel on active duty between FY 1968 and 1973, and of 1,373,000 between FY 1968 and 1974, exceeding the original estimates.[41] Yet, as a result of pay and related increases, there was an expected increase in manpower cost from $32.6 billion, at current prices, in FY 1968 to $41.8 billion in FY 1973 and $43.9 billion in FY 1974.[42] It is not surprising, therefore, that, after deducting this increased manpower cost from a declining defense budget, only a sharply reduced balance is available for all other costs, including construction, procurement, and research and development. At current prices, this balancing item fell from $45.4 billion in FY 1968 to $35.4 billion in FY 1972, and $33.0 billion in FY 1973; it then rose slightly to $35.1 billion in the FY 1974 budget. At constant (FY 1973) prices, the decline would be from $55.3 billion in FY 1968 to $36.4 billion in FY 1972 and $33.0 billion in FY 1973.[43]

In short, the fiscal realities of the Nixon Administration are such that less is available for defense spending on new equipment at a time when the maintenance of the strategic balance vis-à-vis the Soviet Union, already much worse than it was not very long ago, and the replacement and replenishment of conventional forces will clearly demand new defense spending. One speaks of fiscal realities in the sense that defense spending has to accommodate itself to congressional and public sentiments at any given time. That such sentiments might change or be changed is a possibility not to be dismissed offhand. However, a predominantly anti-defense attitude, born of sentiments against U.S. participation in the Vietnam War, has clearly exacted its toll on American security. While budget cutting often follows the path of least resistance when reductions must be made for practical reasons, the trend shown in the preceding discussion is unmistakably a reflection of policy, which in turn mirrors what the U.S. Congress and public seem to demand.

The changing mood of certain American intellectuals seems to have its origin in a number of circumstances. Having become accustomed to relative security, they tend to underrate the need to maintain it. They even question whether past perceptions of threat were real.[44] Fearful of the abuse of power by others, especially the executive branch of government—unfortunately, such abuses have doubtless occurred—they have come, in effect, to extol the virtue of national weakness, almost as if lack of strength could have a spiritually purifying effect. Their frustration and impatience demand instant solutions for complex problems; they refuse to recognize that some problems may even have no complete solutions. Their example, magnified a thousand times as a result of technological advances in television, has contributed to the anti-defense politicization of American society, many segments of which have become impatient and disillusioned with American participation in the Vietnam War. A mass following for half-baked and poorly informed arguments can be created much more rapidly than before and may elicit responses from policy-makers who have themselves become sensitized by the powers of the communications media.

AMERICA'S INCREASING DISINCLINATION TOWARD EXTERNAL ASSISTANCE

The relative and, when measured at constant prices, absolute decline of U.S. defense expenditures has also been accompanied by a worsening balance of payments and growing popular impatience with giving assistance to foreign countries. These developments emerged, however, long before the Nixon Administration.

After World War II, the cumulative total of U.S. Government grants and credits to foreign countries from July 1, 1945, through December 31, 1969, amounted to $121.2 billion.[45] (Of this amount, only $18.7 billion went to countries in the Far East and Western Pacific.) However, if a linear trend is fitted to the annual totals of economic and military aid, including military assistance grants from excess stocks, for the period between 1949 and 1969, there would be a decline of $78.6 million a year. (See Figure II.2.)

This gradual contraction of total aid is the net result of two opposite trends. On the one hand, there is an annual decrease of economic and military

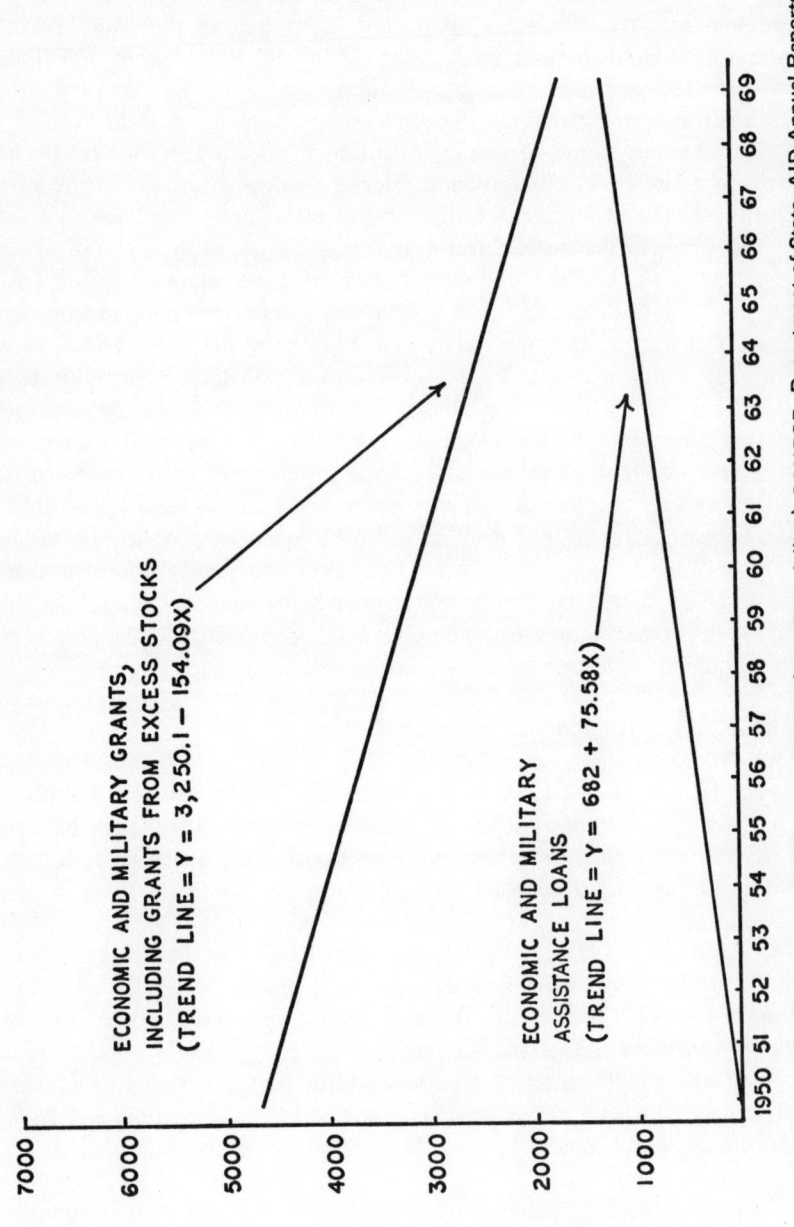

Figure II.2. Foreign Assistance Programs 1950–1969 (in million dollars). SOURCE: Department of State, AID Annual Reports.

grants, including military aid from "long stocks." On the other, there is an annual increase in loans (economic and military). These divergent trends between loans and grants would seem to indicate both an increase in the capacity of the aid-recipient countries to finance their own foreign purchases and a growing disinclination on the part of the United States to offer outright gifts.

A related factor, not directly discernible from the aid figures, is the growing deficit in the U.S. international balance of payments, especially during the 1960s.[46] The latter, calculated on the net liquidity basis, registered annual deficits that rose from $3.7 billion in 1960 to $6.1 billion in 1969, an unprecedented $22 billion in 1971, and, again, $13.9 billion in 1972. Only in two years during the entire decade of the 1960s (1968 and 1969) was there an increase in official reserve assets. The net decline in official reserve during the 1960s was $4.5 billion. When the accelerated deficits of 1970–72 are added to the result of the 1960s, the deplorable state of the external balance of the U.S. economy reaches monumental proportions. The decline in U.S. readiness to extend economic and military assistance abroad has its foundation in the country's reduced capacity to do so. A spectacular landmark in this development was reached on August 15, 1971, when convertibility of the dollar into gold was suspended in international official monetary transactions. An 8 percent devaluation was adopted by the Congress in March, 1972, when the price of gold was increased from $35 to $38 an ounce. Another 10 percent devaluation took place in February, 1973. The fall of the dollar from the seemingly inviolable position it held during the quarter century after World War II again mirrors the changed strategic position of the United States in the world.

A SPECIAL IMPACT OF THE VIETNAM WAR

The deteriorating international economic position of the United States and vociferous animosity toward defense spending were both in part a consequence of the Vietnam War. However, the decision for gradual withdrawal from Indochina and Vietnamization had in their turn two less obvious effects.

First, in order to placate the public and to demonstrate successful disengagement and Vietnamization, U.S. reports on Vietnam during the period of active participation by American forces tended to stress the progressive decrease in the role of U.S. ground forces in combat. Since Vietnamization was held up as an example of the Nixon Doctrine in practice, this had the effect of identifying the Nixon Doctrine with nonparticipation of U.S. ground forces in future conflicts as a matter of policy. Although no such rigid rule was in fact accepted in U.S. defense planning, this popular understanding became a source of confusion and uncertainty. For example, the allied incursion into Cambodia with U.S. participation might have been cited as an example of the flexible employment of U.S. ground forces. The official explanation in 1971, however, chose to stress its merit as a case of not doing the fighting with U.S. forces.[47]

Second, during the Nixon Administration's first term, U.S. force withdrawals from Asia became a consuming preoccupation in the United States. It became politically difficult to contemplate greater burden sharing or increasing financial contributions by America's Asian allies without large U.S. force reductions in areas other than Vietnam where such reductions would be undesirable for security and/or psychological reasons. What was possible in the case of NATO could not even be contemplated in the case of Asia; perhaps for this reason such an alternative received little attention. Given force reductions in Asia and the promise of not doing the same in Europe, at least for the time being, the impression of a downward assessment of America's interest in Asia was created. Thus, reaction to the Vietnam War further narrowed the range of choices available to U.S. defense planners.

NEW SOURCES OF RESTRAINT ON THE BURGEONING SOVIET POWER

The preceding discussion has dealt with the principal reasons why, from the U.S. point of view, additional restraints on Soviet policy had to be found, when the Nixon Administration was first elected, in order to supplement America's own effort to redress the worsening strategic balance. In particular, these new factors must possess the capability of offsetting the larger conventional forces of the Soviet Union without creating any serious net disadvantages to U.S. interests elsewhere. It so happens that two developments in Asia during the last decade seemed to satisfy these requirements, especially if they could be brought into the "strategic environment" in concert. They were, first, the spectacular economic growth of Japan, which made the Japanese economy a potential source of foreign assistance to help bolster economic development and security of countries in Asia, and, second, the escalation of the Sino-Soviet dispute, which made Communist China a potential candidate to balance Soviet power on land.

THE EMERGING POWER OF JAPAN

In contrast to the United States, as of 1969, Japan had already enjoyed a balance of payments surplus for a number of years. Its current account balance rose from under $1 billion in 1965 to $2.1 billion in 1969, $2 billion in 1970, and $5.9 billion in 1971.[48] This impressive record was achieved primarily as a result of the rapid expansion of Japan's exports, which rose from $825 million in 1950 to $4 billion in 1960, $8.3 billion in 1965, $15.7

billion in 1969, $19.0 billion in 1970, and $23.7 billion in 1971.[49] In 1971, Japan's surplus trade balance alone reached $7.9 billion and its official holding of gold and convertible foreign exchange stood at $15.4 billion on December 1, 1971.[50] The rate of growth of Japan's GNP in real terms averaged about 13 percent a year during 1966–70 and 11.5 percent in the entire decade of the 1960s.[51] Japan's GNP had become the third largest in the world, next only to that of the United States and the Soviet Union.

In 1954, when the former Japanese "National Safety Corps" became the "Self-Defense Forces," Japan's defense-related expenditures total ¥ 135 billion; the corresponding amount in 1970 was ¥ 569.5 billion, a little over four times as much. The increase in GNP during the same period was, however, nearly tenfold. As a result, the proportion of defense-related expenditures to GNP declined from 1.75 percent in 1954 to 0.79 percent in 1970.[52] Japan's defense-related expenditures remained below one percent of GNP during the entire decade of the 1960s. Furthermore, defense-related expenditures fell from 13.5 percent of the government budget, or "disbursements on general accounts," in 1954 to 7.2 percent in 1970. An international comparison of 1969 defense expenditures in percent of GNP, presented by the Japanese Defense Agency in October, 1970, placed Japan last, at 0.8 percent, behind even Switzerland, which had 2.2 percent.[53] Although Japan's phenomenal economic growth had been made possible partly because the country had not been forced to divert its resources to defense, there was little doubt that even a substantial rise in defense expenditures could be readily accommodated by the expanding Japanese economy in the 1970s. Japan's fourth five-year defense plan (1972–76) testifies to the country's recent willingness to do more for its own defense. Its Security Treaty with the United States provides, prima facie, a U.S. orientation in the gradual emergence of a role for Japan in safeguarding international security.

That Japan could play a significant role in maintaining international security had, of course, been in the minds of many Americans for quite some time before 1969. However, while most countries in Pacific-Asia with mutual security arrangements with the United States worried about U.S. readiness to provide them with either direct defense or defense assistance in the face of external threat and/or internal insurgency, the attitude of Japan was quite different until recently. Japan was preoccupied with (1) concern that activities of the U.S. military in Japan might infringe upon Japanese sovereignty and the country's peaceful pursuits, (2) the possibility that U.S. military efforts in Japan in conjunction with other U.S. defense commitments might involve Japan in some unwanted conflict, and (3) the particular apprehension that deployment of U.S. forces in and around Japan might bring nuclear weapons into Japanese territory. Secure in its knowledge that the United

States would defend the Japanese islands, Japan was most reluctant to become overtly and more actively involved even in its own defense or to assume the economic burden of a greater defense effort.

The erosion of Japanese psychological resistance to a greater defense role and effort took place with economic growth and the passage of time, and also as a result of American prodding. The Nixon-Sato Joint Communiqué of November, 1969, constituted a significant landmark in this almost imperceptible movement.

"The Prime Minister," according to the joint communiqué,[54] "appreciating the determination of the United States, stressed that it was important for the peace and security of the Far East that the United States should be in a position to carry out fully its obligations referred to by the President. He further stressed his recognition that, in the light of the present situation, the presence of United States forces in the Far East constituted a mainstay for the stability of the area." While this statement served to stress Japan's recognition of the role the United States played in maintaining security in the Pacific, it was immediately followed by a public announcement that U.S. defense efforts in areas adjacent to, albeit outside, Japan were also in Japan's interest. Thus, in the paragraph immediately following the preceding statement, we find the following passage: "The Prime Minister deeply appreciated the peacekeeping efforts of the United Nations in the area [i.e., the Korean Peninsula] and stated that the security of the Republic of Korea was essential to Japan's own security.... The President referred to the treaty obligations of his country to the Republic of China which the United States would uphold. The Prime Minister said that the maintenance of peace and security in the Taiwan areas was also a most important factor for the security of Japan." In connection with the Vietnam War, the communiqué noted that the President and the Prime Minister "agreed that, should peace in Vietnam not have been realized by the time reversion of Okinawa is scheduled to take place, the two governments would fully consult with each other in the light of the situation at that time so that reversion would be accomplished without affecting the United States' efforts to assure the South Vietnamese people the opportunity to determine their own political future without outside interference." Finally, in paragraph 7 of the joint communiqué, Mr. Sato was said to be "of the view that ... the return of the administrative rights over Okinawa ... should not hinder the effective discharge of the international obligations assumed by the United States for the defense of countries in the Far East including Japan." This diplomatic language marked a significant step forward in Japan's recognition of its own involvement in regional security, although all the implications of the statement may not have been fully appreciated at the time by both contracting parties.

The joint communiqué should be read with close reference to Prime

Minister Sato's address to the National Press Club of Washington, D.C.[55] "In particular," said Sato, "if an armed attack against the Republic of Korea were to occur, the security of Japan would be seriously affected. Therefore, should an occasion arise for United States forces in such an eventuality to use facilities and areas within Japan as bases for military combat operations to meet the armed attack, the policy of the Government of Japan towards prior consultation would be to decide its position positively and promptly on the basis of the foregoing recognition.

"The maintenance of peace in the Taiwan area is also a most important factor for our own security. I believe in this regard that the determination of the United States to uphold her treaty commitments to the Republic of China should be fully appreciated.

"However, should, unfortunately, a situation ever occur in which such treaty commitments would actually have to be invoked against an armed attack from the outside, it would be a threat to the peace and security of the Far East, including Japan.

"Therefore, in view of our national interest, we would deal with the situation on the basis of our foregoing recognition, in connection with the fulfillment by the United States of its defense obligations...."

These statements made it clear that Japan would not hinder U.S. defense efforts in the fulfillment of the latter's treaty obligations. Such cooperation, implemented through prior consultation, would seem to involve an implied, albeit not ironclad, promise to allow the free deployment of U.S. forces and weapons systems. However, it should also be noted that the active participation of Japan's own forces in such activities was not promised. Nor was there any clear indication of Japan's own role in defensive operations in such a contingency.[56]

In short, only a few months after Mr. Nixon's foreign policy statement at Guam and still in the first year of the Nixon Administration, Japan was willing to become a "partner" of the United States in maintaining security in the Far East. In return for the promised reversion of Okinawa, Mr. Sato publicly acknowledged Japan's national interest in the security of Korea and Taiwan, thus justifying, vis-à-vis his own electorate, his policy of involvement. It is not clear how much Japanese involvement was foreseen by the parties concerned. However, from the American point of view, a large economic role and a growing but essentially supporting role in international security could be reasonably expected of Japan. The economic role, one would assume, could become especially important in Southeast Asia while the supporting security role would be essentially passive and concentrated in the Korea-Taiwan area. It was, of course, understood that the Japanese Self-Defense Force would be able to expand within limits in an orderly manner so as to promote Japan's own security, which would, however, in the final analysis, continue to be safeguarded by the Mutual Security Treaty with the United States.

THE SINO-SOVIET DISPUTE AND A U.S. VIEW OF THE POTENTIAL ROLE OF PEKING IN THE PACIFIC BALANCE OF POWER

With 179,000 men in some thirteen divisions the Japanese Self-Defense Ground Forces cannot be regarded as a balancing factor vis-à-vis Soviet forces. The Japanese constitution, as well as government policy and popular sentiment, also imposes serious constraints on the effective use of such military power as Japan possesses.

In the circumstances, a most important parameter of America's new approach to international security was provided by the emergence of polycentrism in the Communist camp since World War II. In varying degrees, Albania, Yugoslavia, and Rumania have successfully asserted their resistance to total submission to the Soviet Union in Europe. In the Far East, Communist China has not concealed its dispute with the Soviet Union since the early 1960s.

An open breach between the two principal Communist powers came in 1963, and the increasing bitterness of their mutual accusations rose to a climax in 1969, when a series of border incidents resulted in active local hostilities from Sinkiang to Manchuria. Previously, beginning in the mid-1960s, the Soviet Union had begun a steady reinforcement of its forces on the Sino-Soviet border. This military movement was redoubled during the spring and summer of 1969, accompanied by rumors deliberately spread by the Soviet Union about the possibility of an impending Soviet attack on China. Peking had little choice but to regard these Soviet military moves and their rumored purpose seriously, particularly in the light of the Brezhnev Doctrine and the Soviet invasion of Czechoslovakia in 1968.

The Chinese Cultural Revoltuion, which convulsed mainland China between 1966 and 1969, was brought to a close at about the time of the Damanskiy (or Chenpao) incident. Several months later, following a meeting between Chou En-lai and Kosygin at the Peking airport, the two countries agreed to open border negotiations. This was followed by a sharp reversal of Peking's policy and attitudes toward the West. One after another, Chinese envoys in Western countries, who had been recalled during the Cultural Revolution, were returned to their posts. Selected American correspondents and others, including an American table tennis team, were invited to visit Communist China. Finally, after many preliminary contacts and a secret visit to Peking by Henry A. Kissinger, the President's Special Assistant for National Security Affairs, Mr. Nixon publicly announced on July 15, 1971, that he had accepted an invitation to visit Peking before May 1, 1972. This dramatic announcement was followed, in October, 1971, by the successful entry of Peking into the United Nations. The Nixon visit, which took place in February, 1972, ended the first phase of an American effort to cast Communist China in a new role.

The new U.S. policy toward China would not have been possible without a corresponding new Chinese policy toward the United States. Leaving the detailed discussion to the next chapter, suffice it to point out now that Peking apparently acted out of genuine fear of a Soviet military attack. Peking was, and still is, perhaps, even more anxious than the United States to find a counter to offset the Soviet threat, which appeared far more ominous and immediate in its case.

The shift in Peking's foreign policy since the fall of 1969 and its accelerated nuclear weapons program, accompanied by the steady modernization of its general-purpose forces and its call for all-out defense preparedness, must be interpreted as an integral policy aimed at deterring the Soviet Union. In the end, this Chinese policy may turn out to have been a transitory phenomenon. However, while it lasts, it will have two important consequences from a U.S. viewpoint.

First, unless the Soviet Union acts promptly to eliminate the growing Chinese nuclear capability through a preventive attack, it will find it increasingly difficult and costly to do so. The cost of such Soviet action will increase sharply with the deployment of more and more Chinese nuclear weapons. As discussed in the next chapter, by 1971 Communist China probably had in its possession a few missiles of IRBM range capable of reaching European Russia. In addition, there is the prospect that Peking could have a few ICBMs in operational status by the mid-1970s. Moreover, a number of MRBMs have already been deployed. If Peking can succeed in deterring the Soviet Union from using nuclear weapons in any future hostility between the two countries with a minimum nuclear force of its own, Communist China's large general-purpose forces will become a major factor in Soviet defense planning. This effect will continue as long as the two countries remain highly suspicious of each other.

Second, as long as Peking is uncertain about its ability to deter the Soviet Union because of the small size of its own nuclear deterrent force, it will feel the need for international political support, in particular that of the United States. Such support is more likely to be forthcoming if Peking does not engage in overt aggression. Consequently, the likelihood of Peking's embarking upon open aggression in Asia is quite small during this period of uncertainty.

These two factors serve to make Peking potentially useful as an offsetting force vis-à-vis the Soviet Union without itself becoming a major active threat to its neighbors, at least during the period of real Chinese weakness, whatever Peking's propaganda may proclaim. Besides, to the extent a Chinese threat to its neighbors may develop, Japan and other regional powers can be expected to build up their own defenses. Since it appears reasonable to suppose that the Chinese threat will be limited for a while, time will be available during which the defense capability of Japan and other Asian nations can be developed. The potential for development in the latter is quite large in view of the excellent economic progress scored by South Korea, Taiwan, and Thailand in recent years.

The preceding account probably describes correctly the reasons why the United States could, during the 1969–70, consider the PRC a useful restraining influence on the Soviet Union. There are several implicit assumptions why Communist China will play this assigned role. These are:

1. That the Sino-Soviet dispute and mistrust of each other will continue, even if there is a change of Chinese and/or Soviet leadership;

2. That the effectiveness of the central authority in Peking will not be seriously impaired as a result of regionalism or other forms of political instability, threats which have emerged as a result of the Cultural Revolution and internal disputes among Chinese Communist leaders;

3. That the Chinese nuclear weapons development will continue to make sufficient progress so that it will be pursued relentlessly, but that progress will not be so rapid that an adequate, minimal deterrent can be obtained too soon; and

4. That the Soviet Union will not attack China or otherwise succeed, e.g., through subversion or coup d'etat, in bringing Peking again into the Soviet orbit.

Another indispensable assumption is that Japan and the other Asian countries vitally affected by the new U.S. policy will see the future and their respective roles in the American way and, even if they do not, that they will not, unwittingly or by design, frustrate U.S. plans through their own action, or as a result of interaction with Soviet and/or Chinese policies.

A BALANCE OF POWER SCENARIO: VISION OR ILLUSION?

Given the fact that the Soviet Union has achieved strategic nuclear "parity" and may be aiming at superiority, the United States is faced with the need to maintain its own strategic nuclear position vis-à-vis the Soviet Union. Technological and other uncertainties make this effort indispensable, even if continuing SALT negotiations yield additional agreements. With declining defense budgets and increasing manpower costs it is unlikely that the United States can maintain its general-purpose forces at a level sufficient to offset those of the Soviet Union. Consequently, the maintenance of a stable military balance in Europe, especially in view of the European countries' desire for détente, requires that the Soviet lead in conventional forces be countered in another manner. The Sino-Soviet dispute and the development of Chinese nuclear capability, which may succeed in deterring a Soviet strike against China using nuclear weapons, make the large Chinese conventional forces ideally suited for this potential role, which China will be willing to play because it is equally anxious to use the United States as an offset to the Soviet Union. Japan, by vitue of its economic power and its slowly increasing military strength, could assume some of the functions the United States has performed in maintaining security in Pacific-Asia. It is also conceivable that Japan could simultaneously act as a safeguard against any undue expansion of Chinese power. Japanese cooperation with the United States can be maintained because of Japan's need for U.S. nuclear and conventional protection, even if U.S. forces are reduced. China, on the other hand, is unlikely to pose a serious threat to its Asian neighbors because of its essential weakness and need to avoid open violence. This set of conditions and assumptions constitute the kind of scenario in which U.S. force reductions can be safely made.

In essence, one can envisage:

1. A U.S.-Soviet strategic balance, the maintenance of which would be primarily a U.S. responsibility;

2. A conventional balance between the Soviet Union on the one hand and NATO and Communist China on the other;

3. A militarily more powerful Japan acting as a barrier to Chinese and Soviet expansion but allied with the United States and relying upon the latter for its strategic guarantee; and

4. A mélange of regional and sub-regional defense groupings in the rest of Pacific-Asia which constitute their own barrier to both Soviet and Chinese—possibly even Japanese—expansionism.

Only the policy-makers are in a position to know whether the U.S. consciously sought to bring about such a scenario through the Nixon Doctrine, or is still trying to do so. It appears, though, that this particular scenario would be consistent with the circumstances that gave rise to the Nixon Doctrine. The remaining chapters of this book will examine the feasibility of such a scenario, as well as other alternatives, together with their respective underlying assumptions and uncertainties. Visions must be separated from illusions if both peace and security are indeed to be maintained.

NOTES

1. Mr. Kissinger presumably thought in early 1973 that he could concentrate on redefining the "Atlantic relationship" in that year after having instituted the new Asian and China policy in 1971–72.
2. U.S.-Soviet discussions leading to the 1972 Interim Agreement and the ABM Treaty are known as SALT I in contradistinction to post-1972

discussions on SALT II. Answering some critics of SALT I, Secretary of State Kissinger stated at a press conference on April 26, 1974:

> And I think it is about time that we recognize the fact, first, that at the time the interim agreement was made, the United States had no program for land-based missiles. The United States had no program—was not building any sea-based missiles. The Soviet Union was building 90 land-based missiles a year and 144 sea-based missiles. The United States stopped no program as a result of the interim agreement. The Soviet Union stopped several programs, and on top of it had to remove 209 older missiles from its force.
>
> [Furthermore] it is not true that the interim agreement leaves the United States at a numerical disadvantage. This numerical disadvantage can be computed only if one omits from the calculation the 630 B-52s that were in our force in 1972, and the 452 B-52s that are in our force today. And the fact that there are 180 less in our force today is not a decision of the Soviet Union; it is a unilateral decision of our Administration, proposed by the Joint Chiefs of Staff.
>
> Thirdly, if one looks not at launchers, but at deliverable warheads, the gap between the United States and the Soviet Union has increased during the period of the interim agreement, and will continue to increase during the whole period of the interim agreement. And one is hit by warheads—not by launchers.
>
> Therefore, it is not helpful to us to talk ourselves into a state of mind in which we are strategically inferior.
>
> Therefore, whether or not the interim agreement should be extended depends on an analysis of where the interim agreement leads us and what the projections are. And it further depends on an analysis of what we get in return for it.
>
> The overwhelming issue, as we see it, is the issue of multiple independent warheads whose deployment on the Soviet side is imminent. Once these multiple warheads are fully deployed on both sides, and one has then warheads upward of 10,000 on both sides, or any number that technology can make possible, then we face a situation of unprecedented nuclear plenty and a potentially enormous gap between first- and second-strike capabilities.
>
> That is what we are attempting to reduce in these negotiations. (Here the reference is to SALT II.)

3. It should be noted, however, that this projection of what Soviet planners regard as probable and would tolerate could, of course, be quite erroneous. The risk of unwarranted "mirror-imaging" in such reasoning is quite high.
4. See the 1970 Annual Defense Department Report, p. 35. For details, see Table II.1.
5. International Institute for Strategic Studies (IISS), *The Military Balance, 1971—72*, London, p. 56.
6. According to the IISS, the Soviet Union had only 250 land-based ICBM launchers in mid-1966.
7. It does not, however, follow from this assumption, even if true, that the Soviet Union has no other motivation in entering into strategic arms control negotiations than the stabilization of the nuclear and overall

strategic balance. For an opinion, that the Soviet Union used SALT to stall possible U.S. build-up while increasing its lead before May, 1972, see Peter N. James, "A Systems Analysis of Détente," *Imprimia*, Vol. 3, No. 3, Hillsdale College, Hillsdale, Mich., March 1974.
8. Address by Secretary Melvin R. Laird at the Annual Luncheon of the Associated Press, New York, April 20, 1970. Also quoted in William R. Van Cleave, "Implications of Success or Failure of SALT," paper presented to the Fifth International Arms Control Conference in Philadelphia, October 1971.
9. See President Nixon's *U.S. Foreign Policy in the 1970's*, II, 1971.
10. See Table II.1 for details and sources. Note that comparable figures are also reported by the IISS. Also, according to William Beecher in the *New York Times* (October 11,1971), one estimate of the Soviet ICBM total had already exceeded 1600 by then.
11. See Table II.1 for details and sources.
12. See the Annual Defense Department Report for FY 1972, published in March, 1971, p. 47, and that for FY 1973, pp. 39–40.
13. In the FY 1971 Annual Defense Department Report (p. 105), published in 1970, the Soviet SLBM force was expected to reach 560–800 launchers by 1974–75. The FY 1973 report would point to a submarine construction rate approximating the higher end of the projected range by the mid-1970s.
14. FY 1973 Annual Defense Department Report, p. 59.
15. *Ibid.*, p. 40.
16. Since the 1972 agreement, the Soviet Union also has developed several new ICBM systems (i.e., the SS-X-16, -17, -18, and -19 in U.S. nomenclature) capable of MIRVing, including one that could herald a mobile land-based system. See Admiral Moorer, *op. cit.*, February 1974, p. 15. IOC is estimated to be 1975.
17. *U.S. Foreign Policy in the 1970's*, III, 1972, p. 158.
18. See the Annual Defense Department Report for FY 1973, p. 39.
19. See the *Washington Star*'s report on a study by Dr. Charles S. Sheldon II, Chief of the Science Policy Research Division, February 8, 1972.
20. For instance, in an interview with *U.S. News and World Report* (April 13, 1965), Defense Secretary McNamara was reported to have stated that there was no indication of any Soviet effort to build a strategic force as large as that of the United States.
21. For detailed comments on SALT, see the Stennis hearings, June 6–July 25, 1972, Committee on Armed Services, 92nd Congress.
22. *Military Balance, 1971–72*, p. 77.
23. Secretary Schlesinger's 1974 report, *op. cit.*, pp. 87–88.
24. Associated Press report from the NATO Defense Ministers' meeting at Brussels, June 6, 1973.
25. *Military Balance, 1969–70*, p. 58 and *1971–72*, p. 60.
26. Compiled from *Military Balance, 1972–1973*.

27. IISS, *Strategic Survey, 1972,* 1973, p. 70. See, however, *Military Balance, 1973—74,* p. 76, where an increase was shown for 1968—72 in terms of 1972 dollars, if NATO rather than national definitions of defense spending are used. Furthermore, it appears that the consumer price index may have been used in calculating constant prices.
28. See the Annual Defense Department Report for FY 1973, p. 109.
29. *U.S. Foreign Policy for the 1970's,* III, 1972, p. 45.
30. United Press International report from Washington, November 14, 1970. Cf. also *New York Times,* May 5, 1972.
31. *Eastern Sun,* Singapore, January 16, 1971.
32. *Ibid.*
33. *Straits Times,* Singapore, May 7, 1971.
34. Admiral Moorer, *op. cit.,* February 1974, p. 49.
35. Cf. *Times* (London), June 27, 1969. See Chapter V.
36. 1970—1971, London, p. 82.
37. See Chapter I.
38. All years referred to are fiscal years. For details see Table II.5.
39. Annual Defense Department Report for FY 1973, February 1972, p. 199. An increase of $1.1 billion was reportedly expected in FY 1973, due to the stepped-up air activities in Vietnam as a result of the North's offensive in 1972. Cf. *The Economics of Defense Spending,* 1972.
40. *National Security Strategy of Realistic Deterrence,* February 1972, pp. 185, 197, and 203.
41. Secretary Schlesinger's *Report to the Congress on the FY 1975 Defense Budget and FY 1973—1974 Defense Program,* March 1974, Table 3, p. 237.
42. *Ibid.,* pp. 197 and 199; *Annual Defense Dept. Report, FY 1974,* March 1973, p. 123. "Manpower cost" as used here includes payroll, other military personnel costs, retired pay, and family housing.
43. *Ibid.,* p. 199.
44. An interesting example of this phenomenon may be found in the following statement of Senator J. William Fulbright: "In a decade's perspective—and without the blinders of the Truman Doctrine—" wrote the Chairman of the Senate Foreign Relations Committee in the *New Yorker* of January 8, 1972, "it even seems possible that the Cuban missile crisis was not so enormous a crisis as it then seemed." Again, speaking of America's national purpose, the Senator noted, "Perhaps our national tendency to extoll competition rather than cooperation as a social virtue and our preoccupation with our own primacy—with being the 'biggest,' the 'greatest' nation—suggest ... that unless we are 'No. 1' we will be nothing; worthless and despised, and deservedly so." An important question is: Would Americans who do not care about being "No. 1" still feel the same way, once they are no longer "No. 1" and have had a full taste of their new status, as they do now when America still is "No. 1"? A second question follows: Would it be possible to regain the status of being "No. 1" once it is lost, and, if so, at what cost?

45. Department of Commerce, Office of Business Economics, quoted in the *Statistical Abstract 1970*, Government Printing Office, Washington, D.C., 1970, pp. 769–72.
46. All the figures referred to below are taken from the *Economic Report of the President, January 1972*, Washington, D.C., 1971, Table B-87, p. 297, and the same report in January, 1973, Table C-87, p. 294, and February, 1974, Table C-88, p. 351.
47. Annual Defense Department Report for FY 1973, February 1972, p. 117, quoting President Nixon on November 12, 1971.
48. Bank of Japan, *Balance of Payments Monthly*, No. 42, January 1970, and No. 66, January 1972, pp. 1–2, Table 1. See also Herman Kahn, *The Emerging Japanese Super State*, p. 209, and *Monthly Statistics of Japan*, Bureau of Statistics, Office of the Prime Minister, No. 124, Tokyo, October 1971, p. 77.
49. Warren Hunsberger, "The Japanese Economy: A Continuing Miracle?" *Interplay*, December 1969–January 1970, p. 18.
50. International Monetary Fund, *International Financial Statistics*, supplement 1971 and March 1972. See also note 48.
51. Estimated by the Japanese Economic Research Center and quoted by Herman Kahn, *op. cit.*, p. 209. See also *Monthly Statistics of Japan*, No. 124, October 1971, p. 121, and *Annual Report on National Income Statistics*.
52. Japan Defense Agency, *Japan's Defense*, Tokyo, October 1970, Chart 12.
53. *Ibid.*, p. 45. The original data are taken from the International Institute of Strategic Studies, *The Military Balance, 1970–1971*, but apparently accepted by Japan without demurral.
54. *United States Security Agreements and Commitments Abroad, Japan and Okinawa*, Hearings before the Subcommittee on United States Security Agreements and Commitments Abroad of the Committee on Foreign Relations, United States Senate, Ninety-first Congress, Second Session, Part 5, January 26, 27, 28, and 29, 1970, pp. 1426–27.
55. *Ibid.*, pp. 1428–30.
56. Cf. John K. Emmerson, *Arms, Yen and Power, the Japanese Dilemma*, New York, Dunnellen Co., 1972.

Chapter III

Negotiation with an Adversary

ARGUMENTS FOR THE WASHINGTON-PEKING RAPPROCHEMENT AS SEEN FROM THE AMERICAN SIDE

One component idea of the Nixon Doctrine is negotiation with adversaries. The application of this idea to Pacific-Asia entails negotiation with Communist China. As we have suggested in the preceding chapter, given (1) the geographical position of the PRC, (2) the absolute and relative size of its population in comparison with that of the Soviet Union, (3) the continuing development of its nuclear force, (4) the potential of its conventional armed forces, and (5) its bitter ideological and political dispute under Mao Tse-tung with the Kremlin, Communist China is a natural counterweight against the Soviet Union in any new power balance. One might even argue that in terms of its ramifications the planned rapprochement with Peking may have been the single most important foreign policy move of the Nixon Administration in its first term.

It is common to be able to adduce more than one advantage to a major policy; the new China policy of Washington is no exception. Also, since certain proponents of a policy may desire one or more specific advantages, it is possible for them to look upon some of the advantages as supplying all or most of the necessary motivation. The partisan supporter of the policy is likely to point to those advantages that seem to him to be more important and more probable, have wider appeal, and entail the least cost. The critic will attach less weight to these advantages, while giving greater weight to the costs. A political opponent of the policy-maker will stress those advantages that appear least "worthy" because they benefit the policy-maker in some immediate manner. The objective analyst has to thread through a labyrinth of opinion in order to arrive at a balanced view. He must, at a minimum, examine all the advantages and disadvantages carefully as well as look beyond the policy in the abstract into its all-important practical implementation.

The balance-of-power scenario postulated for Pacific-Asia at the end of the last chapter is predicated on an assumption that the leadership in Peking will be disposed to let Communist China play its role in the world balance of power in a manner agreeable to the United States. In order to test this assumption, an appropriate channel of communication must, therefore, be established between Washington and Peking. Since the prominent Chinese Communist leaders are elderly, and since Westerners have little knowledge about the potential leaders who may soon ascend to power, *other conditions being equal,* it would be advantageous to the United States to establish this contact before too long. This "new generation of leadership argument" is strengthened when it is considered that the United States may wish to influence these new leaders by exposing them to ideas from which they have been shielded by years of isolation. (Whether or not this objective is realistic is a different matter.) To sum up, in order to be able to identify, know, or influence the future generation of Chinese Communist leaders, one must first establish contact with Peking. Rapprochement with Peking was to establish a necessary condition. One must hasten to add, however, that contact is not the only requirement to attain the postulated advantages. Other conditions will have to be satisfied and other steps taken by both sides.

A second set of arguments related to the balance-of-power scenario can be advanced in favor of (1) establishing contact with, and, better still, an American presence in, Peking and (2) rapprochement with Peking. That is, if there is some risk of a preemptive Soviet attack on Communist China, and if the survival of the PRC as a national unit is a sine qua non of the new world balance of power—because the United States needs an additional restraint on Soviet policy and because no other short-term alternatives are believed to exist—then rapprochement between Washington and Peking may reduce this risk. If we assume that both the threat of war and the deterrent effect of a new American attitude toward Peking are real, the urgency of the need for rapprochement will vary directly with the immediacy of the Soviet threat to

Peking. Several points should be noted at this juncture. First, this is not an argument that has been frequently and openly advanced.[1] On the other hand, it is a perfectly logical argument given its premises. Second, rapprochement with Peking will not necessarily lead to the kind of contact or American presence which would deter the hypothetical Soviet attack on Communist China. Here again we are confronted with the distinction between the necessary and the sufficient conditions of an event. Finally, depending upon the reaction of the Soviet Union, it might also be argued that a Washington-Peking rapprochement, if viewed by Moscow as a prelude to an entente, could actually increase the risk of a Soviet attack on mainland China when the probability of success is greater.

Needless to say, the preceding "deterrence of Soviet attack" argument can be readily translated into a "deterrence of war" argument. In this version, it would gain the added advantage that all antiwar policies enjoyed as long as the United States was still involved in the Vietnam War. Both genuine humanitarian reasons and practical political considerations, not the least of which was the policy's public appeal, came into play in the 1972 election year in the United States.

A third set of arguments in favor of rapprochement with the PRC may be called the "bargaining advantage" argument. As the price of its new policy toward Peking, the United States might ask for Communist Chinese concessions which would, for instance, facilitate the satisfactory conclusion of the war in Vietnam, reduce tension in the Taiwan Strait, enable the United States to attain the goals of the Nixon Doctrine faster, etc. Even if none of these concessions can be obtained, active negotiation with Communist China can be used to strengthen the bargaining position of the United States with the Soviet Union. This argument, of course, derives from advantages envisaged in the balance-of-power scenario of the last chapter. If the U.S.S.R. is forced to coexist with Communist China because of the U.S.-Peking rapprochement, Soviet apprehension about closer U.S.-PRC relations might have the desired restraining effect on Soviet policy toward the United States elsewhere. The argument, however, again presupposes the presence of other conditions, including the adoption of appropriate tactics by the United States in actual negotiation and, insofar as the Soviet Union is concerned, the latter's estimate of U.S. "toughness" and of Chinese capability and intentions.

We turn next to the "sentimental argument," which is often publicly advanced in conjunction with one or more of the preceding arguments couched in *Realpolitik* terms. In essence, the proponents of this argument would like the United States to reverse its previous policy toward the Chinese Communists because, in their view, that policy was wrong. A special variant of this argument is that, until July, 1971, the United States had willfully alienated itself from the Chinese Communists whose hostility was nothing more than a natural reaction to American bullheadedness and their perceived American threat. Without going into a discussion of Chinese foreign policy at this point, the argument, even if valid, fails to supply reasons why the United States should desire Peking's friendship. If we omit the explanations of why U.S. policy was wrong, which are really restatements of the previous arguments, the remainder usually boils down to value judgments about the Chinese generally, or about the Chinese Communists, or about the Chinese Nationalists, leading to a conclusion that the United States should support the Chinese Communists, who are allegedly good or progressive or efficient. The alleged facts are normally debatable, and arguments of this nature are not susceptible to objective analysis. They are like affirmations of faith that must be accepted or rejected without logical considerations. They are mentioned here because they are popular and are often advanced in association with arguments based on power politics, apparently to dress up such "crude" arguments with sentimental appeal. In the context of this discussion, they have the same level of relevance as statements often heard a generation ago about how Italian trains ran on time under Mussolini, or how well disciplined the Germans were under the Nazis. That the Chinese Communists can turn the citizens of Peking out of their homes on a winter morning to shovel snow on public streets or that Chou En-lai seems to be "a good man to do business with"[2] have no bearing on American national interests. However, such points can be and have been used to influence American opinion, which makes them important.

Finally, there is the political argument in favor of Washington's rapprochement with Peking, that the policy has popular support. During 1971, the announcement of the new China policy reinforced the image of American policy conveyed by U.S. force withdrawals from Vietnam and reduced heavy domestic pressures at the time to set a "date certain" for ending the U.S. military presence in Vietnam. Rapprochement with Peking provided another safety valve for pent-up political pressures at home and allowed the Administration more room for maneuver, both at home and abroad. This is a political advantage extending beyond any partisan gains possibly expected—and probably realized—in the 1972 presidential election. Its effect continued to be felt during the Nixon Administration's second term when political criticism of Mr. Nixon was usually tempered by approval of his China policy.

It is not possible to determine from U.S. official statements which of the arguments enumerated above was of primary importance in determining the new China policy. Analysis in the preceding chapter suggests that national-interest arguments were reinforced by political considerations, and that political arguments may have played a role in influencing the timing rather than the substance of many policy announcements. However, even in the case of timing, as we have already pointed out, there was good reason to begin negotiation with the PRC before reaching a definite decision on SALT. A determination of Soviet intentions in regard to the U.S.-Soviet strategic balance had to be made before too long. The pace of continued Soviet advances had the effect of setting deadlines for certain U.S. actions. Hence a U.S.-PRC rapprochement should precede the critical stage of negotiations with Moscow.

Commenting on his 1972 visit to Peking, then still in the planning stage, on August 4, 1971, President Nixon remarked, "What it really is, is moving— as we have moved, I believe, in the situation with regard to the Soviet Union—from an era of confrontation without communication to an era of negotiations with discussion."[3] More specifically, he noted, "there cannot be world peace on which all the peoples in the world can rely ... unless there is communication between and some negotiation between these two great *superpowers* [italics added], the People's Republic of China and the United States."

RAPPROCHEMENT WITH THE UNITED STATES AS SEEN FROM PEKING—THE SOVIET THREAT

Mr. Nixon's 1972 foreign policy report lists some of the feelers extended by the United States to Peking during 1969–71 prior to the first Kissinger visit to Communist China in July, 1971. These feelers would not have been reciprocated and, even if reciprocated, would not have led to such a radical change in Chinese policy toward the United States, culminating in the Nixon-Chou talks in February, 1972, if the PRC authorities had not had their own compelling reasons to make the shift. The reasons must have been compelling. Not only was a response to the overtures of the world's leading capitalist nation and long-time number one enemy a radical break with the past, but there were serious risks. U.S. forces were still aiding South Vietnam, and the U.S. Air Force was still actively engaged against North Vietnamese forces. By "consorting with the enemy," Communist China risked its revolutionary purity and its claim to the mantle of leadership of world revolution. Another serious risk was the possibility of provoking greater Soviet hostility. Moreover, there were, and may still be, domestic critics to convince and active opposition to overcome. There is evidence that those who favored Peking's new American policy may have underestimated the opposition initially, but as noted, the arguments for the new policy were compelling enough to carry the day. The single most important factor appears to have been Peking's perception of a serious and imminent Soviet threat to the security of the regime.

Reference was made in Chapter II to the buildup of Soviet forces on the Chinese border during the years of Mao Tse-tung's Cultural Revoltuion. The spring and summer of 1969 witnessed a series of Soviet military and political moves, including an acceleration of reinforcements on the Chinese border and broad hints that the Soviet Union might be seriously contemplating military action against Peking.[4] Since a number of border incidents earlier in 1969 had provided Peking with a sample of Soviet wrath, and also since the memory of Hungary in 1956 and Czechoslovakia in 1968 was probably still fresh, prudence alone justified a policy shift. A series of events took place during 1969, following the border incidents and the conclusion of the Ninth National Congress of the Chinese Communist Party, which elected a new Central Committee and Politburo and designated Lin Piao, then Defense Minister, as heir apparent to Mao Tse-tung. Among these events were the opening of border talks with Moscow, the return of Peking's envoys to their posts in Western countries from which they had been recalled during the Cultural Revolution, and an apparent intensification of the Chinese nuclear weapons program, together with official calls for all-out defense preparations. It is plausible to infer that these Chinese activities were causally related to the Soviet activities noted above.

Peking's response to the Soviet threat, at that point in time, seems to have consisted of several elements. First, once a serious, imminent Soviet threat was perceived, a minimal Chinese nuclear deterrent force had to be developed as soon as possible in order to discourage potential Soviet first use of nuclear weapons in case of hostilities. This was to be accompanied by the continued and accelerated modernization of Peking's conventional forces. Secondly, political deterrence was to be strengthened by expanding the PRC's contact with the rest of the world, especially the West, in order to make it harder for the Soviet Union to initiate any attack. In particular, if contact would be established with the United States, and if, thereby, the Soviet Union could be made to believe that the United States might even lend active support to Peking if the latter were attacked, regardless of the real U.S. attitude, the deterrent effect would be strengthened. At the same time, Moscow was to be warned against precipitate action because the promised Chinese response would be decisive and all-out. Soviet military action would be costly and run the risk of failure. Furthermore, by agreeing to border talks and more normal diplomatic relations, Peking apparently hoped to convince the Russians that there was no need for Soviet military action. While these diplomatic moves were being made, Peking also tried to put its own house in order through restructuring the Communist Party in the provinces and adoption of more pragmatic economic measures.

Did Peking decide in 1969 that its new foreign policy was eventually to include rapprochement with Washington of the kind and degree agreed to in the Nixon-Chou Joint Communiqué of February, 1972, and heralded by the Chou En-lai-Kissinger meeting of mid-1971? One can only speculate on the nature of Chinese deliberations. A priori, however, one would assume that the decision was not made until some time later. The evidence points to the same conclusion. Although the ambassadorial meetings between the two countries were resumed in January, 1970, they were again suspended during the incursion of American and South Vietnamese forces into Cambodia. Besides, additional U.S. signals of American willingness to improve relations were yet to come. Peking's policy shift, like that of the United States, had to take a little time.

Yet Peking did not permit too much time to be lost. In about a year, Peking overcame the sensitivity it exhibited during the Cambodian incursion. The invitation to Mr. Nixon was extended at a time when U.S. air activities in Vietnam were still continuing. The Peking talks of February, 1972, were held under similar conditions. While U.S. gestures during 1970 and 1971 may have assured Peking of promising results, one must not overlook the effect of Peking's perception of the continued Soviet threat. Peking probably came to the conclusion during 1971 that the country was entering a most dangerous period in its relations with the Soviet Union and that the appearance of better understanding with the United States had to be created for the benefit of the Soviet Union.

According to a September, 1970, report in the *International Defense Digest,* Soviet forces on the Sino-Soviet border had been built up, at some unspecified time before September, 1970, to a strength of 35 combat-ready divisions. In addition, there were said to be another 25 divisions in reserve. The Soviet Union also had hundreds of tactical nuclear weapons on the same front, together with a vastly expanded air force. The entire Soviet force was said to exceed what would be required for pure defense, but the buildup apparently continued. A noted U.S. columnist reported in mid-1971 that Soviet strength on the border had risen to 45 divisions at the beginning of the year.[5] Including support troops, the numerical strength was an estimated 800,000 men. In a subsequent report by the same correspondent, the number of Soviet troops was given as 49 divisions in the summer of 1971, plus another 75,000 border guards. The 800,000 Soviet troops on the border were said to be probably intended to serve as a blocking force against Chinese counterattacks if a Soviet "surgical strike" were to take place first.[6] Writing in the *New York Times* on February 2, 1972, James Reston spoke of a million Soviet troops on China's northern frontier. The exact number of Soviet divisions reported in different sources depends partly upon the degree of inclusiveness, e.g., whether Soviet divisions stationed in Mongolia are also counted. However, a continuing Soviet buildup through 1970–71 seems well established.

Statements by Communist China's official spokesmen substantiating a definite perception of Soviet threat can be readily documented. For example, the PRC's Vice Foreign Minister and chief delegate to the United Nations,

Ch'iao Kuan-hua, said in November 1971:[7] "To the north of China, large numbers of Soviet forces, including rocket forces, are stationed in the People's Republic of Mongolia; to the east of China, the United States is maintaining a large number of military bases and nuclear bases in Japan proper and Okinawa." On this occasion, Ch'iao Kuan-hua was accusing the Soviet Union of "singing a duet with U.S. imperialism." Earlier, Chou En-lai was more direct and made no attempt to couple the Soviet threat with a similar perception of U.S. threat. While talking to Reston in Peking, Chou said: "We Chinese are not afraid of atomic bombs. We are prepared against their [Russian] attack, against their preemptive attack on us. That is why we are digging underground tunnels.... The great majority of our big and medium cities now have a net work of underground tunnels."[8]

The Chinese Communists apparently have made substantial progress in their nuclear weapons program, especially since 1969. Without going into their early history, suffice it to point out that the speed of development of these Chinese weapons has been notable from the very beginning and that the program, though possibly slowed during the Cultural Revolution, was not entirely interrupted by it. With the end of the Cultural Revolution and the call for all-out war preparations, two nuclear tests were staged in September, 1969, including one underground. Additional tests were held in 1970, 1971, and 1972. Two successful satellite launches—one in April, 1970, and another in May, 1971—testified to the development of rockets more powerful than those Peking had before 1969. At least one missile test in a flight of 2,200 miles from Manchuria to the Taklamakan Desert, took place in 1970. There is speculation that the test was at reduced range.[9] In short, Peking seems to have given priority to the development of (1) IRBMs that can strike against the European section of the Soviet Union and (2) tactical nuclear weapons that can also be used in defense, including defense against ground attack. The development of pure ICBMs, necessary for any strike against the United States, may have been given lower priority in the time schedule in favor of the more rapid deployment of a minimum, but credible, deterrent force against the Soviet Union. However, one U.S. report speculates that a 3,000 nautical-mile missile might be deployed in limited numbers in 1974, thus putting Alaska as well as all U.S.S.R. within range.[10] In his 1974 report, Admiral Moorer spoke of Chinese deployment of MRBMs and IRBMs, the possible deployment of a limited ICBM in 1974, and a full-range ICBM with possible IOC in 1976 or 1977.[11]

The key to Communist China's military, as against political, deterrence policy is the speed of deployment of nuclear weapons that can strike European Soviet targets and can survive an initial Soviet strike. According to the *New York Times* in February, 1972,[12] the month of Mr. Nixon's visit to Peking, "a handful" of improved IRBMs may have been deployed at that time. These improved missiles are said to use storable liquid propellents and can, therefore, be installed in hardened underground silos. The same report by William Beecher also mentioned—as did the International Institute for Strategic Studies—the deployment over the past several years of some 20 MRBMs which are, however, not particularly dependable or survivable. An earlier report in the American press gave the same estimate for deployed MRBMs, together with a stockpile estimate of 100 to 150 nuclear bombs and other warheads.[13] A *New York Times* report on March 4, 1973, indicates that there was apparently some evidence that could mean a potentially sizable Chinese construction program for missile deployment in silos. A comparable estimate of the warhead stockpile (100 to 200) was given earlier by Istvan Kormendy in a Hungarian source.[14] The Chinese Communists were said, during 1971, to have 25—or about 30 according to the IISS—TU 16s, which they can now produce themselves. Some 60 to 80 new "F9s," a 1,400-mile per hour fighter-bomber, are said to be operational by various sources.[15]

How soon will the Soviet Union feel deterred from using nuclear weapons against Communist China in a preemptive attack? How soon will Peking feel sufficiently confident that it has effectively deterred the Soviet Union from making a preemptive attack? Obviously, the answers to these questions will depend respectively upon Soviet and Chinese perceptions of (1) the number and relative importance of Soviet targets which can be reached by surviving Chinese missiles and other nuclear warhead delivery vehicles after a Soviet preemptive attack and (2) the degree of damage the Soviet Union is prepared to accept from Chinese retaliation. These factors are, in turn, functions of the Chinese deployment rate, the range and other technical characteristics of Chinese weapons, the corresponding characteristics of Soviet offensive and defensive weapons, etc. It is important to realize that both Soviet and Chinese estimates of each other's capabilities and readiness to accept damage are involved. It is entirely conceivable for the Soviet Union to accept a standoff at some point without Peking's realizing this Soviet state of mind. It is equally conceivable that Peking may at some other point in time believe that it has deterred the Soviet Union when, in fact, it has not. However, given the small number of Chinese IRBMs and of the less dependable MRBMs deployed so far, the Soviet Union probably has not yet concluded that mounting a preemptive attack involving first use of nuclear weapons would involve wholly unacceptable risks.[16] One can state even more positively that the Chinese Communists cannot believe that they have already succeeded in deterring the Soviet Union from a possible preemptive attack. These two conditions will doubtless continue in effect for some time, but not indefinitely.

Speaking to Reston on the need to combat the alleged revival of Japanese militarism, Chou En-lai said, "When you oppose a danger, you should oppose it when it is only budding."[17] Surely Chou must be aware that the same reasoning could be applied to the China problem by the Soviet Union. An article in *Red Star,* reported by Tass on February 25, 1972, accused Peking of deliberately fostering militarism in order to maintain the Mao group in power and to pursue great-power, hegemonistic plans abroad. Other Soviet accusations regarding Chinese crimes against the international Communist movement and unity of the socialist system have been reported from time to time. As the Soviet Union approaches a point beyond which the option of military attack must be abandoned, the urge to attack may increase. If Peking is aware of this situation, the degree of uncertainty it feels is bound to rise. This may prompt Peking to turn more decisively toward the West, especially the United States, and to be prepared to offer concessions for a rapprochement. This consideration may in fact explain why Peking seemed so anxious to establish a Liaison Office in Washington following a Kissinger visit to the PRC in February, 1973, in spite of the continued presence of the ROC embassy in Washington and the repeated U.S. profession of its defense commitment to Taiwan.

INTERNAL DISUNITY IN THE PRC AND NEED FOR CONSOLIDATION OF POWER AT HOME

From the Soviet point of view, the preferred objective is to bring about a reorientation of the ideological attitude and policy of Peking; it is not to subdue China by force. Any use of force, therefore, would be a last resort when other options are clearly no longer effective and only if it is deemed vital to the Soviet interest that a potentially hostile and nuclear-armed China which is also strong in conventional weaponry must not be permitted to exist. One of these options is political subversion. While information on this topic is extremely scarce, one gets the impression from spotty evidence that there were in the past a number of instances of Soviet attempts to interfere directly with the leadership of the Chinese Communist Party. Kao Kang of Manchuria in the early 1950s and Peng Teh-huai in 1958 were among outstanding examples. It is plausible to assume that the Soviet Union might pursue the same approach once it has satisfied itself that Peking has chosen a nuclear-weapons development program and a foreign policy which could eventually threaten the Soviet Union, both as the leader of the Communist movement and perhaps even as a nation-state. If this line of reasoning is correct, the need to effect a change in the leadership in Peking must have become an urgent concern for the Soviet Union following the announcement, in July, 1971, of Chou En-lai's invitation to Mr. Nixon.

One can of course do little more than speculate on what actually happened in the period immediately following the announcement. Several known events, however, are well established.[18] First, during the night of September

12-13, 1971, a Chinese plane in an unauthorized flight crashed within the Kentei Aimak Administrative Region in Mongolia, east of Ulan Bator and near the Soviet border. The plane reportedly carried nine persons to death, including one woman.[19] This event was followed by the cancellation of the customary National Day celebration on October 1, at which the Communist hierarchy normally presents itself to the general public. In addition, Lin Piao, the Defense Minister and designated heir apparent to Mao, was not seen after that date. Subsequently, he was denounced as a schemer and an opportunist who had sold out to alien interests. A year later, Lin's death was finally announced officially. With Lin, Huang Yung-sheng, Wu Fa-hsien, Li Tso-peng, and Chiu Hui-tso, respectively Chief of Staff of the PLA and Chiefs of the Air Force, Navy, and Logistics, also disappeared from the scene; they were apparently purged. Finally, the Chinese Communist Air Force was grounded for a prolonged period after the plane incident.

These events are open to different interpretations. All have in common the suggestion that there was an effort by Mao to purge Lin, together with either an unsuccessful coup d'etat against Mao (and Chou) that was discovered before it took place. Peking's official explanation in August, 1972, first issued through its embassy in Algiers, had Lin as the instigator of an assassination attempt against Mao. A document[20] issued by the Central Committee of the Chinese Communist Party trying to explain Lin's fall from power presented an account of a widespread plot, apparently centered in the military, to overthrow Mao. Regardless of whether Lin Piao and his immediate military subordinates were personally involved in the plot against Mao or whether they were removed in a plain power struggle, with Chou En-lai and Chiang Ch'ing, Mao's wife and leader of the "radicals," on the opposite side, disunity obviously existed at the very pinnacle of the Communist dictatorship. Since all these men had been with the Communist Party for many years, following Mao Tse-tung through thick and thin, one can infer further that, if they had become irrevocably opposed to Mao Tse-tung's policy as enunciated through Chou En-lai, the difference between the two sides went to the very foundation of national policy. Since the highest military leaders were victims of the internal purge, there probably was a radical and unbridgeable difference of opinion concerning Communist China's national security, perhaps its very survival, in addition to the power struggle itself. Perhaps the military men were more than a little disturbed by Chou En-lai's invitation to President Nixon and the implications of this policy shift for fear that this very act, while designed to deter the Soviet Union, might actually provoke a Soviet preemptive attack.

In time, the historian may be able to tell us exactly what happened in Peking during this eventful period. For our present purpose, it is sufficient to know that there was strong evidence of internal weakness and disunity, involving the PLA,[21] that basic elements of instability have remained, and that the Soviet Union was more likely than not seriously involved in some of the anti-Mao plots. Finally, the Soviet Union probably will not be easily dissuaded from renewing its effort to change the Chinese Communist leadership.

An examination of the list of persons elected to the Politburo in 1969 yields some very interesting information. Of the twenty-one full and alternate members, Lin, Huang, Wu, Li—the four military members possibly involved in the September, 1971, incident—together with Yeh Chün, wife of Lin Piao, were purged in September, 1971. Somewhat earlier, Ch'en Po-ta, Mao's secretary for many years and radical leader during the Cultural Revolution, had been purged, reportedly through the joint efforts of the military and the group led by Chou En-lai. Age, death, or ill health accounted for the disappearance or inactivity of several others, including Hsieh Fu-chih, Chu Teh, Liu Po-ch'eng, Tung Pi-wu, and K'ang Sheng. This process of elimination leaves us with Mao Tse-tung and Chou En-lai alone as members of the Politburo Standing Committee. Including Mao and Chou, there were at most eight active full members of the original twenty-one in the Politburo of the Ninth Congress. Counting the four alternate members, not more than twelve had survived from among the original twenty-five since their election in 1969. No announcement was made on filling vacancies prior to August, 1973, two years after Mr. Kissinger's first visit to Peking, when the Tenth Party Congress was convened. In addition, the surviving members of the Politburo of the Ninth Congress belonged to different factions. The political mortality rate of the membership, the complexion of the survivors, and the large number of outstanding vacancies suggested strongly that the leaders in Peking did not have, in 1971, enough high-level personnel, especially among the military, in whom they could have full confidence to fill a roster of prominent leaders. At the risk of being unduly speculative, one might even conclude that having committed themselves to the new policy toward the United States, Chou En-lai and his colleagues, if not even Mao Tse-tung himself, needed in 1971–72 the *appearance* of U.S. support in order to consolidate their own hold within the country. The visit by the American President became even more important to the Chinese Communist leaders clinging to power in October, 1971, than in July. The timing of Mr. Kissinger's second visit, which coincided with the ousting of Nationalist China from the United Nations, if requested by Peking, can be partly explained by this Chinese need and by Kissinger's need for a personal assessment of the Lin Piao affair, although it probably redounded to the net benefit of Peking at the expense of Taiwan.

The continuation of internal instability and the precarious balance of viewpoints and interests in anticipation of Mao's ultimate departure continued on the Chinese mainland after 1972 and through the period covered by this study. The Tenth Party Congress which, in August, 1973, elected a nine-member standing committee of a twenty-one-member Politburo, included as the five vice-chairmen of the standing committee a delicate balance of old party and bureaucratic elements represented by Chou En-lai, radical elements represented by Wang Hung-wen, members of the purged military, and the secret police. The two published principal documents adopted by the Congress continued to betray ambivalence characteristic of an unsettled ideological debate. But the transitory accommodation with the United States was not changed in 1973-74.[22]

PEKING'S DOCTRINE OF "REVOLUTIONARY DIPLOMACY"

For the Chinese Communists, it is not sufficient to explain Peking's new America policy in terms of the imminent Soviet threat. Politically, Mao Tse-tung cannot convince his opponents or the Chinese military that he has been forced to alter his policy because of the Soviet threat which his past policy helped bring about. Rather, the present leaders in Peking have to describe the new policy toward the United States as a tactical move based on established doctrine.

When the PRC delegation left Peking for the United Nations in November, 1971, the Chinese military band at the official send-off played under a banner bearing the words: "Long live Chairman Mao's great victory in revolutionary diplomacy!"[23] The contents of Mao's "revolutionary diplomacy" were described in considerable detail in an article in the official organ, the *Red Flag*.[24] In the first place, the article pointed out, present policy is derived from the "United Front" policy of the 1940s, when the Chinese Communists joined the KMT (Kuomintang or Nationalist Party) in an "Anti-Japanese United Front." The erstwhile "United Front" policy was based on three elements: (1) "Developing the people's forces"; (2) "Winning over all the middle forces"; and (3) "Isolating the diehard forces."

Several necessary conditions for "winning over all the middle forces" were present in the 1940s, according to this analysis. These are: (1) "That we have ample strength"; (2) "That we respect their interests"; and (3) "That we are resolute in our struggle against the diehards and steadily win victories."

Again referring to the 1940s, the *Red Flag* authors propounded: "We deal with imperialism in the same way. The Communist Party opposes all imperialism, but we make a distinction between Japanese imperialism, which is now committing aggression against China, and imperialist powers which are not doing so now" and "between the imperialist powers which adopted different policies in different conditions and different periods of time." In order to transpose this discussion to the present time, we only have to read for "Japanese imperialism," "Soviet social imperialism," and for "the imperialist powers not committing aggression against China," "the United States." Mao's theory in the 1940s made a clear distinction between "primary" and "secondary" enemies and between "temporary" and "indirect" allies. Reasoning by analogy is a typical Maoist practice encouraged by Chinese linguistic usage.

These distinctions between different types of enemies and the corresponding appropriate approaches to them can again be made at the present time, according to the *Red Flag* article, because there exist four major "contradictions" in the world. The four are:

(1) Contradictions "between the oppressed nations and imperialism and social imperialism";

(2) Contradictions "between the proletariat and the bourgeoisie in the capitalist and revisionist countries" (e.g., the antiwar sentiments in the United States and internal economic pressures within the Soviet system);

(3) Contradictions "between imperialist nations and social imperialist nations [i.e., the United States and the Soviet Union] and among the imperialist nations [e.g., the United States and Japan]";

(4) Contradictions "between the socialist nations [e.g., North Vietnam and Albania] and imperialism and social imperialism."

In the circumstances, the appropriate Chinese Communist policy is to seize the advantage conferred by the enemy's "contradictions and difficulties, waging a tit-for-tat struggle with them, strive for the basic interests of the people to the maximum extent, and win victories in the struggle against the enemy." The basic policy is that of the "United Front." Its essence consists of "alliance and struggle."

As the same article tried to explain: "Chairman Mao teaches: 'Our policy should be made known not only to leaders and cadres but to the broad masses.' Only by making the policies and tactics of the Party known to them can the broad masses raise their consciousness of implementing Chairman Mao's revolutionary line." There is an apparent need to persuade the opponents and to convince the general public. While Chou En-lai and his supporters were not totally successful, as evidenced by the September, 1971, incident, and their inability to convene a National People's Congress up to this writing (Spring, 1974) or to hold the Tenth Party Congress until August, 1973, Chou consistently expounded the same line. Basically, Peking has tried to explain the Washington-Peking rapprochement in terms of a tactical move based on established doctrine, the success of which had been previously demonstrated in the 1940s. The basic line is to argue that the victory of the people and of world revolution, which the Chinese Communists claim to represent, is inevitable and foreordained. Consequently, tactical shifts that are intended to seize new opportunities should not be construed as retreats brought about by past failures. This appeal to history and to what one might describe as the Hegelian *Gottesgang in der Welt* was most prominently advertised in the Nixon-Chou Joint Communiqué, in which

"The Chinese side stated:

" 'Wherever there is oppression, there is resistance. Countries want independence, nations want liberation and the people want revolution—this has become the irresistible trend of history....' "[25]

Three days before the issuance of this communiqué, Chou En-lai had paraphrased the same statement in his toast to the American visitors:

"The times are advancing and the world changes. We are deeply convinced that the strength of the people is powerful and that whatever zigzags and reverses there may be in the development of history, the general trend of the world is definitely toward light and not darkness...."[26]

The same theme has been carried forward in subsequent statements by the Chinese Communists; it can also be traced to statements made much earlier. For instance, in an article in the *People's Daily*,[27] commemorating Army Day on August 1, 1971, the theme of inevitability was expressed in the following words:

"People want to make revolution, nations want liberation, and countries want independence. This has become the irresistible trend of history."

The same words were paraphrased by Chou En-lai when he appeared at a Cambodian reception on November 9, 1971. His words then were:

"Countries want independence, nations want liberation, and people want revolution—this has become an irresistible trend in the world today."[28]

The sancity of the dogma is presumably to be established by dint of frequent recitation!

To recapitulate, the new foreign policy of the Chinese Communists in the context of the Washington-Peking rapprochement has several different facets:

(1) Policy toward the United States as an "imperialist" nation, but only a secondary enemy for the time being, whose strength must be used and whose "contradiction" with the Soviet Union must be exploited. (As a corollary, struggle against the United States as a capitalist and "oppressive social system" must nevertheless be continued by exploiting internal American weakness.)

(2) Policy toward the socialist nations, such as North Vietnam and North Korea, whose cause Peking espouses and who must be won over from Soviet influence and supported in their struggle against the United States and the latter's allies.

(3) Policy toward certain U.S. allies, such as Japan, Taiwan, and South Korea, whose weakness must be exploited and whose alliances must be eroded.

(4) Policy toward the "revisionist" and "social imperialist" Soviet Union, whose direct military threat has been the primary cause of the Chinese policy change. (Here the enemy must be resisted, deterred, but not provoked to the degree of open hostilities.)

How all these objectives are to be achieved from Peking's point of view deserves careful attention.

WHY THE UNITED STATES POSES NO PRESENT THREAT AS VIEWED FROM PEKING

The Chinese Communists need to assure themselves that their rapprochement with Washington would not enhance any external threat that may be posed by the United States. There is concrete evidence supporting a doctrinal conclusion that the United States is now a secondary enemy. The various unilateral gestures extended by the United States during 1969–71, culminating in the first Kissinger visit to Peking, provided ample ground for Peking to draw the conclusion that the U.S.-Soviet encirclement of China, which it may have believed to be an integral part of the two countries' alleged "nuclear collusion" against China, was about to be broken. The continuing withdrawal of U.S. ground forces from Vietnam, which began long before July 15, 1971, reinforced by the U.S. force reduction in Korea as well as base closings in Japan and elsewhere, may have convinced Peking that the United States was about to, or could be induced to, leave continental Asia. After July 15, 1971, and especially after the defeat of the American-Japanese co-sponsored resolution to retain a seat for Taiwan in the United Nations, the outcry of anguish, resentment, and confusion in the three capitals of America's Northeast Asian allies may have further persuaded Peking that it was possible, perhaps even highly probable, to drive a wedge between the United States and America's three Asian allies, including the Japanese "linchpin" in America's defense system in the Pacific, and between Japan and the two smaller Asian countries.

These concrete developments seem to lend support to the Chinese Communist doctrine that "imperialist" nations are essentially "paper tigers." Early in 1970, when Volume 1 of President Nixon's *Foreign Policy Report for the 1970's* was issued and the Nixon Doctrine was first expounded, the official comment from Peking followed closely the dictates of the "paper tiger" dogma:

"This report," announced the official NCNA on February 28, 1970, "is a record of the overall defeat of the U.S. imperialists' policy of aggression and a revelation of the weakness, the waning and the drastic decline of U.S. imperialism; it is another helpless confession of the U.S. imperialists that at the end of their rope, they are trying futilely to press ahead with their counter revolutionary, two-faced tactics. . . . What has been brazenly lauded by Nixon as the so-called 'Nixon Doctrine' is in fact a prescription made by him for U.S. imperialism, which is sick to the core and in the grip of overall political, economic and military crises, a prescription that is foreordained to failure. This prescription of Nixon's fully reflects the weakness of U.S. imperialism as a *paper tiger*. . . ." (Italics added.)

About three months later, on May 20, 1970, Mao Tse-tung issued a proclamation exhorting "the peoples of the world to unite" in order to "defeat the American aggressors and all their 'running dogs.' " Mao declared in this proclamation that the United States kindled a violent conflagration of internal revolutionary movements as a result of its domestic oppression and that the United States was meeting with external resistance in the entire world. Mao declared further that protracted revolutionary warfare would succeed in overthrowing American "imperialism." On this occasion, Mao was proclaiming Peking's support for this struggle against the United States everywhere, while calling upon the world's revolutionary elements to join the fight. This proclamation was issued at the time of the Vietnamese-U.S. joint incursion into Cambodia, but it was more than a political gesture on the part of the Chinese Communists. It echoes the Maoist thesis, established for some time, that a people's war had long ago started in the United States and that the American system was bound to fail for internal reasons. The *People's Daily* editorial on Army Day, 1971, cited earlier, clearly referred to the May, 1970, statement by Mao as a correct evaluation of the world situation, on the basis of which Chinese policy was formulated. As we pointed out, the policy enunciated by Chou En-lai since his initiation of the rapprochement with Washington has hewed closely to the same line. The United States is not to be feared because it is destined to collapse in the long run and may be about to do so before very long. The internal "revolution" and dissidence within the United States can be increased and encouraged simultaneously with negotiation with Washington at a government level.[29] This dual-level diplomacy is doctrinally sound, from a Chinese Communist point of view, and supported by historical precedent.

HOW PEKING PLACATES ITS SMALLER SOCIALIST NEIGHBORS

Chou En-lai seems well aware of the fact that his claim to doctrinal purity in spite of the zigzags of Peking's practical policy may look less convincing from a different vantage point. This is particularly true in the case of North Vietnam and to a lesser extent in that of North Korea. Partly to offset Soviet efforts to win over North Vietnam at Peking's expense, Pham Van Dong, the Communist North Vietnamese Premier, was invited to Peking in November, 1971. In a joint communiqué issued by Chou En-lai and Pham Van Dong on November 25, 1971, the Chinese Communist side stated:

> To support and assist the Vietnamese and Indochinese peoples in their war against U.S. aggression and for national salvation is the *unshakable established policy* of the Chinese Communist Party and the Chinese Government and the *unshirkable internationalist duty* of the Chinese people. (Italics added.)

In order to carry out this policy, the joint communiqué announced:

> The Chinese people ... will not flinch even from the greatest national sacrifice.[30]

This statement of all-out support for North Vietnam was also made by Chou En-lai in person at a mass rally on November 23, 1971. The joint communiqué further spoke of changes in tactics and methods in the essentially unchanging imperialism espoused by the United States. Another special feature of the Chou-Pham communiqué was its reference to the comradeship "constantly cared for and nurtured by ... Ho Chi Minh ... and Mao Tse-tung." Finally, Peking stated in the communiqué that it was grateful to North Vietnam for the latter's prolonged war against the United States, implying that the Vietnam War was at least partly responsible for those U.S. policies that had up to that point benefited the PRC.

In the case of North Korea, Peking encouraged Pyongyang in propaganda statements which attempted to convey the impression that the Washington-Peking rapprochement was a result of Chinese strength combined with U.S. weakness. There was no intimation of any Soviet threat to Peking. In August, 1971, the Pyongyang radio spoke of Mr. Nixon's then forthcoming visit to Peking as a journey bearing "the white flag of surrender." In February, 1972, the official North Korean radio again spoke of President Nixon's visiting Peking with "white flag in one hand and beggar's bowl in the other."[31]

On the whole, Pyongyang seems to have been less concerned about any compromise that Peking might make at North Korea's expense, although the public statement of the *Rodong Sinmun* on August 10, 1971, "No force can break the great friendship of solidarity sealed in blood between the peoples of Korea and China," gave the impression of whistling in the dark.[32]

Chou En-lai may not have been fully successful in convincing Hanoi of unflinching Chinese support for the latter's cause, although he continued to demand total and unconditional withdrawal of U.S. forces from all of Indochina, the establishment of a final date for such withdrawals, and the cessation of U.S. military activities and support of South Vietnam.[33] Both the Viet Cong and Hanoi have accused the United States of "plotting against socialist unity and practicing splinter tactics."[34] Peking's lack of positive response when the United States mined North Vietnamese harbors and sent B-52s over Hanoi during the final stages of cease-fire negotiations in 1972 provides additional support for such reasoning in North Vietnam. Nor can the latter's experience have escaped the attention of Pyongyang.

As a matter of fact, in the Nixon-Chou Joint Communiqué of February, 1972, while the PRC "expressed its firm support to the peoples of Vietnam, Laos and Cambodia in their efforts for the attainment of their goals and its firm support to the seven-point proposal of the Provisional Revolutionary Government of the Republic of South Vietnam [i.e., the Viet Cong] ... and to the Joint Declaration of the Summit Conference of the Indochinese Peoples," there was no direct mention of Hanoi. Since both the United States and the PRC stated that they were not prepared "to negoitate on behalf of any third party or to enter into agreements or understandings" with each other "directed to other states," one might assume that Peking did not have Hanoi's agreement to act on its behalf.

A fundamental difficulty in its dealings with the United States on Vietnam was, and still is, Peking's difference with the Soviet Union. While Peking would have no objection to a quick defeat of the United States in Vietnam, it probably did not see such a development as an imminent possibility. It may also have felt in 1972 that since the United States was about to withdraw its forces, there was no compelling need to force the issue. Above all, it would be against Peking's interest to have the Soviet presence in Vietnam continued and Soviet support to the North increased. These possibilities would have loomed large if fighting had been further prolonged and increased in intensity, even if the end result should be the ouster of the United States from Indochina. It would be far easier for Peking to compete with the Soviet Union in that area if the North Vietnamese were not fighting with increasing Soviet support. As Peking saw it, other things being equal, the Soviet Union would be more interested in prolonging and intensifying the war in Vietnam with Soviet equipment and aid. It would also be more difficult to oust Soviet influence from the area once the U.S.S.R. had succeeded in replacing the U.S. military presence. From the Soviet point of view, such an intensification of fighting could either have involved the United States in a longer war, which might incidentally have increased possible frictions between Washington and Peking, or it might have brought about the defeat of South Vietnam through Soviet aid to the North, which might then have been interpreted as a clear defeat of the United States by the Soviet Union. The all-out attack by Hanoi's forces across the DMZ in April, 1972, seemed to substantiate this interpretation, although the U.S. response in bombing and mining of North Vietnamese harbors probably caught the Soviet Union by surprise. As a minimum the Soviet Union would wish to exact stiffer terms from the United States for its cooperation to end the Indochina war. This divergence of interests between Peking and Moscow made the former's effort to placate Hanoi more difficult than it was in the case of North Korea.

Additional examples of Peking's problems with its socialist neighbors may be seen through other events or non-events. For instance, there were press reports that Chou En-lai had to go to Hanoi and Pyongyang in person in order to explain the Nixon-Chou Joint Communiqué. Furthermore, there were reportedly only limited broadcasts in Vietnamese by the Peking radio discussing the Nixon visit, and there was no Peking broadcast on the subject in Khmer during the visit.[35]

In summary, Peking's tactics vis-à-vis North Korea and North Vietnam were:

(1) To describe the rapprochement with Washington as a means of exploiting American weakness;

(2) To appeal to the purity of doctrine on which Chinese policy is based and which permits tactical zigzags; and

(3) To invoke the shade of Ho Chi Minh and the authority of Mao Tse-tung as the historical guarantee of Chinese Communist trustworthiness.

The promise of support and greater aid to North Vietnam paralleled Chinese efforts to enchance Peking's leadership in the Third World both through material assistance and by acting as a spokesmen of radical causes. As an example, during 1970 Peking boosted its foreign aid commitments to $709 million, surpassing for the first time the corresponding Soviet figure of only $204 million. Three countries—Pakistan, Tanzania, and Zambia—reportedly received pledges of $200 million each.[36] As an example of championing causes favored by the Third World, Huang Hua attacked the "white regimes..." of South Africa, Rhodesia, and the Portuguese colonies at a United Nations Security Council meeting in Addis Ababa. On the same occasion, Huang also attacked the Soviet Union for trying to contend with both the old colonial powers and the "neo-colonialists" for a sphere of influence. In 1974, Teng Hsiao-p'ing's speech at the special session of the UN General Assembly on the world's raw material problem, which the 1973 energy crisis generated by the Arab oil boycott had brought to focus, followed the same line of attack. These Chinese tactics are part of an effort to preserve Peking's radical image.

HOW PEKING SEEKS TO PLACATE MOSCOW

The Soviet Union was very careful in its comments immediately after the publication of the Shanghai Communiqué. Its relative reticence can be explained in part by the Soviet desire not to tip its hand in advance of the scheduled visit of President Nixon to Moscow in May, 1972. We can, nonetheless, assume that Soviet suspicions were not allayed by the communiqué. Among the points that could create unhappiness in the Kremlin are:

(1) The statement within the communiqué that both the United States and the PRC were "opposed to the efforts by any other country or group of countries to establish... hegemony" in Pacific-Asia;

(2) The Chinese Communist demand for the withdrawal of all foreign troops from countries where they are stationed, thus including by implication Soviet troops now present in Mongolia and Eastern Europe; and

(3) The statement by Mr. Nixon at a dinner in Shanghai that the peoples of the two countries "held the future of the world in their hands."[37]

There were numerous direct and indirect expressions of Soviet misgivings. For instance, the Budapest *Magyar Hirlap* said on August 10, 1971: "The strange searchings of the strange twosome for the establishment of contacts may add to the endeavors of international normalization, but may at the same time come into effect at the cost of others, to the disadvantage of people who are fighting against imperialist aggression.... What might the common basis of the bargain be?"[38] As a matter of fact, the rhetorical question posed in Budapest had been answered a week earlier in Prague, where the official radio noted that "The magnetic force which is drawing the United States and China closer together is anti-Sovietism." In addition, the Soviet Union has been quick to suggest that Peking's invitation to Mr. Nixon has inflicted serious damage on North Vietnam.[39]

The danger to Peking of its rapprochement with Washington does not consist of Soviet suspicion and displeasure. The latter are intended effects. The real danger would be a possible Soviet overreaction and the triggering of a preemptive attack, which Peking's new American policy is meant to avert. In order to create no more than the desired restraining effect on the Soviet Union, Peking has consistently taken a low profile by stressing on every occasion that its objective is limited and defensive in intent. Thus, immediately after the announcement of his invitation to President Nixon, Chou En-lai said, in answer to a question of James Reston, "No, we are not a nuclear power. We are only in the experimental stage."[40] On the same day as the announcement of the Nixon visit, Chou told a Japanese correspondent that Communist China would never seek to become a great power, even if its economy were to develop substantially within the next five or ten years.[41] On this occasion Chou was commenting on Prime Minister Sato's speech of April 6, 1971, naming the PRC as the fifth potential great power center in the world following the United States, Japan, Western Europe, and the Soviet Union. Chou stressed that Communist China would not follow a policy of external economic expansion as obviously does Japan—which would invite militaristic expansion as a matter of course.

Although Peking has been described as a superpower in American statements, the official Chinese statements have taken care to disavow any such predictions or pretensions. Echoing the same line, Chou En-lai's trusted aide, Ch'iao Kuan-hua, stated at the United Nations: "*China will never be a superpower*, pursuing the policies of nuclear monopoly, nuclear threats, and nuclear blackmail either today or even in the future."[42] (Italics added.) The Chinese Communist message to Moscow and, incidentally, to the United States and its allies, is that Chinese nuclear development has yet a long way to go before it can become a significant factor and that the long-run objective of mainland China is non-expansionary and strictly limited. Therefore, there is no need for undue concern on the part of the Soviet Union and certainly no compelling reason to "preempt" through military action. From the Chinese point of view, struggle with the Soviet Union has to be pursued on grounds where Peking is not at such a distinct disadvantage. It is quite conceivable, once Peking is sufficiently confident of its deterrent capability and bargaining position vis-à-vis the Soviet Union through developing relations with Washington, that Chou En-lai or his successors may turn toward Moscow for greater contact and negotiation. The rehabilitation in 1973 of several persons, including Teng Hsiao-p'ing, who were targets of attack during the Cultural Revolution, may herald such a move in view of their past experience in dealing with the Soviet Union.

DIVIDE ET IMPERA—PEKING'S POLICY TOWARD JAPAN, TAIWAN, AND SOUTH KOREA

There are good reasons why Peking would like to bring Japan into closer relations with itself, ready to do its bidding. Japanese industry could greatly assist Chinese economic and defense programs if imports from Japan could be enlarged, especially on the basis of low prices and liberal credit. If Japan should become estranged from the United States, America's defense position in the Western Pacific would be greatly weakened. At the same time, Japan could be made more willing to accept Chinese terms provided the Soviet Union could be prevented from making effective countermoves in the latter's relations with Japan.

Chou En-lai's approach to Japan has therefore included several complementary measures. By attacking Japan under Mr. Sato's regime for its alleged resurgent militarism, Peking hopes to arouse suspicion in the United States about Japan's future intentions. Peking would like to encourage Japan to believe that the Washington-Peking rapprochement is in part directed against Japan. While stressing the continued defense role of the United States in the Western Pacific and the presence of U.S. bases in Japan, including Okinawa, for the benefit of the antiwar elements in Japan, Peking hopes to undermine the confidence of security-conscious Japanese leaders in U.S. ability and willingness to defend Japanese vital interests and to honor its treaty obligations.

Having suggested in so many ways that Japan's alliance with the United States is a mistaken policy, Peking offers Japan an alternative, albeit at a price. As Chou En-lai stated to Reston shortly after the July 15, 1971, announcement of President Nixon's planned visit to Peking, Peking would be ready to conclude a nonaggression pact with Japan if the latter would give up its "ambitions of aggression" against Korea and Taiwan and accept the celebrated "Five Principles of Coexistence."[43] Chou was even more explicit in his interview with Moto Goto of the *Asahi Evening News* in November.[44] He pointed out his readiness to revise Sino-Japanese relations, as well as the need for negotiations at the governmental level in order to accomplish this purpose. He imposed, however, three preconditions for starting negotiations, requiring Japan to take a clear-cut attitude on three points. First, Japan was to recognize Peking as the sole legitimate government of China. Second, Japan was to affirm that it regarded Taiwan as a part of China. Lastly, Japan was to renounce its peace treaty with the Republic of China. Peking has also made it very clear that it lays full claim to Senkaku.[45]

Furthermore, Peking tried to undermine the domestic political position of the mainstream Liberal Democrats headed by the then Prime Minister Sato. For some time during 1971 the Chinese Communists made it clear in various ways that they would not deal with Mr. Sato. At the time of Mr. Nixon's Peking visit, the official New China News Agency denounced some of Sato's more conservative advisers for promoting Taiwan independence.[46] After Mr. Sato's retirement in mid-1972, Chou then invited Prime Minister Tanaka, Sato's successor, to visit Peking before October, 1972, following Tanaka's indication that he would abrogate diplomatic ties with Taiwan as a result of "normalization" of Sino-Japanese relations. Peking therefore tried to exert pressure on the Japanese Government both by dangling the prospect of trade and by exaggerating Japan's need to accept Chinese Communist terms for better relations with Peking now that the United States is supposedly no longer reliable and is potentially hostile to Japan. In this manner, Peking hopes to maximize advantage while following a new America policy that was born essentially of its own weakness.

Once "normalization" of relations between Peking and Tokyo was achieved in September, 1972, Peking assured Japan that it could well understand Japan's need for defense and even its relationship with the United States.[47] As in other areas in Asia, Peking's present paramount concern is to avoid Soviet replacement of U.S. influence. Hence Japan must not be allowed to turn to the Soviet Union for protection. Following the 1973 energy crisis, Peking has further sweetened its trade bait by promising large oil exports, especially to Japan.

In its 1972 New Year's Day Message, Peking reaffirmed its determination to "liberate" Taiwan. Yet in the Nixon-Chou Joint Communiqué Peking gave the impression that it was not about to use force to accomplish this objective. It did so by stressing the principles of peaceful coexistence as a necessary concession to United States obligations under the Mutual Defense Treaty with the Republic of China. While maintaining its official position regarding Taiwan as a part of the China that it controls, Peking obliquely assured the United States that it did not intend to use force against Taiwan. Instead, it has directed political and, increasingly since 1972, economic warfare against Taiwan by trying to undermine the basis of Taiwan's economic prosperity and relations between different segments of the population on the island and to stir dissension within the Nationalist Party. It has tried to create dissension by spreading in Hong Kong rumors about a possible deal with Chiang Kai-shek, understandings with potential leaders in Taiwan in the post-Chiang period, and reports that Peking's real objection is to some of the Generalissimo's anti-Communist advisers rather than to Chiang himself. Internationally, Peking has sought to reduce Taiwan's foreign contacts and support, including individuals and institutions in Japan and the United States which Peking believes to be susceptible to influence. Peking has also suggested that Taiwan has begun negotiations with the Soviet Union that could lead to Soviet naval access to the Pescadores. This is obviously an attempt aimed at arousing Chinese nationalism against the Republic of China government and at alienating U.S-ROC relations. According to visitors from the United States to Peking, Chou En-lai personally took a hand in this ploy. There is, of course, a genuine concern about a possible Soviet-ROC rapprochement. After all, the Chinese Communists were themselves party to such a relationship with the Soviet Union when official Soviet relations were with the Nationalist government. In 1974, Peking was instrumental in causing the rupture of the civil aviation agreement between Japan and Taiwan. This external policy toward Taiwan can be described as one of isolation without invasion.

Similarly, PRC policy toward South Korea seeks to drive a wedge between the Republc of Korea on the one hand and Japan and the United States on the other by stressing Japanese "imperialist" ambitions and U.S. "unreliability." At the same time, pressure has been put on Japanese businesses in order to discourage the continued expansion of Japanese economic interests in South Korea.

THE STYLES OF NEGOTIATION OF PEKING AND WASHINGTON

A careful reading of the Nixon-Chou Joint Communiqué, including both the joint statements of the two parties and the separate Chinese and American statements, clearly demonstrates Peking's objectives, as well as its difficulties. These include the assertion of the inevitability of world revolution; an obvious bid for the leadership and continued confidence of the Third World; the demand for the withdrawal of troops stationed in foreign countries, directed at both the Soviet Union and the United States; the continued Chinese statement of support for their allies in Indochina and North Korea; the denunciation of Japanese militarism; the reiterated claim to Taiwan; the affirmation of the Five Principles of Coexistence especially for the benefit of the United States; and the disavowal of any intention to attain hegemony or to carve out a sphere of influence in Pacific-Asia. The principal purpose of

Peking's diplomacy is to deter a Soviet attack by creating an impression in Soviet minds of possible American support and by assuring other countries, including the United States, and obviously also the Soviet Union, that Communist China is after all quite harmless. This Chinese Communist policy is also intended to maximize advantages for Peking, especially vis-à-vis Taiwan, Japan, and Korea.

The preceding sections have dealt with the individual aspects of Chinese policy in some detail. We turn now to the style of Chou En-lai's operation. Throughout, Chou has tried to convince the world that Peking does not seek rapprochement with Washington out of weakness, but rather out of strength. This tactic can be clearly seen through Peking's handling of President Nixon's visit. Reference has already been made to the New China News Agency reports of North Korean statements that Mr. Nixon's visit was "not the march of a victor but the trip of the defeated."[48]

Furthermore, while talking to Moto Goto of the *Asahi Shimbun,* Chou stated: "Chairman Mao said a long time ago that if President Nixon wanted to come, he could come, whatever reason he wanted to give."[49]

A second tactic is to try to create the impression that there are certain non-negotiable Chinese demands. The purpose, obviously, is again to demonstrate Chinese strength in addition to maximizing possible advantage. Chou has apparently followed the age-old tradition of the bargainer—that you are likely to get more by asking for more. Thus Chou En-lai told Reston before the passage of the Albanian resolution in the United Nations that he would not go to the United Nations as long as Taiwan remained.[50] The ouster of Taiwan from the United Nations was made not only a condition of Peking's participation in the United Nations, which may be necessary for Chou's own domestic political reasons, but also *seemingly* as the condition for Mr. Nixon's visit. Yet, following the defeat of the U.S. resolution and the successful admission of Peking, Ch'iao Kuan-hua reportedly told a foreign envoy that the vote was "unexpected" and that he had been wrong in his estimate.[51] Thus, Peking had apparently been prepared to engage in the rapprochement with Washington whether or not it could enter the United Nations.

In dealing with the United States, Peking has been slow in offering small overt gestures of changing attitude. The gestures are offered as signals that the United States should continue with its effort at rapprochement. They are, however, small in order to give the world the impression Peking desires. For instance, the "Anti-Imperialist Hospital" where a well-known U.S. correspondent was given his first treatment of acupuncture was renamed the "Capital Hospital" a month before Mr. Nixon's visit as a symbolic relaxation of the hard line. This change followed that of the "Anti-Revisionist Hospital" into the "Friendship Hospital." Of course, there was no mention in any Chinese

Communist announcement that the "Anti-Imperialist Hospital" was the former "Peking Union Medical Center," originally financed by the Rockefeller Foundation. Furthermore, according to Reuters, the "Anti-Imperialist Street" and the "Anti-Revisionist Street" were still Peking thoroughfares after the name change of the hospitals.[52] The deliberately cool reception given to President Nixon's party upon its arrival and the subsequent warming up on the following days may also be viewed from the same perspective.

In the circumstances, one can understandably ask whether the United States appreicates the fact that Peking conducts its foreign relations on two different levels. As one China watcher has noted, "The seeming new harmony developing in relations between Washington and Peking should not be allowed to obscure Mao Tse-tung's continuing commitment to targets of opportunity for revolutionary change in the world."[53] It would, perhaps, be even more necessary to ask whether the American public understands Peking's mode of operation. A related question is whether the American public can be made to understand the real nature of the Washington-Peking rapprochement.

One of the difficulties in understanding this issue lies in the ambiguity that has accompanied certain American moves. One common question never fully answered officially is why the United States chose to hold a summit meeting in Peking. A related question has to do with the timing of Kissinger's second Peking visit in 1971, which coincided with the United Nations debate on the China question and the voting on the competing resolutions. Still another question revolves around the seeming slowness in close consultation with Japan after the announcement of July 15, 1971, not to mention the absence of prior consultation. The net result is to multiply the number of diverse interpretations of U.S. policy to America's disadvantage.

As an example, a *New York Times* correspondent wrote on September 26, 1971, a month before the UN vote admitting Peking:

> At first there was a general feeling abroad that the Administration did not mean what it said—that it would go through the motions of saving Taiwan while being careful to let its potential new friends in Peking know that it would not fight harder than was absolutely necessary for appearances' sake.

(These suspicions had been dispelled, according to the same correspondent, as a result of the all-out U.S. effort at the United Nations.) At the same time, Professor James T. C. Liu of Princeton offered the speculation that the United States really intended to save a seat for Taiwan for one more year. This, according to Liu, was to be accomplished by offering Peking the Security Council seat, which gesture would help create a majority in the United Nations for the "reverse important question." The resultant retention of Taiwan in the United Nations would keep Peking out because of the latter's unwillingness to agree to dual representation.[54]

In spite of these evaluations of the true nature of the American effort at the United Nations, a number of commentators continued to interpret the U.S.-Japan joint effort to save a seat for Taiwan as a sham fight. A critic of U.S. policy toward Communist China before the rapprochement wrote three days before the UN vote:

> The timing of the Kissinger trip is auspicious. Secretary of State Rogers may have to play the straight man at the UN and Senator Buckley the bogeyman there, but Kissinger's meetings in Peking further delegitimize the United States and Taiwan Governments' posture at the UN. . . . In fact the Kissinger trip signals to UN delegates that it is only a matter of time before Sino-American relations are "normalized."[55]

On the other side of the political spectrum, William F. Buckley, Jr. wrote in his syndicated column on the U.S. effort to retain a General Assembly seat for Nationalist China, in early October, 1971:

> I do not doubt that he [President Nixon] is watching carefully to judge the American temper on the question. Meanwhile Mr. Bush is charged to Stakhanovite parliamentary endeavor. The appearance has got to be right. . . .[56]

While the remarks of Tretiak were intended to encourage a bandwagon effect in favor of Peking's entry into the United Nations by hinting that the U.S. effort to retain a seat for Taiwan was a sham, the Buckley criticism of the American policy was that the effort was insufficient and the fight should not be a sham. Again, on the other side of the U.S. domestic political arena, Senator Edward R. Kennedy spoke of the second Kissinger visit in the following terms:

> Perhaps the timing was a coincidence, and perhaps not. We shall probably never know whether this was a gesture, exacted by Peking as the price of the President's coming visit.[57]

Columnist Jack Anderson was more explicit. He wrote:

> But the crafty Chou En-lai undercut the U.S. effort by bringing Kissinger to Peking in the middle of the UN debate.[58]

There were other reports that Peking did pick the date and that the United States consented to the proposal.[59]

Other nations saw the U.S. position of supporting dual representation in the United Nations while at the same time seeking a rapprochement with Peking as contradictory. Some of them thought that the United States was actually pursuing only one of the seemingly contradictory objectives. Others were afraid that, while the United States could explain matters to Peking, they themselves were not in this more fortunate position and could not, therefore, play the U.S. game—even if the game was what the American government said it was.

Amidst all these different perceptions of U.S. policy, curiously, no one has raised what would be an equally logical question concerning Peking's unusual conduct rather than that of Washington. Why was Peking prepared to invite Kissinger for a visit ostensibly to make arrangements for the subsequent Nixon-Chou meeting at a time when the United States and Japan were fighting hard in the United Nations to retain a seat for Taiwan in spite of Peking's publicly stated desires? Did Peking really want to prevent the Republic of China from remaining in the United Nations at all cost? Or did Peking value its rapprochement with Washington more than political consistency? Yet all the questioning in the public press was directed at the real intentions of the United States. Why was the United States less credible than Peking?

Perhaps the answer lies in the manner of implementation of the Nixon Doctrine and the divergent perceptions of U.S. policy by different nations from their own vantage points. Perhaps, too, insufficient attention has been given by the United States to the manner in which perceptions are formed.

NOTES

1. In his column in *Newsweek* (August 16, 1971, p. 84), Stewart Alsop wrote: "The President's mission to Peking could also have some marginal cooling off effect on the impulse of at least some of the Soviet military to 'strangle the baby in the bath,' ... There is no doubt at all that the Soviet leadership has at least seriously considered a 'surgical strike' to knock out the growing Chinese nuclear capability...."
2. These observations were made by an American TV commentator who accompanied the Presidential party to Peking in February, 1972.
3. Report on Mr. Nixon's press conference of August 4, 1971, *U.S. News and World Report*, August 16, 1971, p. 76.
4. For some of the particulars, see the author's study on *Communist China and the World Balance of Power*, American Enterprise Institute, Washington, D.C., 1971.
5. Joseph Alsop's column in the *San Francisco Chronicle*, July 19, 1971.
6. Joseph Alsop, October 25, 1971.

7. *New York Times,* November 22, 1971.
8. As reported by the *U.S. News and World Report,* September 27, 1971.
9. *Ibid.*
10. *Annual Defense Department Report, FY1974,* March 1973, p. 37.
11. Admiral Thomas H. Moorer, *U.S. Military Posture for FY1975,* report to the Defense Appropriations Subcommittee of the House Appropriations Committee, February 1974, p.38.
12. Report by William Beecher, February 1, 1972.
13. See note 8 above.
14. *New York Times,* August 8, 1971, quoting the Hungarian *Magyaroszag.*
15. See *New York Times,* January 30, 1972, quoting estimates of the French journal, *Actualité;* also Beecher, note 12 above.
16. The 200 ABM launcher ceiling of the Moscow treaty would nevertheless not seriously weaken the Soviet strategic balance as long as PRC missiles are few in number and not all deployed in hardened sites. The 50 ABM launchers permitted at test sites offer additional leeway.
17. *U.S. News and World Report,* September 29, 1971.
18. See note 4 above.
19. *New York Times* dispatch from Moscow, October 1, 1971.
20. This document, designated as "Chung-fa (1972), No. 4," issued by the CPC on January 13, 1972, concentrated its criticism on Lin's alleged plot. The account of the plot was contained in a memorandum under the code name of the "Summary Report of Engineering Project No. 571." A later CPC Central Committee document ("Chung-fa, 1972, No. 12") contained an account of Mao's discussions on the proper party line between the middle of August and September 12, 1971, that involved Lin Piao and the four military chiefs, suggesting that there was a deliberate effort to purge Lin. Cf. *Central Daily News,* Taipei, August 10, 1972.
21. *Sovietskava Rossiya* reported on December 31, 1971 that there existed in China an opposition group to the Washington-Peking rapprochement, citing as evidence a brochure published in Peking and summarized in the *Shukan Shincho,* a Tokyo literary weekly. See *New York Times,* January 1, 1972.

    China watchers in Hong Kong reported in interviews with the author an apparent slowdown in 1972 of the purge of Lin Piao's followers in the provinces because Peking feared that more precipitate action might provoke general resistance. See also *New York Times,* December 11, 1971.

    However, in 1973 commanders of major military regions were shifted and some were deprived of their concurrent posts in the party and the civilian government. Thus, Mao's and Chou's fear of the regional military and their continued efforts to consolidate never ceased.
22. See *New York Times,* August 30 and 31, 1973; also Yuan-li Wu, "Chinese Technological and Economic Capabilities: Is the PRC a Stabilizing or Destabilizing Influence?" *Orbis,* Vol. XVII, No. 3, Philadelphia, Fall 1973.

23. Reuters, November 9, 1971.
24. Ninth issue, 1971. The authorship of the article is attributed to the Hupeh Communist Party Committee. The article was reported by Peking Radio on August 16, 1971.
25. *New York Times*, February 28, 1972.
26. *New York Times*, February 26, 1972.
27. This is a joint editorial of the *People's Daily*, the *Red Flag*, and the *Liberation Army Daily*, marking the 44th anniversary of the founding of the PLA. The text was broadcast by NCNA on July 31, 1971.
28. Reuters, November 9, 1971.
29. Invitations to visit China, issued to radical and militant critics of U.S. policy in general, are examples of Peking's effort in this direction. Among these groups are, for example, the "Concerned Asian Scholars" and some Black Panther Party leaders.
30. NCNA, Peking, November 27, 1971.
31. *New York Times*, February 23, 1972.
32. NCNA, August 10, 1971.
33. *New York Times*, February 5, 1972.
34. *New York Times*, February 25, 1972.
35. *New York Times*, March 12, 1972.
36. *New York Times*, January 2, 1972.
37. Report on the text of Mr. Nixon's toast at the Shanghai dinner. *New York Times*, February 28, 1972, quoting an Associated Press report.
38. Budapest MTI, August 10, 1971.
39. Georgiy Arbatov, a well-known Soviet America watcher, in *Pravda*, as reported by Tass, August 10, 1971.
40. *New York Times*, August 10, 1971.
41. Report by Minoru Takahashi of the Kyodo News Service, Tokyo, July 15, 1971.
42. *New York Times*, November 25, 1971. See, however, the Wu article referred to in note 22.
43. *New York Times*, August 10, 1971.
44. *Asahi Evening News*, Tokyo, November 9, 1971.
45. Statement of the PRC Foreign Ministry as reported by the *New York Times* on January 2, 1972.
46. *New York Times*, February 21, 1972.
47. See Hisao Iwashima, "Japan's Defense Dilemma: Principles and Realities," paper presented at the 1973 convention of the International Studies Association, New York, March 1973.
48. *New York Times*, August 11, 1971. See also note 31 above.
49. *New York Times*, November 10, 1971.
50. *New York Times*, October 10, 1971.
51. *New York Times*, November 27, 1971, reported by John Burns of the *Toronto Globe and Mail* from Peking.
52. *New York Times*, January 7, 1972.

53. Richard L. Walker, "About Those Meetings in Peking," *New York Times*, October 26, 1971.
54. Letter to the editor, *New York Times*, September 27, 1971.
55. Daniel Tretiak in *New York Times*, October 23, 1971.
56. *San Francisco Examiner*, October 2, 1971.
57. *New York Times*, October 30, 1971.
58. *San Francisco Chronicle*, October 29, 1971.
59. *New York Times*, October 24, 1971.

Chapter IV

Perception and Response I: Toward Realignment in Northeast Asia?

THE DYNAMICS OF REALIGNMENT

Since the Nixon Doctrine, like all policies, must be implemented in the real world, whether the real world and the environment envisaged by the architects of the policy as most conducive to its realization are identical is a critical question. An affirmative answer cannot be taken for granted. Moreover, the answer needs to be considered dynamically. As the various new elements in U.S. foreign and defense policies have gradually unfolded after Mr. Nixon's Guam speech, U.S. actions and statements have been noted by foreign nations. These perceptions in other countries, where the manifestations of U.S. policy are regarded as materially affecting their own national interests, become important factors in determining their own actions. From the U.S. point of view, these actions in turn alter the environment within which U.S. policy must be carried out, and this process is continuing. There is, furthermore, a U.S. counterpart in the perception of and response to the policies of other countries. Only when the U.S. perception and response can make the appropriate adjustments and corrections of previous errors will it be possible to achieve dynamic equilibrium and stability.

Since our subject of inquiry is the U.S. policy, we may conceive the chain of events, beginning with some major U.S. move, as U.S. action → foreign perception → foreign response (and/or initiative) → U.S. perception → U.S. response (and/or initiative) → ... with the arrows denoting both sequence and causation. The interactions involved are, however, not necessarily reactions to specific individual actions; more often than not they are responses to perceived cumulative changes in the entire international environment. Furthermore, more than one such chain of action, perception, and response may be initiated at any given moment; many are, and have been, initiated by other nations. In the continuum of time, new "chains" are initiated continuously; at any given moment, we have an accumulation of the effects of past actions and perceptions to contend with. From the viewpoint of American policy-makers, a significant question is whether perceptions of U.S. policy by foreign countries will lead to actions conducive to the fulfillment of American policy objectives or whether the contrary will be true. Another question is whether American perception of the policies of foreign countries will require adjustments if foreign responses are not all that may be desired. It is important to realize that on both sides perceptions may be blurred or mistaken and that neither perceptions nor responses will be instantaneous. Delayed perception and/or response can give rise to an apparent need for a stronger response, resulting in overcompensation and consequent instability.[1]

The principal U.S. actions during 1969–74 affecting the security interests of countries in Pacific-Asia which could be readily perceived by foreign countries fell into four categories: (1) reductions of U.S. military presence, accompanied by vociferous public and Congressional demands for greater and faster reductions, (2) occasional moves in surprisingly opposite directions, e.g., the incursion into Cambodia in 1970, the mining of Haiphong harbor in 1972, the dispatch of the *Enterprise* to the Gulf of Bengal in the India-Pakistan War, etc., (3) negotiation with Moscow and Communist China, the latter long regarded by the United States as a menace to security in the region and to American security, although this feeling was not necessarily shared to the same degree by all Asian nations, and (4) adverse changes in the strategic balance of the United States versus the Soviet Union. In contrast to these directly observable phenomena, especially those in the first three categories, assertions of U.S. objectives and ultimate intentions were not always susceptible to immediate and full verification by foreign observers. Perceptions of U.S. policy by other countries have, therefore, focused on (1) changes in U.S. capability, (2) the strength of American will, (3) the internal consistency of U.S. policies, both concomitant and over time, and (4) U.S. sincerity and credibility. As a result of their perceptions regarding these points and through interactions among themselves and with Soviet and

Chinese policies, the non-Communist countries of Pacific-Asia have responded and will continue to respond in ways affecting American security interests. The three most important aspects of their responses concern (1) realignment in relation to the Soviet Union, the PRC, and other nations, (2) plans for their own defense, and (3) their views and policies toward the United States.

Whether a foreign country can or will build up its own military strength in response to its perception of the Nixon Doctrine does not provide a basis for conclusions as to the effect on U.S. national interest. One needs to know how the country "aligns" itself. Alignment should be defined in the broad sense: Where does the country stand in relation to other countries? This would include the position of neutrality or "nonalignment." Accordingly, analysis of actual or potential changes in alignment is preliminary to an evaluation of the state of power balance or its stability.[2]

CAPABILITY, THREAT PERCEPTION, AND AVAILABLE OPTIONS

The reactions of the three Northeast Asian countries to U.S. policy should be discussed together for several good reasons. First, the security of Japan is intertwined with that of South Korea and Taiwan. What Mr. Sato stated in his Washington Press Club speech in November, 1969, and in the Nixon-Sato Joint Communiqué reflects both the geographical and economic position of Japan and the historical outlook of the Japanese people. This is true in spite of subsequent developments in U.S.-Japan relations or equivocating statements by Sato and Tanaka in 1972. Second, the security of Taiwan and South Korea can be greatly enhanced with Japanese cooperation, because Japan is in a position to furnish the kind of aid its two smaller neighbors require. Conversely, without Japanese cooperation, their interests and eventually also Japan's interest can be seriously damaged. Third, because both Korea and Taiwan were under Japanese control until 1945, all three nations are especially sensitive to the substance and form of developing Japanese interest in the latter's former colonies. Lastly, in the case of Japanese relations with Taiwan, the basic security problems represented by the "two Chinas" issue cannot be buried by a series of votes taken at the United Nations. These issues remain to be resolved even though Peking has replaced Taipei in the international organization and has greatly extended its diplomatic relations with non-Communist countries.

The three Northeast Asian countries present two major types of Asian responses to the Nixon Doctrine. As we shall see, the responses of Japan are largely shaped by two dominant factors, namely, (1) the country's existing economic and technological capacity and its resultant military potential and (2) its geographical location as an island nation lacking indigenous resources. Because of its productive capacity, Japan is in a position to do a great deal for itself and other nations if importation of raw materials can be assured. It is, therefore, subject to wooing by both the Soviet Union and Communist China. On the other hand, geography and the legacy of World War II seriously constrain Japan's political attitude and freedom to act. Japan is also a target of potential threats emanating from both Moscow and Peking. If the American role in Japan's defense is reduced, Japanese security planning and foreign policy must aim at developing the nation's options by exploiting its advantages under the given constraints.

The *direct* threats to Japanese security, however, are somewhat amorphous. Japan's view of the large Soviet threat is a traditional one. Some even suggest that it is frequently played up for the benefit of the Diet for budgetary purposes.[3] The *direct* threat from mainland China is of lesser proportions although its magnitude will rise as Chinese nuclear weapons development continues and a viable regional nuclear force comes into being, reinforced by a minimal long-range missile deterrent force against the Soviet Union and, worse still for Japan, also against the United States. Neither the Soviet Union nor Communist China has had occasion to threaten the sovereignty and independence of Japan even though the Sino-Soviet Treaty of 1950 was ostensibly aimed at preventing the revival of Japanese aggression.[4] Because it can make itself useful to its potential adversaries through trade, investment, and technology, Japan probably sees little reason why either Peking or Moscow would pose a direct, dire threat to Japanese security.

However, like other nations, Japan does not wish to depend upon the goodwill of others for its own security, although its most immediate concerns in this connection are indirect threats, i.e., to Korea and Taiwan, and to the uninterrupted supply of goods to and from its shores which it feels must be dealt with. Since the problem for Japan is how to remove or reduce these indirect threats to tolerable proportions by optimizing Japan's special advantages under the constraints mentioned above, there is no a priori objection to negotiating with the sources of potential threat, viz., the Soviet Union and the PRC. The level of military strength Japan must acquire as a leverage in these negotiations is, however, a pressing issue.

The same cannot be said of the Republics of Korea and China, whose responses to the Nixon Doctrine are conditioned by the following factors. First, both are "divided nations." As divided nations both face traditionally implacable foes with whom, prima facie, a compromise solution seems impossible. This is particularly true as long as by "solution" we mean the elimination of one of the divided halves as an independent center of authority. A voluntary solution that would preserve two independent centers of authority for one Chinese or one Korean nation would require the acceptance of the status quo by two separate regimes and the abandonment by both of "reunification" as a policy objective.

Second, the vast disparity in size between Taiwan and the Chinese mainland tends to make the smaller contender feel insecure while the larger opponent is likely to harbor the hope of reunification by force.[5] This disparity is absent between the Republic of Korea and North Korea, but South Korea does not yet see itself as an even match of the North in military terms. The perception of implacable enmity from an opponent who is larger and/or stronger makes readjustment to a perceived new American policy of reduced military presence and involvement in Pacific-Asia a traumatic experience for both Seoul and Taipei. Their search for options has required a reexamination of many shibboleths and "conventional wisdoms." This reexamination has been painful and laborious; the readjustment accordingly has been slow and uncertain. Yet, as we shall see, readjustments are being made. The problem, for both South Korea and Taiwan, is to find solutions which dovetail with the plans of Japan and the United States and, one might add, which would be acceptable to the Soviet Union and the PRC. For both, uncertainty about Japanese policy is as disturbing as the uncertainty about U.S. intentions and capability which they share with Japan.

THE NIXON DOCTRINE AND JAPANESE SECURITY
AS SEEN FROM TOKYO (PHASE ONE)

July 15, 1971, was a benchmark date in the perception of U.S. policy by countries in Pacific-Aisa. During the "first phase," i.e., before President Nixon's announcement on July 15 of his planned visit to Peking, Asian perception had been influenced by antiwar statements and demonstrations in the United States, announcements about Vietnamization, actual U.S. force reductions in Vietnam and South Korea, U.S. base closings in Japan and elsewhere in Asia, the promised reversion of Okinawa to Japanese rule and certain indications of change in American policy toward mainland China. During the "second phase," i.e., between July 15, 1971, and the "normalization" of Sino-Japanese relations at the end of September, 1972, changes in U.S. policy appeared to be much more rapid and dramatic than had been earlier anticipated by leaders in Pacific-Asia. A new element of surprise was injected into Japanese relations with the United States—and into Mr. Sato's relations with the American President—as a result of the July announcement. This feeling was reinforced by the August 15, 1971, announcement of a new American economic policy which included the floating of the dollar and suspension of dollar convertibility into gold, the imposition of a 10 percent surtax on imports into the United States, and the exertion of pressure on countries with large balance of payments surpluses, notably Japan, to revalue their currencies upward. In "phase three," which was ushered in by Prime Minister Tanaka's recognition of Peking and the abrogation of Japan's Peace

Treaty with the ROC, Japan has begun to seek new relations simultaneously with Peking, Washington, and Moscow. The process of realignment was further accelerated by the energy crisis in the winter of 1973 and Japan's reaction to it.

During the first phase, one school of thought in Japan saw in American force reductions in Asia in 1970–71 the beginning of a "permanent" return to isolation.[6] Others, who would not go as far as the first group, nevertheless thought that there had been a decisive downward reassessment of American interest in Asia. In opposition to both groups, which shared a common belief that there was a malaise of the American spirit and a loss of direction,[7] a third group regarded U.S. force reductions under the Nixon Doctrine as a transitory phenomenon. In their view, the trend would be reversed during President Nixon's second term if he should successfully bid for reelection. There was an obvious uncertainty about U.S. intentions and the changing capability of American forces in Asia. Such matters as the then proposed closing of certain key bases in Japan, including the Yokosuka naval base,[8] and the extent of force reductions from Okinawa, were regarded as suspicious portents of a reduction of American concern. Many points at issue revolved around assessments of capability of the Seventh Fleet at the level the United States would be prepared to maintain in Pacific waters. To some thoughtful Japanese observers, if the United States was reducing its military muscle in Asia, it was probably doing so because it no longer expected to use its muscle. This cynical inference in turn became the basis for speculations on the extent of real U.S. interest in Asia—versus, for instance, U.S. interest in Europe—and on the probable course of future changes in U.S. defense and foreign policy.

In this first phase, Japan was uneasy about American policy insofar as it affected the future security of Japan, but it was focused more on indirect threats to Japan than on any direct threat which might follow a reduction in the American military presence.[9] As some Japanese political leaders have put it, an island nation such as Japan is totally dependent upon imports of fuel and raw materials which must be supplied by sea. Since Taiwan lies astride the principal sea lanes from the south, Japan is vitally interested in U.S. attitudes toward Taiwan and the PRC. "Does the United States have the will and capability to defend Taiwan against both political and military attacks?" This was a question frequently raised before July, 1971.[10] A second question followed: If the United States would not, or could not, defend Taiwan, then what would or could the United States do about the defense of South Korea?

In the minds of some Japanese leaders close to then Prime Minister Sato, the question of American credibility in the defense of Korea was wrapped up with that of Taiwan, while the political defense of Taiwan was inextricably connected with the China issue in the United Nations. If China's seat in the

United Nations should go to Peking and if Taiwan was to be ousted from the international organization, Japanese leaders were apprehensive that the United States might then no longer consider it an obligation to defend Taiwan. In the latter case, the same Japanese leaders were concerned that Peking might indeed undertake military action against Taiwan.

Such a development would put Japan in a grave dilemma. On the one hand, Japan would not like to see Taiwan in the hands of Peking, which could then threaten to harass Japan's vital sea lanes. On the other hand, Japan could not do much militarily by itself and would, therefore, prefer not to become involved. Any attempt by Japan to oppose the PRC on the Taiwan issue without American support would only incur Chinese Communist wrath and be to no avail. Accordingly, Japanese officials stressed, during this period, the need to maintain close U.S.-Japanese consultations on the two countries' China policies. Japan desired coordination of U.S.-Japanese actions, if not a joint policy and action in concert.[11]

As for South Korea, Japan's principal concern was that there should be an adequate defense of the country in spite of U.S. force withdrawals, which, according to the official announcement, were then placed at 20,000 men, or about one-third of the U.S. military strength in Korea. The issue went beyond the defense of South Korea by U.S. conventional forces. In the event the South Koreans, aided by such U.S. conventional forces as could or would be made available at the time, should find themselves unable to halt a North Korean attack, would the United States be willing and able to employ tactical or theater nuclear weapons against the invaders? Implicit in this question was another, even more fundamental issue, namely, whether South Korea would agree to such use. Here, again, Japan's role would have to be reexamined. Since a major function of U.S. bases in Japan is to provide support for potential U.S. military operations in Korea, and since U.S. forces on Okinawa are also maintained in part for the same purpose, Japan sought to reassure the United States during Prime Minister Sato's negotiations with President Nixon in 1969 that the reversion of Okinawa to Japan would not interfere with U.S. actions in such a contingency.[12] At that time, it was stated that Japan would give a "positive" response to any U.S. request made in the course of prior consultations. Japan's assumption seemed to be that the United States wanted to be able to defend Korea and Taiwan. In contrast, Japan's growing concern in 1970–71, after the announcement of American force reductions in Korea, was that the United States might no longer intend or might find itself unable to do so. Again, what was Japan to do in such a situation? Aside from restrictions of the Japanese Constitution, neither Japan nor South Korea would want to see Japanese troops on the Korean Peninsula. Japan would be willing to provide Seoul with economic aid, perhaps even aid of a kind which would permit the allocation of a greater amount of South Korean resources to national defense, but Japan was powerless to do more. In the circumstances, would economic assistance alone be enough?

TOKYO'S PERCEPTION OF U.S. POLICY AND THE ISSUE OF TAIWAN (PHASE TWO)

The announcement in Washington on July 15, 1971, that the American President had accepted an invitation to visit Peking after prolonged secret bilateral contacts, brought serious domestic political reverberations in Japan, as well as greater long-term security and foreign policy concerns. Since the announcement was made without prior consultation with Japan, it was an obvious departure from the Japanese understanding that there would be U.S.-Japanese coordination of their respective China policies.[13] This lack of prior consultations had the effect of undermining Prime Minister Sato's claim that he had a special relationship with the United States. Since arrangements for the Peking visit were made without the benefit of Japanese intermediaries, the hitherto oft-repeated assertion that, as an Asian power with a special understanding of Chinese affairs, Japan could serve as a bridge between the East and the West, could no longer be made with a ring of conviction.

These political effects, aggravated by the August 15, 1971, American economic policy announcement and the defeat in the UN of the U.S.-Japanese-sponsored resolution to make the expulsion of Taiwan an "important question" requiring a two-thirds majority vote, were probably less potent and more transitory than some contemporary observers had feared. Thanks to Mr. Sato's political agility and authority in the LDP, he was able to weather the immediate domestic political storms, vis-à-vis both the opposition parties and dissident factions within his own party. However, several policy implications of long-term significance to Japan's security, which were for a time overshadowed by the political reverberations, have since become increasingly clear.

First of all, shortly after the U.N. resolution to admit Peking, the Washington-Peking rapprochement was interpreted by some Japanese analysts as a return of American policy to its pre-World War II position of containing Japan through an alliance with China. An alternative interpretation regarded the rapprochement as directed against Moscow but inferred further that the United States really wanted to build up Communist China as an ally and might welcome Japanese cooperation in this effort. The first explanation seems to have been based on growing Japanese concern that the United States might sense in Japanese rearming a revival of militarism, which it might wish to curb. The second interpretation reflects a basic uncertainty in Japan about the degree to which Washington would go in appeasing Peking. Would Mr. Nixon's visit to Peking lead to the abandonment of Taiwan by the United

States? Would it result in wholehearted U.S. support of the Chinese Communists?

In Japanese eyes, the question posed by Japanese leaders before July, 1971, about the willingness and capability of the United States to defend Taiwan both politically and militarily was partly answered in July and October of that year.[14] The defeat of the "reverse important question" resolution in the UN in October and the timing of the second Kissinger visit to Peking were regarded by many Japanese as indications of American willingness to pay a substantial price for rapprochement with Peking, whatever may have motivated America's new China policy. These suspicions probably served to explain the initial reaction of some Japanese leaders[15] to the Shanghai Communiqué, interpreting it as a U.S. acknowledgment that Taiwan was a part of the one China claimed by the Chinese Communists instead of an acknowledgment of the fact that both Chinese Communists and Nationalists claimed the existence of only one China.

The position of Taiwan in relation to the trade lifelines of Japan is of course the crux of the issue from Japan's point of view. Whatever America's real intentions about Taiwan may be, geopolitical facts are not affected. What may change is the defensibility of Taiwan without U.S. support, given Japan's present political and military constraints. According to students of Japan's defense, a change in Taiwan's status could affect several of the lifelines. One such route runs through the Taiwan Strait; a second follows the Japan current to Kyushu along the east coast of Taiwan and west of Okinawa; a third moves up north toward Japan on the Pacific side of Okinawa, somewhat farther away from the east coast of Taiwan. The last two both pass through the Bashi Channel between Taiwan and the Philippines. While the Taiwan Strait can be readily interdicted from the Chinese mainland, harassment and disruption of the other sea lanes would be more easily accomplished from Taiwan. Should these sea lanes become insecure, traffic would have to be diverted eastward, following routes from Australia or Indonesia via Saipan, resulting in considerably longer shipping time.[16]

In the mid-1960s, one-third of Japan's imports came from non-Communist countries in Western Europe, the Middle East, South Asia, and Africa. In addition, another 24 percent came from countries in the Western Pacific, east of Singapore, and three percent was from the U.S.S.R.[17] Allowing for the fact that some imports from the U.S.S.R. and from other Asian Communist countries (also about three percent) may reach Japan from north of Taiwan, while imports from Eastern Europe, not included in the above statistics, came from west of Singapore and south of Taiwan, it is probably fair to estimate Japan's dependence for imports on shipments from west of Singapore at one-third of the total, and on shipments from south of Taiwan, including the previous one-third, at up to 60 percent of the total. The degree of dependence is even greater in the case of energy resources, such as petroleum of which about 90 percent is derived from the Middle East, with most of the balance coming from Indonesia. Some projections for 1975 estimate Japan's dependence upon imports for certain raw materials as follows: aluminum, 100 percent; nickel, 100 percent; uranium, 100 percent; petroleum, 99.9 percent; coking coal, 92 percent; iron ore, 91 percent; copper, 82 percent; natural gas, 74 percent. Taiwan and Singapore are the two "choke points" which could be used by a hostile power to cut off these imports. For the same reason they should be denied to potentially hostile powers interested in undermining the U.S.-Japanese alliance.

Would Japan go to war if these lifelines were seriously threatened? No maritime power could suffer such a serious threat without responding, but military action requires the existence of an adequate military capability on the part of the victim, as well as the absence of vulnerabilities that might make the end results disastrous. Japanese students of security affairs are, of course, aware of the need to maintain security of the sea lanes, as well as the threat posed by harassment and possible hit-and-run attacks by naval guerrillas.[18] The defense zone of the Japanese Navy now extends about 1,000 nautical miles to the south of the main islands. However, Japan's present naval strength is far from adequate to protect its sea lanes even in the immediate area of Taiwan and the Philippines. The situation is not expected to improve significantly even with the addition of a fifth destroyer squadron under the fourth defense plan (1972-76).

In the event of U.S. unwillingness or inability to come to Japan's aid when these sea lanes are threatened, how would Japan then respond? The replies of Japanese strategic analysts to this question suggest that the responses would vary with the scale of the threat. Small conventional threats to the sea lanes and minor harassments would be endured. Larger threats would have to be met with greater Japanese naval expansion. Still larger threats would have to be "countered" by negotiation and compromise. What level of threat would be regarded as unmanageable? The answer obviously depends on Japan's military capability at the time such a threat materializes; by extension, it will be a function of the rate and nature of Japanese rearmament up to that time. Japan's concern, following its perception of new developments in America's China policy, punctuated by the July 15, 1971 announcement, the defeat of the UN resolution cosponsored with the United States, and the ambiguity of the language of the Shanghai Communiqué, is that the threat may materialize too soon. In Japan's view, should the United States intend to abandon Taiwan before Japan is stronger militarily, it would be impossible for Japan to restrain Communist China by military means. Japan would not, therefore, wish to incur Peking's hostility by making a futile attempt. As long as Japan is uncertain as to the real intentions of the United States about

Taiwan, or because, in view of its recent experience, it does not fully trust U.S. explanations, Japan would not wish to offend Peking by an openly pro-Taiwan policy. On the other hand, since it is in Japan's strategic interest to have Taiwan remain in potentially non-hostile hands, Japan would not wish to see the existence of Taiwan as a separate entity jeopardized. The repeated U.S. statements that it will honor its commitment under the 1954 Mutual Defense Treaty with the Republic of China are of course, welcome, and the missions of Marshall Green, Kissinger, and others to Japan in 1972 helped to allay some but not all concerns. At the same time, the Republic of China itself does not see any serious Chinese Communist military threat to the security of Taiwan in the early 1970s. The net result of these conflicting considerations and uncertainties was a deliberately ambiguous and ambivalent Japanese policy toward Peking and Taipei between July, 1971, and July, 1972, when Mr. Sato resigned.

This attitude was clearly expressed by Mr. Sato at a press conference after his meeting with President Nixon at San Clemente in January, 1972: "Japan and the U.S. are not necessarily in complete agreement, because each has its independent thinking as an independent state."[19] This assertion of independence was neatly balanced at the other end by the report that Secretary of State Rogers and Foreign Minister Fukuda had agreed to a "joint Japan-U.S. attitude on the Taiwan problem" at their concurrent meeting in California. Again, in presenting a "unified view" of the Japanese government on the Taiwan issue after the initial confusion following the Shanghai Communiqué, the official Japanese position was reported by the *New York Times* as follows: "The government is in no position to speak about Taiwan's legal status since it renounced all right, title and claim to Taiwan and the Pescadores under the San Francisco peace treaty of 1951. However, the government can understand the claim of the People's Republic of China that Taiwan is part of its territory in the light of the circumstances under which China was admitted to the United Nations, and other developments. The government will, on this understanding, make all efforts to normalize relations with China."[20]

Partly for the security reasons analyzed above and partly as a reaction to the style of American diplomacy as seen by Japan's leaders, Japan has talked about "normalization" of relations with Peking and has expanded its relations with Hanoi and Mongolia.[21] Yet, prior to the Tanaka premiership, Japan did not accept Peking's *pre-conditions* for discussions on "normalization." Mr. Tanaka, who was invited to visit Peking in September, 1971, went further, however, by announcing that Japan would not be able to maintain diplomatic relations with Taiwan if it should finally "normalize" its relations with the PRC. A Nixon-Tanaka meeting preceding the Tanaka visit to Peking failed to influence Tanaka's position.

Under Sato, the Japanese tactic had been to win more time during which developments in mainland China, Taiwan, America's China policy, the Soviet Union's position in Asia, and Japanese military capability could all change. This tactic could, however, be upset by precipitate action on the part of either the United States or Japan. In the eyes of Tokyo's leaders, the United States might concede more to Peking either in continuation of its "withdrawal" from Asia or as a gesture toward Peking, in order to create a greater restraining effect (a) on Soviet behavior, or, according to some Japanese, (b) on Japanese rearming. As for Japan itself, some post-Sato Japanese leaders seem to assess the strategic situation differently. Some are more inclined toward Peking for a number of reasons, such as ideological predisposition, real or imaginary prospects of greater trade, and, for at least a few, a sentimental desire for reconciliation with the mainland Chinese against whom the Imperial Army committed many grievous wrongs during the last Sino-Japanese War. In addition, the post-Sato leaders may wish to demonstrate their "independence," in contrast to the "pro-American" Sato policy. The same "pro-American" label was probably to a degree responsible for Tanaka's victory over Fukuda, Sato's Foreign Minister, in their contest for LDP leadership. By the summer of 1972, some LDP leaders were probably more apprehensive about the effect of these internal pressures on Japanese policy than they were about untoward effects of U.S. actions.

JAPAN'S SEARCH FOR A NEW EXTERNAL EQUILIBRIUM (PHASE THREE)

The third phase of Japanese reaction to the Nixon Doctrine may be said to have begun with the "normalization" of relations with the PRC in the fall of 1972. Premier Tanaka's visit to Peking led to Japan's acceptance of two of the three preconditions stipulated by Chou En-lai for restoration of diplomatic relations. The first condition was fully accepted when Japan recognized Peking as the sole government of China. Chou's third condition that Japan abrogate its peace treaty with the ROC was accepted de facto. The Japanese argued that with the derecognition of the ROC government, a treaty with a non-existing government could no longer be valid! Japan, however, did not acknowledge that Taiwan was a part of mainland China. While professing its understanding of Peking's position, Japan insisted that by accepting the Potsdam Declaration, which referred to the earlier Cairo Declaration requiring Japan to relinquish all territories taken from China, Japan had nothing to say about the matter any further. In short, as of September, 1972, Japan was still unwilling to help the PRC consolidate its claim to Taiwan beyond the diplomatic derecognition of the ROC government.

It should be borne in mind that Mr. Tanaka's visit to Peking came not only after that of Mr. Nixon, but also after the latter's visit to Moscow. The ABM Treaty and the U.S.-Soviet executive agreement on strategic offensive weapons had been announced, with their implications for the greatly altered U.S.-Soviet strategic balance and America's apparent willingness to accept in some respects an inferior position. If agreement with the Soviet Union was so important to Washington, should not Tokyo begin to think of a different relationship with the Soviet Union? Soviet offers of economic cooperation for the development of Siberian oil and other resources in return for their future supply to Japan were certainly worth considering especially if the United States could no longer be depended upon to shield Japan. Like the United States, Japan should try to take advantage of Sino-Soviet differences and mutual suspicions. From Japan's point of view, Chou En-lai's expressed understanding of Japan's need for greater defense and even U.S. military support was apparently a welcome result of the Sino-Soviet dispute. It was perhaps directly responsible for the final adoption of the fourth defense plan.

Yet the Soviet Union had not always been accommodating. Nor had been Peking. The volume of Japan's China trade had not grown sharply. Domestic opposition to the new China policy was still vociferous. Two major politicians who were extreme advocates of the PRC were defeated in the 1972 general election. Yet the Japanese Communist Party had greatly increased its representation in the Diet. The consensus Japan needed had eluded its leaders thus far. As for Washington, its economic demands on Japan in contrast to its statement about Japan's role as a linchpin of U.S. defense plans were rather confusing. The typical Japanese complaint was "What does the United States want of us?"[22]

THE AFTERMATH OF THE 1973 ENERGY CRISIS (PHASE IV)

As of the summer of 1973, the Tanaka government had made no readily perceptible shift in its U.S.-oriented alignment beyond the derecognition of Taiwan and the establishment of diplomatic relations with Peking a year earlier. The energy crisis in the winter of 1973–74, however, constituted a new benchmark. It focused attention on the economic vulnerability of Japan, accentuating one of the dimensions of the country's security problem.

In mid-1973 Japan still regarded the Soviet Union as by far the most potent source of threat to its security in the long run. This traditional perception had not changed. Japan hoped, however, to secure the return of its four northern islands during the forthcoming peace treaty negotiations with Moscow. In order to placate the Soviet Union, Japan would try to make itself economically useful to the former by agreeing to invest in the development of Siberian resources. However, in order to reduce the risk to Japanese investors and to increase the security of supply of the developed resources to Japan in the future, U.S. participation in this investment would continue to be solicited. Regarding the PRC, the Japanese view was that it was important for both the United States and Japan that the present Sino-Soviet conflict continue. Hence aid should be extended to Peking to shore up the latter's ability to stand up to the Soviet Union because of the PRC's relative weakness. This Japanese argument served both to rationalize Japan's obvious effort to expand its export to mainland China and to make Export-Import Bank credit easier for Chinese plant purchases, and to allay U.S. concern about Japan's over-zealousness in dealing with Peking and in competing with American business on the Chinese market. A third point in Japanese policy relates to Japan's acknowledged inability to defend its sea lanes and its dependence on the Seventh Fleet for as long as the latter would be available in the area. A sizable expansion of Japan's own defense budget above the level of the Fourth Defense Plan (1972–76) seemed most improbable at the time. For "defense" against Japan's two nuclear neighbors, the obvious policy was to make Japan economically useful to both on the theory that no rational adversary would wish to destroy Japan's industrial capacity, the goose that lays the golden egg for both Peking and Moscow.

Japan's own economic well-being and its economic usefulness to others as a supplier of goods are predicated upon the maintenance of a high level of output and continued growth. As a highly developed island economy deficient in indigenous resources, Japan can maintain its economic activity at a high output level only if an unimpeded flow of import of resources and export of manufactures and semiprocessed goods can be fully assured. Full assurance implies that it must exist at the sources of supply, along the routes of transportation, on the home market of production and consumption in Japan, and in foreign countries where Japanese goods are sold. What the energy crisis did was to demonstrate the importance of some of these factors other than the security of the sea lanes themselves on which attention had been concentrated heretofore.

The gist of Japan's approach to securing raw material supply during the pre-"1973 crisis" period consisted essentially of the following points: (1) diversification of external sources of supply, (2) diversification of transportation routes, (3) expansion of long-term purchasing contracts from foreign suppliers, (4) increased Japanese participation and investment in the exploration and development of mineral and other resources with host countries possessing these resources, and (5) greater offers of Japanese capital and technology to developing countries for general economic development that may be tied to (3) and (4). Although these factors have both economic and security aspects, it was not clear to the outside observer that they were well coordinated. While the Foreign Office and the defense-oriented segment of the Liberal Democratic Party were very security conscious, the Ministry of Industry and Trade seemed to see its task as primarily economic and was seemingly oblivious of security concerns at times. The trend toward more and more Japanese investment in raw material supply in foreign countries, such as the expansion of Japanese-owned oil concessions, was partly motivated by a desire to become independent of Western-owned major international oil companies and other Western interests and by innate Japanese competitiveness that simply abhors being left out of any important economic sphere.

On the other hand, for those who were conscious of security implications of Japan's raw material policy, their principal concerns before the winter of 1973 were (1) how to balance the advantage of securing more raw material supplies from places in the Soviet Union and mainland China that are nearer to Japan against certain strategic disadvantages, (2) how to balance involvement with the Soviet Union against involvement with the PRC in the light of the continuing hostility between Peking and Moscow, and (3) how to secure the sea routes south of Japan leading to the Indian Ocean and beyond. The strategic disadvantage of helping the Soviet Union develop its Siberian resources, especially the development of Tyumen oil and the Soviet-proposed construction of a pipe line to bring this oil to Nakhodka, is to give the armed forces, including the Soviet Pacific Fleet, a greater oil supply and even more mobility and flexibility of deployment than they already possess. In addition, any increase in dependence on the Soviet Union for key raw materials would enhance the latter's leverage on Japan. By the same token, similar arrangements between Japan and Peking would impart a corresponding strategic advantage to the PRC. These considerations of bilateral relations between Japan on the one hand and the Soviet Union or the PRC on the other are further complicated by the displeasure Moscow or Peking might show Japan, each as a result of Japan's economic cooperation with the other. These security concerns were tied to the worries of Japanese businessmen as potential investors. In the Soviet case, since the amount of Japanese investment called for would be exceedingly large, and since Japan has little leverage vis-à-vis the Soviet Union, Japanese businessmen were afraid of losing their investments through expropriation. The private Japanese businessmen might be satisfied with a solution based on guarantees of the Japanese Export-Import Bank. For the government, however, such risk could be reduced only through U.S. participation in a joint development of Siberian resources. From the Japanese point of view, the risk of expropriation or of Soviet stoppage of promised supply might be lowered by involving the United States. The same considerations also apply to Japanese-PRC cooperation to develop resources that could be sold to Japan. In the Chinese case, however, because of the relatively weaker position of Communist China, Japan views the United States more as a competitor than a sharer of risk.

In any event, however, the continued military presence of the United States in the Western Pacific, though on a substantially reduced scale after the completion of the withdrawal of U.S. ground forces from Vietnam in March, 1973, would help keep the sea lanes open. Furthermore, Peking's general need to retain the good will of the United States because of the Chinese perception of the Soviet threat would exert a restraining effect on the PRC. In both respects, Japan would stand to benefit. Hence Japan's raw material policy also supported the continuation of the U.S.-Japan mutual security arrangement.

The Arab oil embargo, however, greatly altered the situation. First, the embargo showed that to be on the side of the United States in an international political alignment could be a disadvantage of imminently disastrous proportions for Japan. Second, in Japanese eyes, the U.S. reaction to the embargo demonstrated the American inability to shield Japan from such a threat at the source of supply, as distinct from any threat to the sea routes, as well as American unwillingness to soften the immediate impact on the Japanese economy by sharing its own available supply. Granted that the embargo was not watertight, and its effect on the United States was not sufficiently painful to call for drastic U.S. countermeasures against some of the Arab countries, the U.S. inability to offer an immediately effective, automatic response could not but convince the Japanese that even U.S. participation with Japan in the joint development of Siberian or Chinese resources would, under these circumstances, add little to the restraint either of the Kremlin or of Peking. Third, because the settlement of the October War would lead to the ultimate reopening of the Suez Canal, thus making the Indian Ocean more accessible to the Soviet Fleet based on Black Sea ports, the Soviet naval presence in both the Indian Ocean and the Pacific would be increased. This factor would have to be weighed by Japan in conjunction with the degree of assurance that the Malacca Straits would always remain open to all shipping against the possibility that selected countries might on occasion be denied the right of transit as a result of pressures similar to the Arab oil embargo.

Indicative of a new trend in Japanese policy following the Arab oil embargo were the reported Japanese willingness to provide the long-sought credit of over one billion dollars to the Soviet Union[23] and the concession to Peking for the conclusion of a civil aviation agreement at the cost of severing a similar agreement with Taiwan. The establishment of closer links with Moscow and Peking in 1974 indicated the shape of events toward a gradual realignment.

KOREA AND JAPANESE SECURITY AFTER JULY, 1971

Japanese policy after July, 1971, did not develop the same degree of ambivalence in regard to South Korea as it did with respect to Taiwan, principally because there was no significant change in U.S. policy toward Korea. What uneasiness there was about Japan's relations with the Republic of Korea derived from anxiety in business circles about the effect of their having business interests in South Korea on the prospects of doing business with mainland China. According to the *New York Times*,[24] such well-known firms as Nippon Steel, Hitachi, Toyota, the Fuji Bank, the Mitsubishi Bank, and the Itoh and Marubeni trading companies all absented themselves from a routine business conference, in early 1972, of Japanese and South Korean businessmen for this very reason. The government, however, has remained forthright in assessing Japan's strategic interest in a friendly Korea serving as a buffer zone for Japan, if not an area of forward defense.

Japan's official concern about South Korea continues to focus on the rate of U.S. troop withdrawals and the growth of the ROK's defense capability. A potentially far-reaching development was the reported U.S. policy decision at the time of the mining of Haiphong that the United States would refrain from using ground forces or nuclear weapons in combat.[25] If this self-imposed restriction was applicable to Korea, it would go a long way to answer Japanese questions about potential U.S. first use of nuclear weapons in defense of its Northeast Asian allies.

THE EXTENT OF JAPAN'S DEFENSE BUILDUP

A question uppermost in the minds of students of security problems in the Western Pacific is whether Japan will go beyond a modest expansion of its conventional forces. More specifically, will Japan go nuclear? How has the Nixon Doctrine influenced some of the determinants of Japan's position on this matter?

In January, 1964, nine months before the first test firing of a nuclear device by Communist China, the French General Gallois, famous advocate of the national nuclear deterrent principle, stated in an interview with *Mainichi Shimbun* that Japan would be faced with three alternatives if Peking should develop nuclear weapons.[26] The first would be to strengthen the country's security ties with the United States and to remain under the protection of the American nuclear umbrella. The second would be to enter into closer relationship with Peking, or to establish some degree of neutrality with Peking's blessing. The third would be to develop Japan's own nuclear force so as to remain independent of China while emerging out of the shadow of the U.S. umbrella. Some initial comments should be made on the Gallois alternatives.

The first alternative presupposes that the U.S. nuclear umbrella will continue to be credible in Japanese eyes, a point directly related to the estimate by Japanese decision-makers of U.S. intentions and capability vis-à-vis those of the Soviet Union and the PRC. Second, in view of the Soviet effort to loosen, if not to "decouple," Japan from the latter's U.S. ties, of which Gromyko's Tokyo visit in January, 1972, was an early indication and the invitation to Prime Minister Tanaka to visit Moscow in the summer of 1973 a strong follow-up, a fourth alternative available to Japan, which Gallois failed to mention, would be to enter into a closer relationship with the Soviet

Union. Lastly, not all the alternatives are mutually exclusive. A country does not have to depend upon negotiations in order to have a better relationship with one or more of its neighbors, who may otherwise pose a threat to its security, as a trade-off for an arms buildup. It is necessary, generally speaking, to have sufficient military strength before one can negotiate effectively. Looking at the same proposition the other way, an arms buildup could be a prelude to negotiation for coexistence; armed neutrality could be another end result.

One tenet of the Nixon Doctrine is to negotiate with one's adversary while maintaining one's strength. From a Japanese standpoint, if its strength has decreased because of perceived, actual, or probable changes in policy of its American ally, it will be necessary to develop its own military capability. The question still open is how far Japan has to and can go. As we have pointed out, it is improbable, according to one theory, that the Soviet Union would have consented to SALT if it had not greatly improved its strategic nuclear position vis-à-vis the United States. There is a corollary theory of more recent origin, which envisages a continuation of SALT on a tripartite basis once the PRC has reached a level of nuclear deterrence, vis-à-vis both the Soviet Union and the United States, which it deems satisfactory. Since Japan has the economic and technological capability to engage in a substantial arms buildup, could not the same principle apply, making Japanese rearmament a prelude to negotiations? Would not going nuclear, in essence, be a special application of an arms buildup and no more than that? A militarily stronger Japan, which may be synonymous with a Japan armed with nuclear weapons, would, in Japanese eyes, be a more effective and independent negotiator with other countries. In terms of the diagrams introduced in the Appendix to this chapter, for Japan to become a "balancing power" the Japanese may believe it necessary to build up Japanese arms, perhaps including nuclear arms. As a balancing power, Japan will then be able to choose the order of closeness of its relationships with the United States, the Soviet Union, and the PRC.

The seemingly mutually exclusive alternatives posed by General Gallois should be modified from another point of view. In practical terms, while the decision to go nuclear or to rearm in general may be an act that takes but an instant, however long it may take to reach that decision, implementation of the decision will necessarily be time-consuming. It is entirely plausible, for instance, for Japan to wish to build up its arms while remaining under the U.S. strategic nuclear umbrella. Doing so may even be regarded as a necessary means of reducing the risk of energetic countermeasures by other nuclear powers, even if continued United States goodwill can be assured.

Obviously, the Japanese perception of threat and of the appropriate means to deal with it, together with the "nuclear allergy" Japan developed after World War II as a result of its experience with Hiroshima and Nagasaki, stands at the core of Japan's decision on this matter—that is to say, if Japan is not "inadvertently" swept into such a course of development by events. Before the appearance of Mr. Nakasone's "White Paper" on Japan's Defense in late 1970, the standard answer to inquiries about Japan's attitude toward nuclear weapons consisted of the following two points: (1) Japan would not possess or manufacture nuclear weapons or allow them to be introduced into Japan. (2) Constitutional restrictions and Japanese public opinion would make the development of nuclear weapons unthinkable. A noticeable change, however, took place following the publication of the above "White Paper," and certain passages were often referred to by the Japanese themselves. In a discussion on "limits of defense power" the report distinguished between "constitutional limits" and "policy limits."

> Since our military power is intended for self-defense, its size and scale must be that which is proper and necessary. What degree of defense power this means in concrete terms cannot be described categorically because of various conditions—such as the progress and development of science and technology at a given time; . . .
>
> With regard to nuclear weapons, we adopt the three-point nuclear principle. Even though it would be possible to say that in legal and theoretical sense, possession of small nuclear weapons, falling within the minimum requirement for capacity necessary for self-defense and not posing a threat of aggression to other countries, would be permissible, the government, as its policy, adopts the principle of not attempting at nuclear armament which might be possible under the Constitution. . . .[27]

Official expressions of policy have not changed in spite of the "Nixon shocks" of 1971 and President Nixon's discussions in Peking and Moscow in 1972. In line with established policy, Japan sought reassurance from the United States following the reversion of Okinawa that American nuclear weapons had been withdrawn from the island.[28] The fourth defense plan already envisages an expansion of the conventional navy and air force, increases in which are deemed "proper and necessary for self-defense." There has not been any official statement on a new assessment of the need for nuclear weapons. However, the perception of threat, U.S. credibility, and Japan's needs have all changed.

According to what might be called a "counter-base" strategy for the joint defense of Japan by U.S. and Japanese forces put forward by some Japanese analysts,[29] Japanese defenders would be assigned the responsibility of protecting the home islands in the event of an external attack, whereas U.S. defenders would be responsible for mounting a counterattack against the bases of the attacking enemy. The reduction of U.S. forces indicated in 1970 under the Nixon Doctrine prompted the same Japanese analysts to question the effect of any reduction of this U.S. counter-base capability and its replacement by a Japanese equivalent. Regardless of whether or not American forces expected to use nuclear weapons in carrying out their mission, some Japanese may have expected "nuclear first use" by U.S. forces. A legitimate question about the need for nuclear weapons in the event that conventional defense measures fail cannot, therefore, be dismissed. Moreover, if the attacking force is capable of initiating use of, say, tactical nuclear weapons against Japan's conventional defense force, and if an adequate U.S. response cannot be taken for granted, would not the availability of an appropriate Japanese substitute, or that of a new ally, be required? Thus, with the reduction of U.S. forces from Asia, even before July, 1971, some aspects of the tactical defensive use of nuclear weapons had already become a matter of interest in some Japanese quarters. American renunciation of the use of nuclear weapons in South Vietnam in order to halt the massive attack by the North in the spring of 1972 doubtless introduced a new factor for serious thought in Japan.

As for the U.S. "guarantee" under both the Nixon Doctrine,[30] which promises a "shield" against attack or blackmail by a nuclear power, and the specific terms of the U.S.-Japan treaty,[31] several developments have affected or may affect Japanese perception. First, some Japanese seem to hold the view that the U.S. announcement of July, 1971, on China policy could and, perhaps, should be treated as a precedent indicating that in matters of vital U.S. national interest the United States would act unilaterally without prior consultation with Japan even though vital Japanese national interests are also involved. Consequently, the United States must be expected all the more to act unilaterally on the basis of its own perception of national interests if it is called upon to honor its nuclear guarantee in behalf of Japan against another nuclear power which might retaliate in kind, whether or not on the same scale. In fact, Japan cannot expect or, even more so, count upon the United States to act otherwise.

This viewpoint was expressed prior to Mr. Nixon's meetings at Peking and Moscow in February and May, 1972. As Peking begins to develop even a small number of ICBMs or other delivery means capable of reaching the continental United States in the next few years, in addition to a minimal deterrent against the U.S.S.R., the above perception of the unreliability of the U.S. nuclear umbrella can become even more convincing to Japan's leaders. The same conclusion is likely if the Soviet Union achieves a substantial lead over the United States in the number of both land-based and sea-based ICBMs within the foreseeable future taking full advantage of the leeway permitted under the SALT I agreement.

A Japanese analyst, writing in the *Daily Yomiuri* on August 19, 1971, stated bluntly,[32] "No longer can Japan count on the U.S. nuclear umbrella that had already been folded quietly as a strategic signal to China.... No U.S. president, many have long suspected, would ever risk 150 million American lives just to honor his—or more precisely his predecessors'—treaty commitments. No, he would not. No more umbrella for a total 44 allies, including Japan and 35 NATO and Rio treaty nations." The linkage of the credibility of the U.S. "nuclear umbrella" to this particular view of America's new China policy may have been weakened by subsequent U.S. efforts to reassure Japan. However, the more lasting effect of the altered strategic balance between the United States and the Soviet Union can hardly be dispelled in the eyes of U.S. allies; Japan is no exception.

A scenario painted in the same *Yomiuri* article, perhaps intentionally fanciful for effect, deserves quoting.

> In the Asian scene, the no-more-umbrella principle might produce the following result in a hypothetical war.
>
> Phase I—a civil strife of indigenous origin in a U.S. ally X escalates to a chaotic political-social crisis that in turn provokes a non-ally Y to extend subversive aid to X's anti-government elements; the U.S. gives no aid openly to X but alerts its token treaty forces in the region.
>
> Phase II—the escalated contingency leads to an open local, conventional war between X and Y, both non-nuclear; the Soviet Union covertly intervenes to *preempt* China's initiative.
>
> Phase III—The Soviet Union intervenes openly and threatens to overrun X; this forces the U.S. to use a limited number of tactical nuclear arms, primarily to protect its own forces and their withdrawal.
>
> Phase IV—the Soviet Union, in retaliation, uses tactical nuclear arms with an explicit warning that a further nuclear escalation will lead to a "direct attack" on U.S. cities.
>
> The question: Would the U.S. president order the firing of ICBMs on the Soviet Union to defend the ally, knowing that a Soviet retaliation might kill 150 million Americans?
>
> The answer: No.
>
> The result: The ally X is wiped off the map; the conflict is over in a few days.[33]

What is the Japanese capability to go nuclear? Japan is, of course, already familiar with tactical defensive weapons using conventional warheads. Would it be technologically too difficult for Japan to take the further step of developing nuclear warheads? The correct answer is: Probably not. Japan envisages a sizable expansion of its civilian nuclear power capacity from 45 to 65 million kilowatts by the 1980s.[34] According to one Japanese analyst who is opposed to Japan's development of nuclear weapons, the transformation from civilian nuclear power reactor technology to weapons technology will not be unduly difficult. A need for power will demand the development of nuclear reactors and this expansion of nuclear power will automatically lead to the training of a large pool of technical labor accustomed to handling nuclear equipment. Fast-breeder reactors may also enable Japan to resolve the problem posed by lack of any domestic source of fissionable materials.[35] In addition, the same technical preparation could have the effect of neutralizing such "nuclear allergy" as may still remain. This assessment, however, may overrate the stage of development of fast-breeder technology and difficulties inherent in assuring a secure and adequate supply of enriched uranium, proper test sites, etc.

How much of Japan's nuclear allergy does remain is an unresolved question. The results of public opinion polls vary, depending partly upon how the question is phrased.[36] More people are opposed to Japan's going nuclear than to the expansion of Japanese defense capability. At the same time, an increasing number of people seem to believe that Japan will eventually have nuclear weapons. More and more people seem to care less and less should Japan manage to acquire them somehow. What is wanting is a consensus, and a consensus may develop, according to knowledgeable Japanese observers, if there is a suddenly heightened sense of threat to Japan's security. Sharp reverses suffered by the United States in international affairs, drastic further reductions of U.S. military presence, further downgrading of U.S. credibility in Pacific-Asia, or other developments adverse to Japanese interests in the Western Pacific will all have this effect. Other developments which may be essentially unrelated to defense at the outset, such as expressions of economic nationalism on the part of both Japan and the United States, but which may serve to exacerbate relations, could so condition the perception and response of Japanese leaders with respect to the United States that the nuclear question may even become "academic." A decade hence, students of Japanese affairs may well wonder why anyone bothered to ask the question: Would Japan go nuclear or would Japan go beyond the bounds of a conventional arms buildup? To them it may appear that the proper question should have been: Why did Japan choose to follow this or that route in developing sophisticated weaponry, which, incidentally, may not be the same as going nuclear?

Psychological aversion to nuclear weapons is not the only constraint that has affected Japanese decision-making. Lack of convenient test sites is, for example, a practical obstacle. Also, because of the large size of the Soviet Union and Communist China, two of Japan's potential adversaries, even a minimal deterrent capability may require a sizable nuclear force. This would increase both cost and lead time. Because of the lead time required between a decision to go nuclear and the development of an adequate deterrent force, it might appear prudent for Japan to develop a substantial conventional force first. Hence, any decision to go nuclear, even if politically feasible, cannot be taken until later in the 1970s. Until the reversion of Okinawa on May 15, 1972, concern about America's adverse reaction to the character of Japan's arms buildup may have acted as an additional constraint. After this date, however, concern about Soviet and PRC reaction may increasingly become a more potent factor in Japan's decision-making. This consideration would increase in importance if the Soviet Union and/or the PRC can acquire greater leverage against Japan in regard to Japan's trade lifelines, for instance, with respect to the supply of petroleum, and/or if the two countries can improve their respective strategic capability to a point where each, alone or jointly, can take unilateral preemptive action against an emerging nuclear power, even in the face of U.S. opposition.

To recapitulate, Japan's policy toward nuclear weapons, like Japan's China policy, may be characterized as one of "deliberate indecision." It is a policy of not "taking the plunge" unless circumstances become too compelling. It is not the policy of resurgent militarism suggested by Japan's detractors in Peking and elsewhere. Nor is it a policy that will develop as an afterthought or appendage to Japan's economic growth. At the same time, it is definitely a policy of self-interest based on the assumption that, by postponing the fateful decision, Japan will gain more options than it will lose or that the options gained will at least be better. Until the Nixon-Brezhnev agreement in SALT I, this potential gain in postponing the nuclear decision seemed primarily to consist of a possible shortening of lead time before deployment through discovery of new techniques some of which might enable a technologically advanced but non-nuclear power to bypass the entire nuclear weapons phase. Following the Moscow agreement on SALT, the potentially much larger say Moscow may gain over future Japanese decisions in this matter may further narrow Japan's choice and reduce the flexibility of its timing. It may not be possible for Japan to hold its options open indefinitely. Developments after the 1973 energy crisis have further narrowed Japan's range of choices. The technical possibility of bypassing the "nuclear phase" is, of course, fraught with uncertainties.

Finally, one should bear in mind that until Japan has a viable substitute for the mutual defense treaty with the United States, maintenance of the treaty still serves a very important purpose. Even in the case of the nuclear guarantee, lack of credibility in Japanese eyes does not mean that a potential adversary can totally disregard it. As long as an adversary is not certain that the United States will not honor the guarantee, the hypothetical "shield" will continue to have a deterrent value. It would behoove Japan, therefore, not to question the guarantee officially. Some protestations of Japanese leaders that the defense treaty with the United States still is the cornerstone of Japanese policy can be credited to this highly practical consideration.

A somewhat cynical view of the U.S. "shield" is that, in the event of a grave, imminent threat to Japanese security, the existence of the security treaty will give Japan an opportunity to use the United States as an intermediary in negotiating with the source of threat. A past example of such an attempt, which failed, was Japan's last-minute effort toward the end of World War II to solicit Soviet help in order to secure better terms from the United States than unconditional surrender.

SOUTH KOREA'S PERCEPTION OF THE NIXON DOCTRINE

The Korean perceptions of the Nixon Doctrine and reaction to it have been much simpler than in Japan. Before July, 1971, the withdrawal of one of the two U.S. divisions from Korea for budgetary and other U.S. domestic reasons provided the first shock to the Koreans. The U.S. decision to withdraw troops from Korea was compared with the assurance Washington had given Europe that there would not be any withdrawal from there, at least for some time to come; it was regarded by Koreans as evidence of the downgrading of U.S. interest in Korea, as well as in Asia generally. Given the ROK's perception of threat from the north and its estimate of its own defense capability, South Korea was concerned that U.S. forces would not be willing or able to return in adequate numbers to defend Korea in the event of an attack. Potential congressional opposition and adverse U.S. public opinion were frequently cited as reasons for this concern, regardless of repeated American assurances.

The threat perception was generally based on comparisons showing North Korea to be considerably stronger than the South in military expenditure, industrial output, and the potential for arms production.[37] Projected to the mid-1970s, the imbalance appeared to be such that it could be offset only by increasing the fire power of the ROK forces and the country's own capacity to produce arms. All this provided a good case for a five-year program to modernize Korean forces with U.S. assistance.

While the provision of U.S. military assistance to bolster the capability of an ally willing to defend itself coincides with one of the tenets of the Nixon Doctrine, and while priority was actually given to military aid to Korea by the Nixon administration,[38] actual performance tended to fall short of both promise and expectation. Some of the psychological impact of the withdrawal of the one American division was relieved by the acquisition, after long delays, of a new plant to produce M16 rifles, but uncertainty in funding and delay in both funding and delivery greatly weakened the positive aspect of the Nixon Doctrine in Korea in 1970–71. The situation did not seem to have materially improved in 1971–72. These practical problems of implementation during Mr. Nixon's first term reduced U.S. credibility in Korean eyes.

After July, 1971, South Korea's perception of the Nixon Doctrine, like that of other Asian nations, was dominated by U.S. negotiations with Peking. The immediate Korean concerns were the following: First, how would developing relations between Communist China and the United States affect the triangular U.S.-Soviet-China relationships on the Korean peninsula? Would the Soviet Union and China find it in their mutual interest to maintain peace in Korea? Or would Moscow wish to goad Pyongyang into an attack on the South, hoping thus to embroil the Chinese Communists with the United States? This possible Soviet gambit was frequently suggested before Mr. Nixon's Peking visit as a means the Soviet Union might employ to break up the Washington-Peking rapprochement. Still another view, more optimistic than the other, suggested that Peking might actually desire an American presence in South Korea as an offset to potential Soviet dominance. All these speculations were focused on one point, namely, that the Korean peninsula might become a theater of conflict involving at least two of the big powers as a result of big-power machinations outside Korea.

On the other hand, some South Koreans also feared that Kim Il-sung might act on his own, choosing to attack the South before it would be too late. This possibility relied on the assumption that both Moscow and Peking would wish to maintain the South Korean buffer and restrain Kim Il-sung, thus thwarting the latter's ambition to unite all Korea under him. For a time in the winter of 1971–72, this possibility was presented in a short-war scenario in which the North Koreans would descend upon Seoul with light infantry and wreak havoc on the country before UN forces could intervene. The same possibility was also advanced by South Koreans as an explanation of President Park's proclamation of a state of national emergency on December 6, 1971. In their view, while the weakening of the ROK's diplomatic and military position "may be more apparent than real, . . . it is quite likely that dictator Kim Il-sung in North Korea will interpret the situation this way, and his error would be a disastrous one for him and for us as well."[39] The reference to Kim Il-sung's potential "error" in perception reminds one of the line drawn by Dean Acheson shortly before the outbreak of the Korean War, which left South Korea on the other side of the American defense perimeter in the Western Pacific.

Finally, the fate of Taiwan in the United Nations presaged trouble for South Korea. The latter feared that Pyongyang might be invited by the United Nations to participate in discussions on the Korean Resolution without having first to acknowledge UN authority. Since the ROK was established under UN auspices, such a development could become a threat to the

ROK government's legitimacy and to its claim to rule over all Korea. Besides, a resolution might be passed in the U.N., for instance, under Peking's sponsorship calling for the removal of all foreign troops from the Korean peninsula in order to let the Koreans settle their own problems. At a minimum, the passage of such a resolution would remove the justification for a United Nations Command in Korea. Worse still, so the South Koreans fear, the remaining American troops might then find it opportune to withdraw, whether required to or not. To some Koreans proof that these sentiments were correct was provided by Kim Il-sung's call in May, 1972, for direct discussions and troop withdrawals by the United States.[40]

KOREA'S PROBE FOR OPTIONS

The partial U.S. force withdrawal had the effect of making South Koreans think about the hitherto unthinkable. The U.S. alliance and dependence upon U.S. participation and full support under the UN command for the defense of Korea had become a habit. Once it was realized that sizable U.S. force reductions would actually take place, "non-U.S. options" had to be examined more carefully. After July, 1971, most South Koreans became convinced that all U.S. forces were likely to be withdrawn before very long. Some observers then set the date in the mid-1970s when the "modernization" of Korean forces is scheduled for completion. Among options being considered are the following.

The first option is the opening of a dialogue with the North. To begin with, during 1971, South Korea entered into direct "Red Cross negotiations" with North Korea on the subject of separated families. While the subject was non-political and the negotiators were ostensibly all Red Cross representatives—the South, however, complained about political exploitation of the talks by the North—the significant points were (1) that the talks were held, thus setting a precedent for direct negotiations; (2) that both sides agreed to continue future discussions, moving the location of the meetings from Panmunjon to Seoul and Pyongyang on an alternate basis. Moreover, some ROK observers credited the talks with a favorable modification of Seoul's international image, making it less intransigent and militantly anti-Communist than before. The direct talks were also a contributing factor to the postponement of discussion of the Korean issue in the United Nations by a year. To allow the issue to be aired immediately after the passage of the Albanian resolution to oust Taiwan, according to most Koreans, would have been far too risky. In July, 1972, exploration of this option was brought another step forward by a joint ROK-DRK announcement that they would try to avoid accidental war, seek reunification through talks, and cease hostile acts against each other. The North-South Accord, announced on July 4, 1972, came at the end of a series of secret meetings in Seoul and Pyongyang. However, although the bilateral

Coordinating Committee met several times during the twelve months after the Accord, no further significant agreement was reached until 1973.

A few months after President Nixon's second inauguration, an ROK government statement on June 23, 1973, suggested the representation of both North and South Korea at the United Nations. The principal points of the June, 1973, statement were:[41]

1) "The peaceful unification of the fatherland is the supreme task of the Korean people...." (Point I)

2) "Peace must be maintained in the Korean peninsula by all means. The south and the north should neither interfere with each other's internal affairs nor commit aggression against each other." (Point II)

3) "We shall not oppose North Korea's participation with us in international organizations, if it is conducive to easing of tension and the furtherance of international cooperation." (Point IV)

4) "We shall not object to our admittance into the United Nations together with North Korea, if the majority of the member-states of the United Nations so wish, provided that it does not cause hindrance to our national unification."

"Even before our admittance into the United Nations as a member, we shall not be opposed to North Korea also being invited at the time of the UN General Assembly's deliberation of 'the Korean question' in which the representative of the Republic of Korea is invited to participate." (Point V)

5) "The Republic of Korea will open its door to all the nations of the world on the basis of the principles of reciprocity and equality. At the same time, we urge those countries whose ideologies and social institutions are different from ours to open their doors likewise to us." (Point VI)

6) "Peace and good-neighborliness are the firm basis of the foreign policy of the Republic of Korea. It is reaffirmed that we will continue to further strengthen the ties of friendship existing between friendly nations and our country." (Point VII)

An upshot of the June, 1973, statement was the virtually open official acknowledgment that Seoul now expected to have two Koreas for an indefinite period. While the remote goal of reunification had not been totally abandoned, it was openly admitted in government and informed circles that reunification could not be achieved since neither side was willing to discard its own social and political system. The continuation of talks between the two sides may yield certain minor agreements on cultural (including sport) matters and humane issues, but is unlikely to bring about any real political agreement barring a major change of heart on both sides or in the international situation.

Seoul's proposal in June, 1973, like the announcement of the North-South Communiqué a year earlier, had the immediate purpose of forestalling any Communist proposal in the UN that might lead to the dissolution of the UN Command and a consequent upsurge of international pressure, as well as internal pressure within the United States, to withdraw the remaining U.S. forces from Korea.

Actually Seoul's proposal might not be able to forestall such a development unless both the PRC and the Soviet Union would like to see U.S. forces remain in South Korea for the time being. One hypothesis is that the PRC may wish to keep U.S. forces in Korea for now in order to preclude Soviet efforts to dominate the area. On the other hand, the Soviet Union may also wish to preclude a possible injection of PRC military presence into the peninsula in the absence of U.S. troops in the South. The Chinese threat to the Soviet Maritime Province would be increased otherwise. South Korea may be banking on such mutual Soviet and Chinese reluctance to see American forces leave too soon. As a minimum, the position Seoul has taken has enhanced the possibility that any discussion of the Korean question in the UN will not be a one-sided affair.

Acknowledgment of the likelihood of long-term division of the country has, however, raised certain political problems. Internationally, reconciliation of the present official position of allowing for the coexistence of two Koreas in international dealings with the ROK government's past position of insisting on its own sole legitimacy is accomplished by a bit of sophistry. In the words of one Korean, "We cannot control the policies of foreign countries that wish to deal with both North and South Korea. We are now telling these nations that it is all right with us if they wish to do so. However, internally, we are not about to recognize the North as a separate state and have not done so."[42]

The issue is, however, more difficult to resolve in terms of domestic politics. The government has made such a point on reunification and for so long—and the general public, especially perhaps in the rural areas, is still yearning for a united Korea—that it is hard for the leaders now to tell the people that this goal must be abandoned for the foreseeable future. How to do so is an art of domestic politics which the Korean government has yet to master.

A second new departure is to explore the possibility of contacts with other "non-hostile" nations. In part, this has been accomplished by stating South Korea's willingness to trade with all such countries, including non-hostile Communist countries. Presumably, even trade with Peking would not be barred. South Korea is ready also to admit visitors from Communist countries. However, some Koreans believe that both Communist powers are still being reluctant to approach Seoul because each is afraid of being accused by the other to have sold out to the capitalist West in seemingly abandoning Pyongyang.

South Koreans have not yet forgotten Japan's previous imperial role and are suspicious of Japanese intentions. Among young Koreans, nationalistic sentiments and antipathy toward Japan continue to be strong. Nor do Koreans have much confidence in Japan's present military capability. Thus, South Korea is not particularly happy to have to consider Japan as a potential big power to fill the role the United States seems about to vacate. In Korean eyes, the presence of U.S. forces in Korea is not only a deterrent to the North but also a check to the undue expansion of Japanese influence. For these reasons, South Korea sees its "Japan option" primarily in terms of Japanese economic assistance and would not welcome any direct Japanese military assistance at the present time. Economic assistance, too, is viewed with reserve; the proportion of Japanese capital in foreign investment in Korea is said to exceed 50 percent. Many Koreans regard this ratio as too high. They become disturbed, however, when they find Japanese businessmen ambivalent about doing business in South Korea in the face of Chou En-lai's threats, and the new Tanaka shift in Japan's China policy is a source of apprehension. Finally, the South Koreans would be pleased to see a greater Japanese financial contribution to a collective defense arrangement also involving the United States.

The last point leads to the fourth option, namely, regional defense cooperation, an old standby. Before the open shift of America's China policy in July, 1971, certain ROK leaders favored a Northeast Asia regional cooperative arrangement, including South Korea, Japan, and Taiwan, but the proposed inclusion of Japan posed considerable difficulty. Past discussions between Seoul and Taipei, even on such "low-profile" matters as repair and maintenance of military equipment received from the United States, had not been particularly fruitful for want of more active American participation. Because of these and other factors, the regional concept seems to have become even less viable after July, 1971. Since the ROK may find it necessary to deal with Peking, there are indications that it may be ready to weaken its ties with Taipei. South Korea, like Japan, is afraid of becoming the unprotected object of wrath of a powerful Communist China. The notion that regional defense arrangements could substitute for American military presence or even supplement a reduced U.S. military presence is regarded by Koreans as unrealistic. The general feeling is that the Nixon Doctrine is essentially an American retreat, not an American search for a new and stable equilibrium.

In diplomatic language, the official attitude toward the United States may be summarized as follows: "Korea has realized that there are limits to what the United States may be expected to do, limits imposed not by lack of good will or good faith, but by changes in the times and circumstances. The United States is now in the midst of a difficult situation internally and externally. Therefore, she must look after her own interests and this is what Korea ... must do."[43]

THE REPUBLIC OF CHINA'S PERCEPTION OF THREAT

The 100-mile-wide Taiwan Strait presents serious difficulties to a potential invader who must establish air and naval superiority as a prerequisite to establishing local superiority on the ground. There is only a token American military presence, the U.S.-ROC Joint Taiwan Defense Command; most American air force personnel on the island were involved in supporting operations in Vietnam. Even U.S. military assistance, especially grants in aid, has been at a minimum for quite some time. These points were often cited by Nationalist Chinese leaders in order to explain their relative equanimity about the Nixon Doctrine at the time of the President's Guam Speech. Taiwan would remain as secure or insecure, depending on the way the issue was examined, as it had always been. A condition was always attached to this statement; the joint defense command should remain lest there be some fundamental question about the U.S. intention to defend Taiwan.

The July 15, 1971, statement was a Nixon "shock" in Taiwan as it was in Japan and South Korea. However, from the military point of view, it was quickly recognized that Taiwan's position had in no way worsened. In fact, if Peking's own strategic position was such that it had to come to terms with the United States in order to restrain the Soviet Union, the Chinese Communists' physical threat to Taiwan, in a sense, had actually lessened. Accordingly, as long as the U.S. would honor its treaty commitment to defend Taiwan as a part of the Republic of China, Taiwan's relative security in a physical sense may even have changed slightly for the better. In addition, the Nationalist Chinese forces have not stopped building, and the morale of their reserves is said to have improved as a result of new welfare provisions.

Even the Shanghai Communiqué did not immediately result in greater military insecurity for Taiwan. While Peking did not give up its claim to Taiwan as a part of China, the Chinese Communists did renounce the use of force as a method of settling international issues. Since the United States did not promise to withdraw its forces from Taiwan before conditions in the *region*—a rather vague term—became, in the American view, sufficiently stable, this was tantamount to an indirect assurance by the Chinese Communists that they would not use force to try to take over Taiwan. There was no hint of the length of time during which this condition of restraint would last, or what might happen if the leadership of a unified PRC should change.

However, Peking had renounced the use of force in the Taiwan Strait for as long as the U.S. defense guarantee would be honored, even though no pledge had been made not to take action against Taiwan as an "internal issue." Again, this situation seemed to be understood by ROC leaders. The purely military threat would increase only with a substantial change in the strategic relationships among the United States, the Soviet Union, and the PRC or if the United States should choose to denounce its defense commitment or consider it invalid. The latter possibilities appear small as long as the United States sees the need to deny Taiwan's strategic position on Japan's lifeline to either the Soviet Union or the PRC, quite apart from the desirability of maintaining a separate "China option" in case the PRC-Soviet rift is fully mended or if the PRC needs additional restraints itself.

THE ROC'S PERCEPTION OF POLITICAL THREAT

From Taipei's point of view, with a direct assault from the mainland unlikely, the only military threat would be internal. Since security against subversion is more than adequate under present conditions, only a collapse of morale and political cohesion or a substantial rise of dissidence because of economic difficulties, combined with social discontent, could give rise to serious problems. The Chinese Nationalists' perception of political threat rests primarily on an assumption that Taiwan's economic growth, which is dependent upon the continued expansion of international trade, could falter as a result of economic isolation. Economic isolation, they fear, could result from political isolation and the undermining of the international standing of the regime through derecognition, exclusion, or expulsion from international organizations, and, above all, the positions taken by the United States and Japan that might hamper trade. Hence, the PRC occupation of the Paracels in 1974 and the disruption of the civil aviation agreement with Japan in the same year were both disturbing developments. As for the United States, the Chinese Nationalists are probably less concerned that the former may not honor a valid commitment in practice than that it may no longer consider the commitment valid. To Taiwan, the Peking visit in 1972 and the establishment of U.S. and PRC Liaison offices appear as progressive steps leading to eventual diplomatic recognition. The ROC leaders fear that for domestic reasons or through miscalculation the United States may believe it necessary to give in more to Peking than it, in their view, has to. In addition, they are worried that, even if the United States should steer a very careful and correct path, the complex maneuvers of the American foreign policy under Kissinger's stewardship may not be understood by other countries so that the latter may take steps detrimental to Taiwan's interest. This seems to have already happened in post-Sato Japan. It could well happen with Korea, Thailand, Malaysia, and the Philippines, to mention a few others. They cite a temporary falling-off of Japanese investments in Taiwan after October, 1971, as evidence of the dangers of Japanese misperception. Simultaneously, though, they can point to a statement in Taiwan by Mr. Kearns, then President of the Export-Import Bank, in early 1972 on American intentions to continue extending loans to Taiwan, as well as the actual growth of such loans, as a demonstration that the United States is far from giving up Taiwan gratuitously. Washington's appointment of a new ambassador to Taipei in 1974 was greeted in the same manner.

Perceptions of U.S. policy by ROC leaders were initially influenced by the following major events.[44] First, the speech by U.S. Deputy Representative to the United Nations, Mr. Phillips, in 1970 to the effect that the United States was more opposed to the expulsion of the ROC from, than the admission of the PRC to, the United Nations was one of the earliest indications of a change in America's China policy. This statement, however, then seemed to be the result of a possible divergence of views in different parts of the U.S. government. This problem facing Taiwan is the same as that facing other nations. To use a metaphor, there are too many "blips" on the radar screen of communications emanating from the United States. Foreign observers are sometimes at a loss to separate the real "incoming vehicles" from the "chaff," some of which may even be broadcast inadvertently.

Secondly, the opinion of ROC observers of U.S. policy has been affected by seeming contradictions and allegedly frequent changes in U.S. positions preceding the failure of the U.S.-Japan cosponsored "reverse important question resolution." As in Japan, there was lingering doubt about the "real reason" for the timing of the second Kissinger visit to Peking.

Lastly, the Shanghai Communiqué and its language about "one China" is susceptible to more than one interpretation. Chinese Nationalists share with the Japanese and others the same uncertainty about the correct interpretation of U.S. intentions or even whether the United States has made up its mind at all. The English-language version of the relevant passage in the Shanghai Communiqué describing the U.S. position on the one-China issue speaks of the U.S. as "not challenging" the mainland Chinese position. The Chinese version of the same document describes the United States as, *literally*, "not holding a different opinion." Neither reading was designed to assuage Taiwan concerns, but the apparent ambiguity when the two versions are compared tends to erode confidence in the credibility of U.S. policy statements.

ROC OPTIONS AND SOME NECESSARY CONDITIONS

As in South Korea, the Nixon Doctrine has forced Taiwan to reexamine its options. Some Chinese Nationalists believe that the United States may have opted for the specific alternative of "one China, but not now." An additional view held by others is that the United States would prefer that the Chinese Communists and Nationalists engage in direct negotiations for a settlement giving Taiwan a high degree of autonomy within a one-China framework. Theoretically, the remaining alternatives would be "association with Japan," an "independent Taiwan" in one form or another, and, lastly, the adoption of an intermediate political adjustment with a broadening representation in the Central Government, within the present structure, of "native Taiwanese" elements.

Nationalist Chinese leaders insist that the option of "negotiation with the adversary" is ruled out for them because of (1) their conviction that it would be futile on the basis of past experience, (2) the predictably adverse effect, because of this very experience, both within the government and among different elements of the public, (3) their basic anti-Communist ideology, and (4) their belief that the Chinese Communists really have not changed. Equally emphatically, they have ruled out "return to Japan," although they would welcome some form of defense cooperation with Japan, South Korea, and others. Lastly, they have consistently maintained an official position that they do not advocate independence because the legitimacy of the ROC government rests on the concept of one-China, which includes Taiwan. Underlying this position, one would surmise, is the continued hope nurtured by some that the Chinese Communist central authority may collapse with the death of Mao and/or Chou. Choosing an irreversible alternative, therefore, would be premature.

It should be noted that some of these choices are not mutually exclusive. In fact, Taiwan can improve its prospect of being able to choose from among the available options and make the choices more meaningful if it can increase internal unity and economic well-being while safeguarding and expanding the island's external connections.

Like South Korea, Taiwan has increased its trade volume and other economic and cultural ties with many countires. Very preliminary gestures of non-hostility toward Taiwan have also emanated from the Soviet Union, but the ROC, on its part, has so far maintained an official aloofness toward Communist countries.

The ROC no longer insists that diplomatic recognition of Taipei by another country is a sine-qua-non of mutual trade. Nor will Taiwan automatically withdraw its diplomatic or other missions from another country if the latter recognizes Peking but does not derecognize Taipei or otherwise request the removal of Taipei's personnel. Persons who have visited the Chinese mainland are no longer excluded from Taiwan. The principle seems to be: "We want to be your friends unless you insist on being our enemies."

This attitude, of course, is calculated to expand external trade and foreign investments in Taiwan. It is also a means to combat the PRC's campaign to isolate Taiwan. Economically, Taiwan has further liberalized its regulations governing foreign investments.[45] On the political scene, the National Assembly and the Legislative and Control Yuan were expanded in size in the spring of 1972 in order to accommodate increased "native Taiwanese" representation.[46] The new Cabinet formed by Premier Chiang Ching-kuo included five ministers of Taiwanese origin. Frank discussion of the various alternatives for Taiwan is no longer taboo. Information on the Chinese mainland is allowed to be distributed more freely. All these measures are calculated to give Taiwan a greater degree of freedom in choosing from among available and desirable alternatives. More likely than not, the growth in the Chinese economy will affect the nature of the choice itself. The drift toward a state legally separate from mainland China and recognized as such by others, within the concept, but not structure, of a single Chinese nation, appears almost inexorable. Among the determining factors will be the attitudes of the United States, the Soviet Union, and Japan. If these are favorable, the PRC may have little to say about the matter in the end.

NOTES

1. Students of business cycle theory will readily recognize the effect of delayed perceptions and responses on stability in the economic sphere.
2. A diagrammatic analysis of realignment possibilities is presented in the Appendix to this chapter. For simplicity, we have omitted from these figures such collective defense arrangements as SEATO and ANZUS, as well as other non-defense groupings such as ASEAN, ASPAC, etc.
3. A substantial portion of this and the next chapter is based on personal interviews conducted by the author during the winters of 1970–71 and 1971–72, and again in the summer of 1973.
4. Japan is, however, quite conscious of the intermittent activities of potentially hostile aircraft and naval vessels near Japan. Listed among such military activities of "unidentified nationalities" in Chart 6 of the Nakasone White Paper, *The Defense of Japan*, issued by the Japan Defense Agency in October 1970, were the "Tokyo Express" flights (5 to 20 times a year), naval vessels passing through the Tsushima Strait (2 to 7 times a year), etc. *Op. cit.*, p. 83.

In addition, the following data on comparative military strength "in the vicinity of Japan" was presented by the 1970 report on Japan's defense:

	Army		Navy		Air Force
	Number of:		Number of:		Number of
	Divisions	Men	Naval ships[1]	Men	Planes
Soviet Far Eastern Forces*	17	240,000	600	600,000	2,000
Communist Chinese Forces	118	2,450,000	940[2]	200,000	2,800

	Army		Navy		Air Force
	Number of:		Number of:		Number of
	Divisions	Men	Naval ships[1]	Men	Planes
North Korean Forces	22 (plus 5 brigades)	370,000	120	14,000	580
U.S., Far Eastern Forces*	2	65,000	150[3]	550,000	400
Japan	13	179,000	210	125,000	450

SOURCE: *Op. cit.*, pp. 78–79 and 82.
1. About 20 nuclear-powered submarines and 80 conventional ones; plus about 250 planes.
2. About 33 conventional submarines; about 28,000 marines.
3. 10 to 12 submarines of which more than 3 are SSNs; about 550 planes; about 61,000 men.
*The estimates of Soviet and U.S. forces were made by the Defense Agency. Many changes have taken place since 1970. The Soviet figures also do not seem to reflect development on the Chinese border. The U.S. figures are exclusive of the ground forces then in Indochina.

5. According to *The Military Balance, 1971–72*, published by the International Institute of Strategic Studies (London), the relative military strength of the PRC and the ROC are as follows:

	Communist China*	Republic of China
Army	2,550,000 Number of divisions: infantry 110 armor 5 cavalry 3 airborne 2 artillery 20 Of the above, excluding artillery, only 25 are in East and Southeast China [Tsinan, Nanking and Foochow (opposite Taiwan) Military Regions]. These are the forces normally facing Taiwan.	390,000 Number of divisions: infantry 14 armor 2 armored cavalry regiments 3 light divisions 6 airborne brigades 2
Navy	150,000 (including 28,000 marines) 1 Soviet G-class submarine and 32 fleet submarines 3 coastal submarines 4 destroyers 4 destroyer escorts	35,000 (plus 35,000 marines) 10 destroyers 6 destroyer escorts 12 frigates 12 submarine chasers 12 patrol vessels

Continued on page 124

	Communist China*	Republic of China
Navy	11 patrol escorts 24 submarine chasers 15 missile patrol boats 30 minesweepers 45 auxiliary minesweepers 220 MTB and hydrofoils (under 100 tons) 320 motor gunboats (many under 100 tons) 530 landing craft	3 fleet minesweepers 17 other minesweepers 21 tank landing ships 9 medium landing ships 30 landing craft
Air Force	180,000 (including 85,000 air defense personnel) 2,800 combat aircraft	80,000 385 combat aircraft

SOURCE: *Op. cit.*, pp. 41–42 and 45–46.
*The Chinese figures presented here differ in details from the more aggregated Japanese estimates in note 4 above.

6. The following discussion is largely based on personal interviews.
7. One of the most notable statements in this vein may be found in Professor Yonosuke Nagai's article, "Disintegrating America—Ecology of Crisis," published in the September 1970 issue of *Chuo Koron*. According to Professor Nagai, "The forces which are moving America today are not the President, or a handful of leaders, or experts. They are rowing the boat desperately, frantically trying not to be carried away by the waves of a huge racial change. However, the boat is going around in a circle, or is being pulled back." In regard to the formulation of Japan's foreign policy, "the United States today is becoming a divided nation," warns the author, "which cannot be called a nation with a unified general will."
8. The plan to transfer U.S. facilities from Yokosuka to Sasebo was rescinded subsequently.
9. The generally low popular perception of threat in Japan during this period may be seen in the results of various polls. A July, 1970, poll reported in *Seron Chosa* showed only 11.8 percent of the respondents rating the risk that Japan might be attacked by a foreign country to be high, while the risk was rated low by 18.8 percent, and slight by 46.9 percent. In a poll conducted by *Yomiuri* on May 31, 1970, 7.6 percent of the respondents thought the danger of war between Japan and another country in the near future to be "very great"; 37.9 percent saw some danger; 28.7 percent, little danger; 11.3 percent, no danger. The *Yomiuri* poll was taken shortly after the first successful launch of a Communist Chinese satellite. In the same poll, 18.6 percent of the respondents registered the perception of a strong Chinese threat and 39.8 percent felt some threat. When the two polls are taken together, they gave the

impression that some of those who perceived a strong Chinese threat did not consider it sufficient to result in war.
10. Based on personal interviews in Japan.
11. Japan's desire to have close U.S.-Japanese consultation and coordination in order to promote détente and dialogue with Peking while maintaining security in Asia was clearly voiced by the Japanese ambassador to the United States on July 9, 1971. In a speech at Georgetown University, Ambassador Nobuhiko Ushiba stated: "One of the basic principles in dealing with a Communist country in your past experience in Europe has been the necessity of close coordination and cooperation among the policies of Western nations. In Asia, such close contact and coordination between the U.S. and Japan is even more necessary in regard to China." Less than a week after the speech came the July 15 statement from Washington about the Kissinger visit to Peking, a prime example of lack of prior consultation. Mr. Kissinger was actually in Peking at the time of Ambassador Ushiba's address calling for close consultation between Japan and the United States.
12. According to some Japanese analysts, the 1970s should witness another revision of the strategic relationship between the United States and Japan, leading to the inauguration of a "cooperative strategy," which would recognize Japan's growing importance as a U.S. partner. *In their view, there would be no U.S. forces stationed in mainland Japan on a permanent basis beyond the mid-1970s.* The strategy would be based on the mobility of U.S. forces and reentry of the bases in an emergency. Representative of this view is the Study Committee on National Security Problems whose members include Tadao Kuzumi, Shinkichi Eto, Kiichi Saeki, Kei Wakaizumi, Hidejiro Kotani, Ichiro Suetzugu, and others, many of whom are well known.
13. In his July 9, 1971, speech, Ambassador Ushiba stated that Japan would "provide the U.S. with bases for U.S. actions in the Far East for the common cause of the two countries." The word "common" should probably be italicized.
14. On the basis of interviews, it seemed that Japanese analysts were most reluctant to accept U.S. arguments in favor of not consulting even Mr. Sato prior to the July 15 announcement and U.S. explanation of the timing of Mr. Kissinger's second visit to Peking in October, 1971, when the "reverse important question" was being debated in the U.N., especially after Japan, in their view, had been pressured by the United States into cosponsoring the resolution.
15. Speaking in the Diet on February 23, 1972, prior to a meeting in the same evening between Foreign Minister Fukuda and Assistant Secretary of State Marshall Green who had come directly from Shanghai to brief the Japanese government on the Peking conversations, Mr. Sato said in response to questioning, "Based on this situation, i.e., Peking's admission to the U.N., we can say Taiwan is part of the PRC. It is a natural assertion that the Chinese mainland and Taiwan are inseparable and it is not a

question a third country argues." *New York Times*, February 29, 1972.
16. For a discussion of the sea lanes and the key roles played by both Taiwan and Singapore, see the author's article on "Planning Security for a Small Nation: Lessons from Singapore," *Pacific Community*, Tokyo, July 1972.
17. *Ibid*. For some of the specific commodities cited below, see "Japanese Trading and Investment Patterns," *Strategic Survey, 1971*, London, IISS, p. 60. See also Yuan-li Wu, *Raw Material Supply in a Multipolar World*, National Strategic Information Center, New York, 1973.
18. One such discussion links the sea guerrillas to other insurgency operations that could threaten Japan. "Seizing a freighter there and sinking a tanker here," writes M. Yasuda (pseudonym) in the *Daily Yomiuri* (January 6, 1971), sea guerrillas could wreck Japan's communication lines without even giving Japan a chance to retaliate. "Witness the Pueblo, the EC121, or a second Yodo." An interesting discussion of the same problems was also presented by Shinsaku Hogen of the Japanese Foreign Office at an Indian Ocean conference sponsored by the Center for Strategic and International Studies of Georgetown University in March, 1971.
19. *Asahi Evening News*, Tokyo, January 10, 1972.
20. *New York Times*, March 6, 1972.
21. Japan dispatched an economic mission to Hanoi on February, 1972. The mission was headed by a member of the Asian Affairs Bureau of the Foreign Ministry. See *New York Times*, February 13, 1972.
22. Cf. Hisao Iwashima, *op. cit.*, March 1973.
23. Associated Press report from Tokyo, April 23, 1974.
24. March 11, 1972.
25. Secretary of State William P. Rogers, speaking before the North Atlantic Treaty Organization Council on May 5, 1972, said, according to the *New York Times* quoting an American official, that in attempting to stop the North Vietnamese, the United States would take whatever military action was necessary and "that he excluded only the use of nuclear weapons and the reintroduction of U.S. ground forces." *New York Times*, May 6, 1972, reported from Brussels by Bernard Gwertzman.
26. *Mainichi Shimbun*, Tokyo, January 30, 1964, quoted in John Welfield, *Japan and Nuclear China*, Canberra Papers on Strategy and Defense, Australian National University, Canberra, 1970.
27. The above passage is from the official translation, Japan Defense Agency, *The Defense of Japan*, October 1970, pp. 39—40.
28. Prime Minister Sato stated on June 17, 1971, at the time of the signing of the reversion agreement that ". . . fundamental agreement was reached in the Joint Communiqué issued in the fall of 1969 which called for the reversion of Okinawa during 1972, free of nuclear weapons on the same level as mainland Japan. . . ." At the same time, U.S. Ambassador Armin H. Meyer stated: "The Joint Communiqué and this Agreement make clear that the U.S. fully recognizes the Japanese Government's policy and the sentiments of the Japanese people with regard to nuclear weapons. The return of Okinawa will be on a completely homeland level. . . ." Embassy

of the U.S.A., Tokyo, Japan, *Okinawa Reversion Agreement of June 17, 1971 and Related Documents*, June 1, 1971, pp. 48 and 51.
29. Based on personal interviews.
30. See Chapter I above.
31. The U.S.-Japan Treaty of Mutual Cooperation and Security of 1960, like all other similar treaties, stipulated that each contracting party "would act to meet the common danger in accordance with its constitutional processes." None of the treaties actually spells out the exact means each party would adopt in meeting "the common danger."
32. The article by M. Yasuda is entitled "U.S. Nuclear Umbrella No Longer Credible."
33. *Ibid.*
34. This capacity may be boosted further.
35. Japan signed the Non-proliferation Treaty (NPT) in 1970 but did not ratify it. Enriched uranium obtained from abroad to fuel Japanese reactors is presumably subject to "safeguard" measures and cannot be diverted to other use. In February, 1972, Japan and France signed a ten-year agreement on cooperation in industrial use of nuclear energy. According to the *Wall Street Journal* of February 28, 1972, an immediate effect of the agreement is to accelerate Japanese studies of fast-breeder reactors which can produce more fissile material than they consume as fuel.
36. The results of some samples were as follows:

	Yomiuri Poll of:	Percent of Those In Favor	Against
Should Japan have nuclear weapons?	August 7, 1969	16.1	71.8
	May 31, 1970	7.7	67.6
Will Japan have nuclear weapons in ten years?	August 7, 1969	32.1	35.5

37. According to *Military Balance, 1971–72* (pp. 47–48), the following comparative statistics are available:

	Republic of Korea	North Korea
GNP ($ billion)	1970–8.3	...
Defense budget ($ million)	1971–411 (129 billion won)	1971–849 (2.183 billion North Korean won)
Army	560,000 men (including 29 infantry divisions of which 10 in cadre only, and 2 armored brigades)	360,000 men (including 2 armored divisions and 20 infantry divisions)

Continued on page 128

	Republic of Korea	North Korea
Navy	16,750 men	11,000 men
Air Force	24,500 men; 235 combat planes	30,000 men; 555 combat planes

38. In terms of net obligations and loan authorizations, U.S. military assistance to the ROK in fiscal years 1970 and 1971 was as follows:

(in millions of $)	1970	1971
Military grants (Military Assistance Program grants and service funded grants)	369.7	506.1
Grants from Excess Stocks	10.7	15.0
Military Credit Sales	–	15.0
Military Cash Sales	–	0.8
Total	380.4	536.9

SOURCE: Department of State, *United States Foreign Policy, 1971*, p. 411.

39. Ministry of Culture and Information, *Thaw versus Freeze in Korea*, Seoul, p. 8.
40. The preceding analysis of the ROK's concerns and North Korean intentions, based on personal interviews in Korea in 1971 and early 1972, was amply confirmed in the following statement by Kim Il-sung in an interview with Harrison E. Salisbury and John M. Lee of the *New York Times:*

> From our point of view it is very simple. Everything entirely depends on the United States Government. If the United States Government changes its policy toward us we will also change ours toward it. The most important thing is to leave the Koreans to unify their country by themselves and not interfere in the internal affairs of the Korean people.
>
> Nearly 20 years have passed since the signing of the armistice agreement, and what kind of necessity do you have for stationing forces in South Korea under the signboard of the United Nations forces?
>
> Some people say you are staying in South Korea to protect the South Koreans because we want to invade South Korea. But we have declared time and time again we have no intention at all of invading South Korea. Therefore I think it is high time for you to put an end to your role of police. If you withdraw, we Koreans can do things in common for peaceful unification.
>
> What the United States Government does that displeases us is not only station its troops in South Korea but helps the revival of Japanese militarists. So we see the joint communiqué of 1969 between Nixon and Sato, and Nixon put forward the so-called Nixon Doctrine under which he instigated Japanese militarists so as to replace the United States in South Korea so as to interfere in the internal affairs of the Korean people.

After the joint communiqué Sato claimed he would interfere in the internal affairs of the Korean question. We cannot but describe this as an unfriendly attitude of the United States Government toward us.

The American attitude toward us at the United Nations is not justified either. Why do they attach conditions to inviting us to the United Nations while they invite the South Koreans without any conditions? They insisted we recognize the legality of the resolutions adopted at the United Nations against us. How can we go under such preconditions?

And you also instigate the so-called United Nations Commission for the Unification and Rehabilitation of Korea to make an annual report full of lies and falsifications against our country and make unfriendly false propaganda against us.

You should withdraw United States forces, dissolve the United Nations Commission for the Unification and Rehabilitation of Korea and not encourage the division of the Korean nation but help the reunification. If there is no interference of outside forces, the Koreans can seek common points for unification of the country.

When President Nixon visited China, he said while looking at the Great Wall of China that there should be no divided countries—no barriers. If the United States Government wants to put this into practice, it must begin with Korea.

President Nixon said he wanted to improve relations with China, and while visiting the Soviet Union he said he wants to have improved relations with the Soviet Union. We say, why should he continue to have military bases in South Korea and the Korean peninsula?

If in the past you said you needed military bases in South Korea to prevent the expansion of Communism, now that you have good relations with the big powers, why is there any necessity of having military bases in South Korea?

What can you benefit by asking Japan to replace the United States in South Korea to invade South Korea and turn South Korea into a market for Japanese goods and turning it into an appendage of Japan?

The Korean nation is a single nation. We must unify this nation.

Many North Koreans have relations in South Korea and many South Koreans have relations in North Korea. So we should remove this barrier of long standing and eradicate the tragedy of Korea.

Our policy toward the United States is as follows: If the United States Government stops its unfriendly attitude toward us and stops obstructing the unification of our country, then there is no reason why we should have a hostile attitude toward the United States. So I should say relations between ourselves and the United States entirely depend on the United States and not on us.

41. ROK Ministry of Culture and Information.
42. Based on personal interviews in 1973.
43. ROK Ministry of Culture and Information.
44. Based on personal interviews.
45. The ROC's external trade reached a total turnover of $4.1 billion in 1971; in 1972, the volume reached $5.7 billion. The upward trend continued in 1973, which recorded a total turnover of $8.3 billion. There has been a substantial increase in European and U.S. direct investments in Taiwan since 1971.

46. According to the final official announcement reported by the Central News Agency, the increase in local representation in terms of the numbers of members of the Legislative Yuan and the Control Yuan who were in Taiwan in 1972 were as follows:

	The Legislative Yuan	The Control Yuan
Number of original members in 1972	425	66
Increase in 1972 of Taiwan members	36[1]	10
Percent of increase	8.4	15.1

[1] Including 8 from professional groups and 28 selected on the basis of residence.

APPENDIX: A Diagrammatic Presentation of Alignment Patterns

For those who prefer to see the discussion in this chapter more graphically, the diagram on page 131 may help.

In addition to the "balancing" or "equilibrating" big powers—the United States, the Soviet Union, and Communist China—Figure IV.1 contains two outer groups of nations which we have labeled as "allies" and "neutrals." The "allies" are divided into two subgroups: those allied with X, the United States, and those allied with the Soviet Union and/or Communist China. The alliance relationship indicated here is not exclusively with one country (Y or Z), although it is definitely not with X. Dotted lines with arrows denote the directions in which any country may shift its "alignment" or group allegiance. A neutral may become allied to (1) X or (2) Y and Z, or (3) Y or Z. (The combination, alliance with Y or Z alone is not shown.) Conversely, a nation allied with X or with Y and Z may become a neutral. Theoretically, a nation in the "allies" category, as well as a neutral, may also become an "equilibrating" power; in practice, size, available resources, and military capability will strictly limit this type of realignment.

In contrast to Figure IV.1, which describes the alignment pattern at the inception of the Nixon Doctrine and the potential directions of realignment, Figure IV.2a shows what seems to be the alignment pattern desired by the United States under the Nixon Doctrine in the short run, while Figure IV.2b shows the pattern envisaged for the long term.

In Figure IV.2a Japan (J) has moved from the position of an ally to that of an equilibrating power still in alliance with the United States. In Figure IV.2b, an additional "balancing power" consisting of a group of regional nations (R), including Indonesia, has entered the arena. Japan may be a part of this regional group or it may be in alliance with such a group if arrangements of this nature are permissible under the then Japanese Constitution. The arrows with continuous lines in both Figures IV.2a and IV.2b denote the directions of the shifts from one group to another that will have already occurred. The arrow with a dotted line in Figure IV.2b indicates, as in Figure IV.1, the

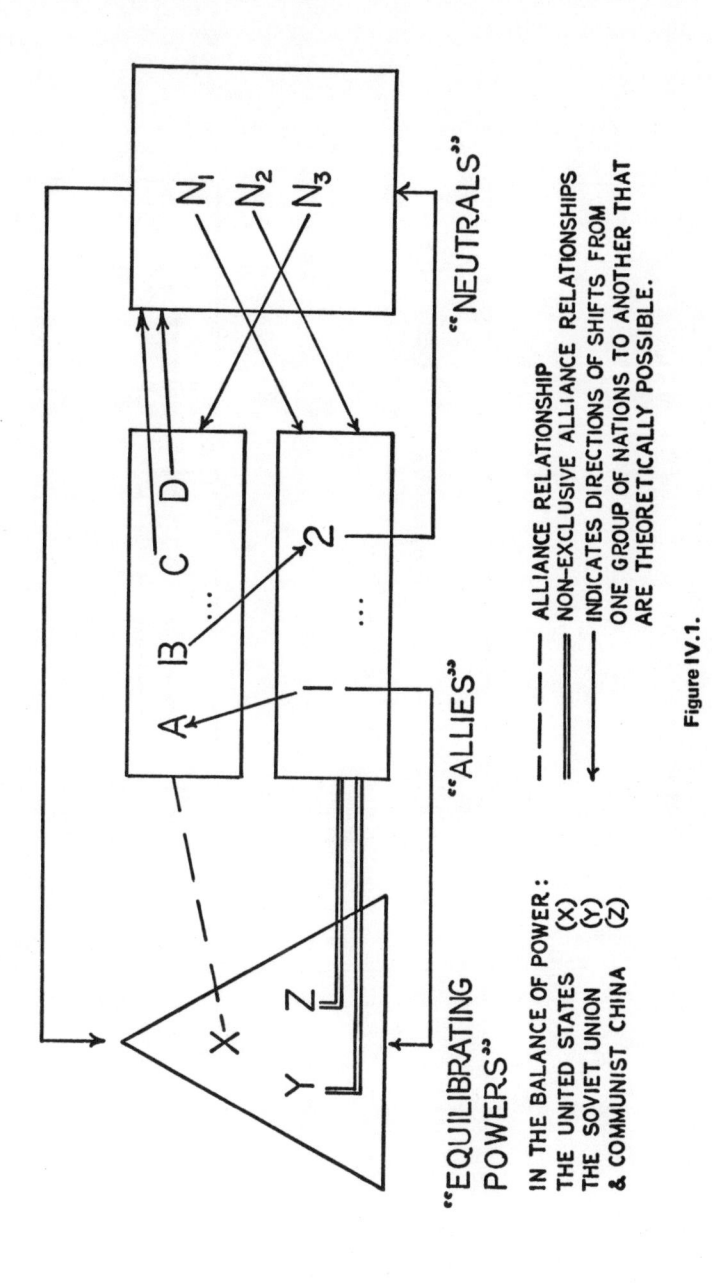

Perception and Response I

Figure IV.1.

Figure IV.2a.

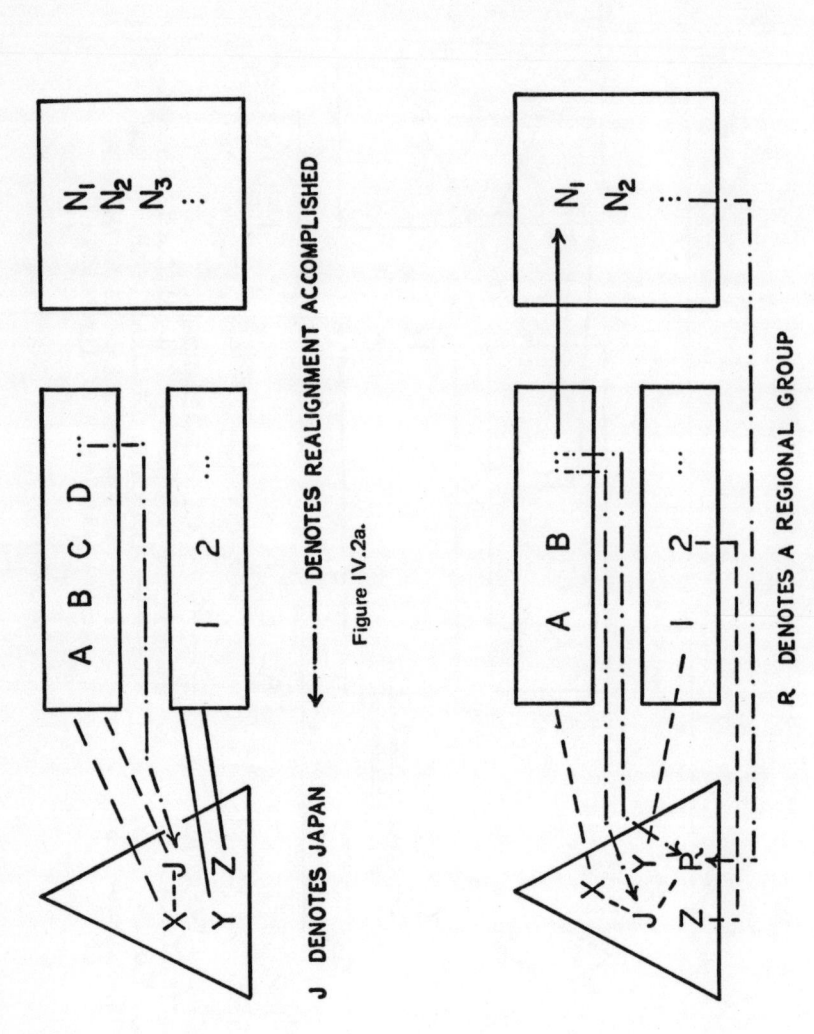

J DENOTES JAPAN — — — DENOTES REALIGNMENT ACCOMPLISHED

Figure IV.2b.

R DENOTES A REGIONAL GROUP

direction of shifts that *may* occur. Although Figure IV.2b shows some possible shifts by allied nations to the neutral group, the pattern may still be labeled as "preferred" (that is, by the United States) by assuming that the net benefit from the shifts of J and R to the group of balancing powers will more than compensate for the loss of one or more small allies to neutrality. The real emerging pattern could, of course, turn out to be quite different, barring new U.S. initiatives, as has been pointed out in this chapter.

Chapter V

Perception and Response II: From Indochina to the Indian Ocean

DIFFERENCES AND SIMILARITIES AMONG THE INDIVIDUAL COUNTRIES

Outside Northeast Asia, the remaining countries of the Western Pacific affected by the gradual unveiling of the Nixon Doctrine constitute a most diverse group. Their interpretations of U.S. policy and their reactions to its effects accordingly vary a great deal, although they do share a few common characteristics. Some principal factors underlying these differences and common features are outlined below.

First of all, within this vast region, which includes for our purposes Australia and New Zealand, South Vietnam, Cambodia, and Laos have been involved in a protracted conflict. The eventual outcome will necessarily remain uncertain for some time even after the cessation of direct U.S. involvement in large-scale hostilities in the winter of 1972–73. Standing at the opposite pole to these war-torn countries, Australia and New Zealand are good examples of countries at peace, abstracting from small-scale participation in the Korean and Vietnam Wars. In the group of countries more or less at peace at present, insofar as *direct overt aggression by a foreign power* is concerned, we can include nearly all the other countries of Southeast Asia—Indonesia, Singapore, and the Philippines. Thailand and Malaysia are marginal cases because of foreign-supported insurgency operations in the North and Northeast of Thailand, on the Thai-Malaysian border, and in Sarawak in East Malaysia, as well as use of Thai bases by U.S. forces in the Vietnam War and in policing the Indochina cease-fire. The situation in the Philippines, as of this writing, also raises some questions because of possible foreign intervention in the Moslem insurgency.

Second, few countries in the region, however, have been *fully* at peace for very long. Thailand, Malaysia, and the Philippines are vivid illustrations of another factor, the degree of actual or threatened insurgency, including past experience in unrest or insurgency. All three have to contend with insurgency as a current problem of varying but significant proportions. Add Indonesia and Singapore essentially because of their past experience and only Australia and New Zealand within this group of Pacific-Asian countries are free from the experience of significant levels of insurgent activities of their own. Moreover, the majority of nations suffering from insurgency concerns are under the justified impression that they can trace the actual or potential antigovernment forces facing them to the inspiration and/or support of Peking and its allies. This is not to say that, in the absence of domestic discontent, exhortation by Asian Communist powers alone could have led to insurgency. However, examples of Peking's involvement can be found in the Free Thai Movement, the Maoist New People's Army of the Philippines, the Barisan Socialis of Singapore, and the Malaysian insurgents reportedly still operating under the command of Chin Peng.[1]

Third, geographical influences are felt in several ways. As one moves southward and farther away from mainland China, or as one crosses the sea, concern about a direct threat from the PRC, still primarily a land power, decreases. The Chinese threat is felt more keenly in Thailand than in the Philippines, more immediately in Thailand than in Malaysia and Singapore and least of all in Australia and New Zealand. As an archipelago at a considerable distance from mainland China, Indonesia should have little to fear from Communist China. This geographical fact could help explain Sukarno's readiness to erect a Peking-Djakarta axis. On the other hand, the 1965 coup undertaken by the Indonesian Communists (PKI) with Peking's support have shaken the sense of security from the Chinese threat that distance would otherwise impart.[2]

Until recently, the same geographical yardstick could have been applied to the perception of Soviet threat. If the Soviet Union is considered a land power alone, China constitutes a barrier to possible Soviet ambitions in the area. The recently rapid and still continuing expansion of the Soviet navy, together with the increasingly prominent role Soviet warships have played in the Indian Ocean, have altered this situation rather fundamentally. The Indian Ocean, especially in the post-1973 energy crisis period, it seems, is emerging as an arena of big power competition. From the point of view of the present study, its littoral countries that simultaneously face the Pacific in another direction must now consider the Soviet Union from two points of view: (1) a potential force which may be adroitly utilized in order to offset the influence of Peking and, on occasion, also of Washington; (2) a potential source of threat to their own security. Furthermore, the interests of the Soviet Union must be analyzed in terms of (1) its general expansion as a world power, (2) specific Soviet interests in the Indian Ocean, and (3) Soviet policy in the Western Pacific.

The last point is, of course, related to Soviet policies toward mainland China and Japan. The encirclement of China from south, east, and southeast, rapprochement with Japan and its attempted alienation from the United States, and potentially from the PRC, and the acquisition of suitable leverages that might be employed against Peking, Washington, and Tokyo are among the Soviet Union's possible objectives. Soviet activities will, therefore, affect all the countries in the region, especially Malaysia, Singapore, Indonesia, and Australia-New Zealand; to these we might add Thailand, which is in a similar position. But for its Moslem dissidents and possible involvement of such militant Arabs as al-Qadhafi of Libya, the country perhaps least immediately affected by external involvement is the Philippines, which is also relatively insulated from a mainland Chinese threat as long as Taiwan is securely outside the influence of Peking.

One geographical characteristic lends special importance to the Malay Peninsula at the tip of which stands the island Republic of Singapore, with the populous and rich islands of Indonesia just beyond. The Malacca Straits, together with the shipbuilding, repair, and trading facilities of Singapore, provide a vital passageway between the Pacific and Indian Oceans. When the map is viewed vertically, the Malay Peninsula appears as a land bridge between the Asian mainland and the Indonesian archipelago, in addition to being a barrier between the two oceans. Nations with maritime traffic in the Malacca Straits or those that wish to overfly the Peninsula, perhaps to reach Indonesia from the direction of the Peninsula, have strong interests in the area.

Fourth, countries in the area share differing degrees of mutual distrust. For example, Malaysia and Singapore were both targets of Sukarno's "confrontation"; there is a continuing uneasiness between Malaysia and Singapore that the governments of both are anxious to reduce; Malaysia and the Philippines have certain unsettled territorial issues between them; Australia is still mindful of the fact that Indonesia was at one time quite vociferous in its demands on New Guinea, an area of Australian interest.

Fifth, with the exception of Australia and New Zealand, the countries in question all have large Chinese minorities who wield substantial influence, especially economic, in their respective countries of residence.[3] These minorities are not fully absorbed into the host societies. Accordingly, Chinese ethnic groups, the definition of which is often arbitrary because of intermarriage and adoption of local names, may be regarded by the "local" population as China-oriented in loyalty. Hence the host countries may be interested in having more than one source of Chinese influence to balance against each other. Rightly or wrongly, such perceptions may influence the assessment of the Communist Chinese threat on the part of countries in the region. The same perception, if held by Peking, might raise the latter's estimate of its own prospects for influence in the area. In Singapore, where the Chinese ethnic group is actually a majority, the issue greatly complicates the difficult task of creating a sense of identity for a new multiracial nation.

Finally, external alliance and alignment patterns vary considerably from country to country. As active participants in the Vietnam War, the Indochina states (including Cambodia after Sinanouk and from time to time the Laotian government) are in effect aligned with the United States, although the multilateral SEATO Treaty is the basic instrument on which initial U.S. intervention in Vietnam rested. Among the countries within the area under study, and leaving out the three Indochina states, Thailand, the Philippines, Australia, and New Zealand are members of SEATO[4] and, therefore, America's allies. The United States, Australia, and New Zealand are also allies under the ANZUS Treaty. In addition to a bilateral defense treaty between the United States and the Philippines, various agreements have been concluded by the United States with the Philippines, Thailand, Indonesia, Australia, and New Zealand governing U.S. military assistance and, in some cases, military bases for U.S. use. Malaysia, Singapore, Australia, and New Zealand, together with the United Kingdom, are members of a Five-Power Defense Arrangement designed primarily for the defense of Malaysia and Singapore, which have no direct defense relationship with the United States. Indonesia, too, has no defense commitment from the United States.

The above discussion has only pointed to the principal political and strategic considerations underlying the different reactions in these countries to perception of threat and with particular reference to concern about changes in U. S. policy. The diversity we have noted would be compounded if we took into account differences in the present status and rate of economic development of these countries—hence, in their ability to bear the defense burden—as well as differences in their forms of government, leadership, and traditions—therefore, in their ability to plan and organize their own security within a given time.

Table V.1 shows that the two nations with the largest populations (Indonesia and the Philippines) were economically among the slowest growing

Table V.1 Comparative Statistics of Economic Growth and Defense Expenditure in Southeast Asia and Australia-New Zealand

	Annual Growth Rate of GNP per Capita (%) (1961–68)	GNP per Capita	Annual Growth Rate of Gross Domestic Product	GNP at Current Prices (in million dollars*)	Defense Expenditures (1970)	Defense Expenditures in % of GNP 1969	Defense Expenditures in % of GNP 1970	Population (1970, in million persons)
South Vietnam	1.9	150	3.7 (1960–70)	4,000	1,028	...	25.7	3.0
Cambodia	0.6	120	3.6 (1960–69)	910	115	1.9	2.0	7.0
Laos	0.2	100	...	200	22	...	10.8	3.0
Thailand	4.6	150	8.0 (1960–70)	6,100	240	3.7	3.9	35.0
Malaysia	4.3	330	5.8 (1960–68)	3,950	183	3.6	4.6	11.2
Singapore	3.8	700	10.5 (1960–70)	1,820	106	4.9	5.8	2.1
Indonesia	0.8	100	3.0 (1963–67)	11,600	272	2.3	2.3	114.5
Philippines	0.8	180	4.9 (1960–70)	5,900	110	1.5	1.5	39.8
Australia	2.4	2,070	...	34,400	1,261	4.0	3.6	12.8
New Zealand	1.7	2,000	...	5,770	115	1.9	2.0	2.9

SOURCES: The annual growth rates and values of per capita GNP (1960–68) are taken from the *World Bank Atlas* of 1970. The GDP annual growth rates are from Asian Development Bank, *Annual Report*, 1971, p. 137. All the other data are taken from IISS, *Military Balance, 1971–72*.

*U.S. dollar estimates are converted from the original currencies at the following rates per dollar: 275 piastres (117.5 piastres before October 4, 1970), 55.5 riels, 500 kip, 20.8 baht, 3.06 Malaysian and Singapore dollars, 378 rupiahs, 6.43 pesos (3.9 pesos before February, 1970), and 1.12 Australian dollars.

countries in the 1960s. On the other hand, the highest per capita GNP growth rates were registered by Thailand, Malaysia, and Singapore. In 1970, these three countries also devoted a greater portion of their total output to defense than other countries in the region, except, of course, the three Indochina states. Furthermore, during 1969-70, with the exception of Australia and Indonesia, the five countries for which data are available all raised their defense expenditures to GNP ratios. In the absence of war the amount of national output that can be allotted to defense is clearly a function of the per capita GNP growth rate. Disparate rates of growth are in turn an obstacle to regional cooperation and important factors in fostering economic nationalism.

In absolute terms, the present national outputs of the countries in the region and their defense efforts are all far too small for them to defend themselves on an individual basis against either Communist China or the Soviet Union. (See Table V.2.) In terms of population and potential resources, Indonesia may constitute a future exception, especially following the post-1973 rise of the crude oil price. If the Australian population could be multiplied several times, it could become another. At the present time, the possibilities of "autonomous defense," to use Mr. Nakasone's phrase for Japan, against the two potential sources of external threat are, however, out of the question and will remain so for some years to come. Successful defense against Communist China and/or the Soviet Union can be achieved by

Table V.2 Comparative Military Strength of Selected Non-Communist Countries in Southeast Asia and Oceania

	Army	Navy	Air Force
South Vietnam	414,000 men (see, however, Table V.3)	31,000 men plus 15,000 marines 1 destroyer 3 destroyer escorts 6 patrol escorts 72 patrol boats 3 coastal minesweepers many other vessels	40,000 men 275 combat aircraft
Thailand	130,000 men plus 10,000 in Volunteer Defense Corps and 8,000 in Border Police	21,500 men 1 destroyer escort 3 frigates and 3 on order 1 escort minesweeper 4 coastal minesweepers 17 submarine chasers and various other vessels	23,500 men 144 combat aircraft

Table V.2—Continued

	Army	Navy	Air Force
Malaysia	43,000 men plus 50,000 reservists	3,000 men plus 600 reservists 2 ASW frigates 6 minesweepers and 28 patrol boats	4,000 men 30 combat aircraft
Singapore	14,000 men plus 7,000 reservists (planned to rise to 9,000 at 1971 year end)	500 men 3 patrol boats and another 3 on order	1,500 men 36 combat aircraft
Indonesia	250,000 men	34,000 men 12 submarines 1 cruiser 4 destroyers 11 frigates 6 fleet minesweepers and many other vessels	35,000 men 122 combat aircraft
Australia	47,800 plus 36,000 in the Citizens Reserve Force	17,800 men plus 4,300 in the Navy Citizens Military Force 1 ASW aircraft carrier 3 destroyers with SAM 5 destroyers 6 destroyer escorts 2 minehunters 4 coastal minesweepers 20 patrol boats other vessels	22,700 men 210 combat aircraft
New Zealand	51,600 men plus 11,300 territorials	2,900 men 600 in reserve 1 frigate with SAM 2 ASW frigates with SAM 2 escort minesweepers	4,250 men 27 combat aircraft

SOURCE: IISS, *Military Balance, 1971–72.*

(a) collective defense, (b) alliance with one or more big powers, or (c) a combination of both. Still another approach in these circumstances is to look for security without relying upon an appropriate national defense capability. Complete success using this tactic would depend in large part on the attainment of equilibrium in a balance of big powers and acceptance of the status as neutral or nonaligned nations.

A common characteristic of these countries is experience with Japanese militarism during World War II. Some underwent a brutal Japanese occupation; others perhaps regarded the occupation as a transitional phase between colonialism and independence, and two, Australia and New Zealand, succeeded in preventing invasion. None of the informed leaders in these countries, however, could lack a degree of apprehension about the potential consequences of an effectively rearmed Japan accompanied by resurgent militarism. Hence, among the three defense-oriented alternatives to achieve national security the preferred one probably would be to ally with the United States.

The fact that Indonesia, Malaysia, and Singapore did not seek a U.S. alliance in the past can be explained by history and the absence of a perceived threat which would have required alliance with a superpower. Until Britain's decision in 1967 to withdraw from East of Suez, British protection of Malaysia and Singapore was sufficient to inhibit Indonesia. In the case of Indonesia itself, the policies and predilections of Sukarno could go a long way to explain the country's attitude up to the 1965 coup. Circumstances, however, are changing. If U.S. military presence in the Western Pacific is regarded as no longer adequate because of force reductions, can Japan play the role of the benevolent big power envisaged by the United States and required in alternative (b) in the face of Soviet and/or PRC threat? Would Japan be willing and able to rearm adequately in time? Once rearmed, would Japan behave as a benevolent big power? Would concern on the part of the weaker nations about Japan's past behavior undermine the latter's ability to play such a role? Would Japanese fear that this may turn out to be the case inhibit Japan from rearming to the degree necessary for this role? Would aggressive Japanese economic behavior as investors and traders spoil the taste for noneconomic cooperation? Above all, what the Japanese decision will be on nuclear or other sophisticated weapons systems will affect the number of viable options available to countries in the area.

If both the United States and Japan are ruled out as candidates for the mantle of the protective big power in alternative (b), another way out would be for each of the countries in the region to seek on an individual basis either Soviet or Chinese protection, depending upon whether Communist China or the Soviet Union is perceived to be the greater threat. This is where a

Soviet-sponsored Asian collective security arrangement would become relevant.

On the basis of our preliminary analysis, one can presume that, with the possible exception of Australia (especially under the Labor government which recognized Peking) and New Zealand, most countries still see the Chinese Communists as the greater present threat. Yet the Soviet Union does not enjoy the reputation of extreme benevolence toward smaller nations. Neither choice is likely to be regarded as desirable.

The remaining alternatives are (1) collective defense, with or without big power participation, and (2) security through balance of power. It should be noted at this juncture that collective defense and security through balancing a few big powers are not mutually exclusive, even if a big power is also involved in the collective defense arrangement. The group as a whole can still seek to gain security through balancing the other big powers as long as the particular big power (e.g., Japan) is not itself in diametric opposition to another big power. Which arrangement is the most profitable will depend on a complex of factors, including each country's general outlook. The primary criterion, however, may be simple feasibility. The heterogeneous background of the countries in this region and their divergent interests do not warrant great optimism about the short-run likelihood of regional defense arrangements including more than a few member countries. Furthermore, a logical view is that a collective regional defense arrangement is more meaningful and likely to succeed only if there are big power leadership and participation.

Again, would Japan be able and willing to play such a role? If so, participation in a collective arrangement in defense, including its own defense, may even have some additional restraining effect on Japan. Such a restraining effect may be beneficial from the point of view of both Japan and the smaller powers if it can help allay domestic Japanese concern of the antimilitary segments of the population and external fear that rearming will lead to the resurgence of militarism in Japan. If Japan is not ready or able to play such a role, would the United States be in a position to provide leadership in a regional defense arrangement at least on an interim basis? Would the United States continue as a participant even with Japanese membership, with the American role, in time, decreasing as that of Japan increases?

If we rule out both U.S. and Japanese participation in a regional defense arrangement, after having ruled out earlier the alliance alternative, what will be left? Some analysts maintain that the only viable alternative then would be for each country to try to balance the big powers against one another in order to create a new equilibrium. Others are not yet prepared to give up the collective defense alternative, albeit without big power participation. As a matter of fact, one can point to ASEAN, a regional organization of Thailand, Malaysia, Singapore, Indonesia, and the Philippines for economic and other non-military cooperation, as the potential base for a collective defense arrangement. Some broadening of the organization's original functions and membership would eventually have to take place. For all the countries the choice is a hard one; nor do they have the same options.

All the countries in this part of Pacific-Asia are, therefore, in the position of having to study the evolution of American policy and the changing strategic balance. The success Vietnamization demonstrates in the battlefield and in civilian administration in the mid-1970s, together with U.S. statements and actual conduct in both negotiation and war, including the muscle it uses in policing the cease-fire in Vietnam and in attempting to establish stability in Cambodia and Laos, will serve as an uncertain weathervane of the future winds of change. Since all these indicators are not wholly reliable, it is easy to understand why the perception of U.S. policy is ambiguous and occasionally contradictory even for the same nation, not to mention for the region as a whole.[5]

THE SIGNIFICANCE OF VIETNAM TO THE PERCEPTION OF AMERICAN POLICY

As already pointed out, American policy is always perceived through the filter, as it were, of each country's individual problems and interests. What happens to Vietnamization and eventually to Vietnam constitutes an acid test of American policy and a crucial determinant of the international environment other nations in the area will have to face. The perception of Vietnamization by Southeast Asian nations is subject to the same general rules. "Vietnamization" as employed here should be understood in two different ways. In a narrower sense, it means the substitution of Vietnamese defense effort for U.S. effort, especially on the ground, in a manner that would make it possible, while U.S. ground forces were being withdrawn, to (1) stabilize the fronts vis-à-vis North Vietnamese (NVN) or NVN-supported forces and (2) progressively eradicate the influence of the Viet Cong. In a broader sense, and in the long run, it means that South Vietnam will be enabled to continue the necessary level of military effort while simultaneously pursuing nation-building under a non-Communist government even after the withdrawal of U.S. ground troops and with diminishing U.S. support.[6] It is possible for Vietnamization to be successful in both ways. It is also conceivable that Vietnamization, while successful in the first sense, will nevertheless fail in the second.

Whether Vietnamization can succeed or not in the first sense depends upon four variables—how South Vietnam performs in combat and in building up both its defense effort and the necessary political and economic support; the level and nature of U.S. support; the policy and performance of North

Vietnam and the Viet Cong both in Vietnam and in Cambodia and Laos, and the nature and level of Soviet and Chinese Communist support to North Vietnam. While the net result of the interactionn of these four variables concerns the very existence of South Vietnam as an independent nation, the perception of American policy by other nations in the area is especially focused on the net result in relation to U.S. policy, the second variable.

Until the all-out attack mounted by North Vietnam against the South in April, 1972, and President Nixon's response in May, the nature and scale of the U.S. effort in such a contingency could not be clearly discerned. This point was made clear only when U.S. naval and air efforts over Vietnam were redoubled in an attempt to cut off Soviet and Chinese supplies through the mining of Haiphong and other North Vietnamese harbors and severance of land links between North Vietnam and Communist China. Whatever may be the eventual outcome in Vietnam, these developments had certain short-run effects. First, they showed that as far as the United States was concerned, Vietnamization was not a code word for withdrawal of U.S. forces regardless of the end result in Vietnam. Rather it was intended from the beginning as a means to readjust the American defense effort both in Vietnam and globally. Second, these events showed that large air and naval support, when combined with the effort of local forces, could in fact halt an all-out conventional attack such as that of North Vietnam. Third, the events showed that South Vietnamese forces were by and large able to fight quite well in spite of unfavorable and even alarmist prognostications at the time.[7] Fourth, the train of events in Vietnam also gave rise to Secretary of State Rogers's reported statement that the United States did not intend to employ nuclear weapons in order to change the tide of battle in Vietnam.[8] Fifth, President Nixon's announcement on May 8, 1972, made it clear that the United States was now prepared to withdraw *all* its forces from Vietnam within four months from the enforcement of an internationally supervised cease-fire in all Indochina and the release of American POWs.[9] Sixth, there was ample evidence that neither the Soviet Union nor Communist China was prepared to challenge openly American efforts to interdict the flow of external supplies to North Vietnam,[10] even though, as we have argued, it would have been in Soviet interest to prolong the drain of U.S. resources through Vietnam. Finally, in spite of the fact that the battles in Vietnam were fought out at the very time Democratic and Republican delegates to their respective party conventions were gathering in Miami in order to nominate candidates for the 1972 American Presidential election, there were notably fewer antiwar protests in 1972 than in 1968. The reduction of U.S. ground forces in Vietnam not only lowered U.S. battle casualties, it also curtailed battle reporting. Both developments were, inter alia, responsible for cooling antiwar emotions.

In summary, all these consequences had certain effects on the perception of U.S. policy in Pacific-Asia. First, in like circumstances in the future, if the United States should act with its air and naval forces in support of an ally, as it did in Vietnam in 1972, the combined defense effort may again be quite effective, as long as the Soviet navy is unwilling or unable to spoil U.S. activities. Second, the United States could again act decisively in a future contingency, especially if the American domestic political scene and the total strategic environment are improved, or if they do not worsen. Granted that there are serious uncertainties on both counts as of this writing, other nations in the area cannot fail to note that the United States definitely has not opted out of Southeast Asia. This was the minimum accomplishment of the battle of Vietnam in the summer of 1972.

The B-52 bombing of North Vietnam toward the end of 1972 followed the same pattern of U.S. response earlier in the year and was clearly responsible for the final agreement by Hanoi to a cease-fire. However, the long-run question about Vietnamization has not been answered. Nor can it be. Hanoi and the Viet Cong are bound to test the strength of U.S. will and the stamina of South Vietnam. The fighting in Cambodia in 1973-74 is one of such tests. Aside from questions about the extent of U.S. defense participation through air and naval forces in similar future contingencies and the likelihood of a repetition of the 1972 contingency, we are faced with the familiar difficulty of building a viable economic and political structure in a newly independent and economically underdeveloped country which also has to maintain a large military establishment.

It should be recalled in this connection that the dominant philosophy underlying the Marshall Plan a quarter of a century ago was that Western Europe should be allowed to rebuild its war-torn economy without having to resort to domestic controls and privations to a degree that might have fanned internal unrest. In addition, following a precipitate American demobilization, security was provided for Western Europe through the formation of NATO. The same general philosophy was adopted for American aid to Japan under occupation, with the Americans simultaneously providing total military protection. Again, following the Korean armistice in 1953, U.S. military and economic assistance to Korea was continued for two decades. What is expected of South Vietnam and Vietnamization in the long run may, therefore, exceed what some other nations have been asked to accomplish in the past.

SOME ECONOMIC FACTORS IN LONG-TERM VIETNAMIZATION

The nature of the task facing South Vietnam is only too familiar. It may be viewed as a matter of acquiring and applying sufficient resources to meet competing claims. On the basis of year-end figures, the payroll of the

Vietnamese government numbered 817,900 in 1965, 1,138,200 in 1968, and 1,396,000 in 1971. (See Table V.3.)

The expansion of government payroll, which was as much as 25 percent in 1969–71, especially in the size of the armed forces and the police, unmistakably reflected the assumption of wider defense functions by the Vietnamese. This development had both a manpower aspect and a financial aspect. Total GVN military expenditures amounted to 72 billion piastres in 1968, when the U.S. ground effort was at its peak, and 128 billion piastres in 1970.[11] These figures represented 62.8 percent and 63.7 percent of total government expenditures (including extra budgetary expenditures) in the two years in question. On the other hand, government revenue from its own sources amounted to 54.2 billion piastres in 1968 while another 24.2 billion constituted local currency made available from U.S. sources. The combined total barely covered total military expenditures alone. In 1970, 125.7 billion piastres of government revenue were derived from the government's own sources while U.S. sources supplied 27 billion piastres, the two together exceeding total GVN military expenditures by only a small proportion. Following the completion of scheduled U.S. force withdrawals, the cost of equipment purchase and maintenance that must be paid by Vietnam may well increase, quite apart from any operation and replacement costs incurred in combat.

The South Vietnamese balance of international payments is another

Table V.3 Number of Persons on Government of Vietnam Payroll (in thousands)

	1965	1968	1971
Armed forces	571.2	819.0	1,090.0
Para-military	68.0	102.6	41.0
Police	52.2	78.4	120.0
	691.4	1,000.0	1,251.0
Civilian employees	126.5	138.2	145.0
Total	817.9	1,138.2	1,396.0

SOURCE: Office of Economic Policy, Bureau for Vietnam, Agency for International Development, *Summary of Monthly Economic Data*, September-October, 1971.

long-term Vietnamization problem. In 1970, for instance, total exports from Vietnam, based on the exchange record, were U.S. $13 million[12] while total imports were $850 million. Invisible export income from services was $315 million. The large deficit in the trade account was offset principally by imports financed by the Agency for International Development (AID), including agricultural products imported under Public Law 480. In 1968, for example, $331.8 million out of $668.8 million total imports were financed by AID. Invisible service exports will obviously decline sharply with the withdrawal of U.S. forces. In addition, the above figures probably do not reflect all direct imports of military end items. One should, therefore, expect a serious balance of payments disequilibrium unless adequate military and economic aid continues.

The large transfer of American resources which enabled South Vietnam to carry on its war while maintaining other resource uses must be replaced. If the adjustment is to be successful, replacement must be carried out in step with the reduction of the inflow of U.S. resources. As one 1970 study on the subject puts it, "The major task facing Vietnam now is to expand her exports and cut down unnecessary imports so that by 1974 she will be able to finance her trade deficit out of a reduced flow of aid. In order to be able to carry out this task, she will need appropriate economic policies (1) to control domestic inflation; (2) to correct her grossly overvalued exchange rate of VN $118 to U.S. $1; and (3) to replace her existing system of import licensing which is a major force of inefficiency and distortions in her economic system."[13] In October, 1970, an exchange rate of VN $275 to $1 was introduced for financial transfers, exports, invisibles, certain luxury imports, and piastre purchases of U.S. civilian and military personnel from American disbursing officers. A year later, in November, 1971, three new rates were adopted: VN $275 per American dollar for U.S.-financed imports, VN $400 for GVN-financed imports and VN $410 for invisibles and exports.[14] The nature of the problems of stabilization, adjustment, and development appears well recognized by an increasing number of both Vietnamese and American policy-makers. The experience of Taiwan and Korea suggests that the prospect is by no means hopeless, provided both time and effort are available under conditions of relative security. The presence of serious uncertainty on both points can hardly be denied. What would happen if in the long run South Vietnam should find itself unable to resist pressure from the Communist North, or if it should find the dual task of nation building and maintaining security beyond its capability? What if other external assistance on "Marshall Plan terms" are unavailable to substitute for U.S. assistance? These, of course, are questions that plague the Vietnamese and other Asian nations.

The South Vietnamese are concerned because their very national existence is at stake. Yet, faced with an enemy that has never ceased to call for its total surrender, the GVN can hardly do other than continue its fight for survival. As long as Vietnamization in the narrow sense was still incomplete, the only real choice was to continue the war with whatever level of assistance the United States, operating under the latter's own set of constraints, can offer. In short, the American option was the only option available. As long as conditions in Cambodia and Laos are not stabilized, it is most improbable that other choices will present themselves to South Vietnam for the latter's free decision.[15]

For the other Asian countries, the long-term results of Vietnamization, as measured by their effect on the status and policy of South Vietnam, will affect them in several ways. If the outcome is such that North Vietnam can continue or even expand its role as a secure source of supply and sanctuary to insurgents operating in adjacent countries,[16] it would tend to encourage insurgency in Thailand and Malaysia. The same conditions that would permit North Vietnam to play this role would enable Peking to do the same in both Thailand and Malaysia, and beyond Pacific-Asia, in Burma. Needless to say, Cambodia and Laos can hardly escape the same fate, should South Vietnam prove to be not viable in the long run. Conversely, South Vietnam's viability may be adversely affected by the fall of Cambodia and Laos to Communist control.

PERCEPTION OF AMERICAN POLICY IN THE REST OF PACIFIC-ASIA

With the exception of the three Indochina states, the countries of Southeast Asia are not involved in external conflicts with implacable enemies. To them other alternatives are available even though some choices may be unattractive.

Thailand. Thailand's initial perception of the Nixon Doctrine came in a period when inquiries were being made in the U.S. Congress and elsewhere about America's external commitments, the operations of the military assistance program, and the implications of American military bases abroad.[17] The Thais were quick to point out that, under the Nixon Doctrine, countries receiving U.S. military assistance and faced with internal insurgency should be primarily responsible for providing the manpower in their own defense and that this had been Thai policy for a long time. U.S. criticisms of their handling of American aid, as well as the high cost of American bases in their country, caused the Thai leaders some unhappiness as the new era began. They were able to reply, however, that U.S. air bases in Thailand were constructed to support American operations in Vietnam and that costs incurred for building and manning these bases should not be lumped together with military assistance for the direct benefit of Thailand.[18] However, natural resentment against what was genuinely felt to be unfair criticism was combined with a growing concern that Thailand's past unstintingly pro-

American policy had placed the country in an exposed position vis-à-vis its Communist neighbors. Consequently, long before the July, 1971, announcement of America's new China policy, there was a tendency to describe U.S. force reductions in the rest of Asia as examples of American willingness to "cut and run." In the face of this presumed trend in American policy, a widespread reaction in Thailand was to look for other more promising alternatives.

For a small country like Thailand recognition of its own limitations is realistic. Whether being realistic necessarily implies immediate acceptance of what seems to be inevitable and whether it precludes "unrealistic" efforts to alter "the inevitable" are, of course, open to question. During the Japanese invasion of Indochina in World War II, Thailand accepted an undesirable arrangement because of its "inevitability" in order to escape a worse outcome. Is there to be a historical parallel for the future?

Views favoring an active search for an alternative solution seemed to be gaining support in 1970 and in the first half of 1971. However, it was not until after July, 1971, that proposals for accommodation with the Communist powers and trying to balance them against one another received more public attention. Mr. Nixon's announced plan to visit Peking was reported in the Thai press as an admission of failure of American policy both in Vietnam and toward Communist China. A common reaction was similar to that in Japan, i.e. suggestions that a Peking-Bangkok dialogue should be initiated immediately and that the Thai Prime Minister should try to visit Peking.[19] The survival of Thailand appeared at stake, and a policy change seemed impending.

However, there were no rapid changes in external policy in 1971–72. A change in government did come in November, 1971, but there was no change in leadership, and the first effect was a tightening of internal control not unlike the Korean model of the same era. Prime Minister Thanom Kittikachorn himself headed a "coup" which dissolved the parliament, abolished the constitution, disbanded the cabinet, and instituted martial law.[20] As reported in the *New York Times*,[21] Marshal Thanom, now Chairman of the new National Executive Council, believed that the "pre-revolution" governmental machinery was inadequate to deal with the situation following Peking's entry into the United Nations. He needed new powers in order to forestall the leftists' "rush to make peace with Peking even while Peking continues to support terrorism and subversion in Thailand."[22]

Immediately after Thailand's change of government, a conference of ASEAN foreign ministers meeting in Kuala Lumpur announced that the five member countries were determined to undertake "initially necessary efforts to secure the recognition of ... Southeast Asia as a zone of peace, freedom and neutrality."[23] "Neutralization" was reportedly defined by Thailand as "freedom from interference by other countries,"[24] presumably along with noninterference with other countries. Marshal Thanom agreed with the declaration of Southeast Asia as a "zone of peace and neutrality" and called upon the Soviet Union and the PRC as "nations concerned with this region" to guarantee the ASEAN agreement.[25] Speaking in Singapore at another meeting of ASEAN foreign ministers, Dr. Thanat said, "It seems that smaller countries should ... refrain from being proxies of others and engage in performing such work as doing the fighting for them, and North Vietnam would be well to take cognizance of this new trend,"[26] referring here to the new invasion of South Vietnam by the North.

It is quite clear that Thailand would like the Communist powers to leave it alone. The Thai leaders, however, realized that Thailand was not about to be left alone. According to the Thai military, the number of armed insurgents in Thailand increased by 15–20 percent between late 1970 and early 1972. In March, 1972,[27] three thousand armed Meo tribesmen, under Thai and ethnic Chinese leadership, operated in the North; 1,500 armed insurgents were in the Northeast, centered around the Phu Phan Mountains; 500 Thai guerrillas were believed to be near the Malaysian border in the South. In the circumstances, an attempt to establish neutrality as a national policy appeared impractical or premature.[28]

The Thanom government was ousted in a student-led revolt in late 1973. However, Thailand has continued to move very cautiously toward Peking. Trade missions and visits by athletic teams have been exchanged, accompanied by government officials. But Thailand has not been willing to accept PRC assurance of noninterference in Thai internal affairs at face value and the anti-Communist counterinsurgency effort has continued.

U.S. air bases in Thailand in support of operations in Vietnam and, later, in enforcing the cease-fire agreement provide a source of invisible export income. Although implementation of the Nixon Doctrine and reduction of the American base structure in Asia would threaten the Thai balance of payments, this is not an immediate concern. With the removal of U.S. ground forces from Vietnam and stepped-up dependence on the air force, especially after the start of the North Vietnamese offensive in April, 1972, the air bases in Thailand have assumed greater importance than before. Instead of reduction, there was even initial expansion during this period[29] although a force reduction agreement was concluded between the United States and Thailand in early 1974. In addition to the original six air bases—Takhli, Utapao, Udorn, Ubon, Nakorn Phanom, and Korat—whose usefulness and implications were the subject of debate in the Symington Subcommittee, when the Nixon Doctrine was still in its initial stage of development, a seventh base was made ready in mid-1972 at Nam Phong in Northeast Thailand.

In addition to the new U.S. base, Thailand also undertook to increase the strength of its armed forces with American military assistance. Although there were complaints of inadequate funding and slow delivery, U.S. military assistance to Thailand held up reasonably well in 1970–71. In terms of new obligations, U.S. military grants to Thailand amount to $95.5 million in FY 1970 and $89.1 million in FY 1971. (See Table V.4.) These were supplemented in FY 1970 by $21.2 million of cash sales and $2.7 million in "long supply" (i.e. excess stock). In FY 1971, $3.9 million in "long supply" were provided.[30] Economic adjustments incidental to reductions of U.S. military assistance and spending derived from American bases, in terms of balance of payments and domestic budgetary and employment problems, could be serious.

Malaysia. The trend of Thai policy in 1970–72 and its underlying factors were not lost upon Thailand's neighbors not directly involved in the Vietnam War. Such a neighbor is Malaysia, which has no defense arrangement with the United States but which would be shielded from the potential consequences of the extension of Chinese and other Communist influence from the north as long as South Vietnam and Thailand remained as effective buffers. Malaysia, therefore, is free to act without the "onus" of having been a U.S. ally. Not surprisingly, the Malaysian Prime Minister, Tun Razak, was one of the first, since the announcement of the Nixon Doctrine, to call for the neutralization of Southeast Asia with big power guarantees. While visiting Indonesia in December, 1970, he expressed hope that Communist China would change its policy of supporting revolution in the smaller nations.[31] This was followed by soundings of possible Chinese reaction to additional Malaysian overtures, the dispatch of a Malaysian trade mission to Peking, the reception in Malaysia of a return visit by a Peking trade group, the prompt conclusion thereafter of a Sino-Malaysian trade agreement in August, 1971, and withdrawal from ASPAC of which the ROC is a member. The trade agreement followed on the heels of the announcement of Mr. Nixon's planned trip to China and was a clear indication of a Malaysian effort to seek accommodation with Peking. The opening of the U.S.-Peking dialogue was apparently viewed in Malaysia as an indication of the impending end of the Vietnam War and the withdrawal of the U.S. presence from Asia in a manner that would presage a potential upsurge of Peking's influence.[32]

It should be noted, however, that Malaysia's move toward accommodating Peking was made with considerable caution. Malaysia was very much aware of the threat of subversion and the potential danger from Chinese Communist support of domestic insurgents. Malaysian authorities took note of the fact that radio broadcasts emanating from China constantly aimed their propaganda against the Malaysian government.[33] The New China News Agency, Peking's official news service, often relays reports of allegedly successful operations of the insurgent Malayan National Liberation Army

Table V.4 U.S. Military Transfers to Southeast Pacific-Asia (Excluding Indochina)
(Net obligations and loan authorizations in millions of dollars)

	Grants FY 70	Grants FY 71	Long Supply FY 70	Long Supply FY 71	Credit Sales FY 70	Credit Sales FY 71	Cash Sales FY 70	Cash Sales FY 71	Total FY 70	Total FY 71	FY 72**
Thailand	95.5	89.1	2.7	3.9	—	—	21.2	*	119.4	93.0	40
Malaysia	0.2	0.2	—	—	—	2.2	2.1	0.2	2.3	2.6	7
Singapore	—	—	—	—	—	—	5.9	5.1	5.9	5.1	7
Indonesia	5.8	16.8	0.4	1.3	—	—	*	—	6.2	18.1	28
Philippines	18.7	17.0	1.1	1.3	—	—	0.7	1.4	20.5	19.7	...
Australia[1]	—	—	—	—	—	—	58.5	55.2	58.5	55.2	...
New Zealand[2]	—	—	—	—	—	—	5.3	7.0	5.3	7.0	...

SOURCES: *United States Foreign Policy, 1971. A Report of the Secretary of State*, Dept. of State Publication 8634, Washington, D.C., March 1972, pp. 410–11. For FY 72, See the *New York Times*, July 9, 1972.
1. Plus Export-Import Bank military loans of $128.4 million in FY 1970 and $123.0 million in FY 1971.
2. Plus Export-Import Bank military loans of $10 million in FY 1971.
*Negligible
**Proposed

originally broadcast by the "Voice of Malayan Revolution," a clandestine radio based in China.[34]

The Malaysian authorities have been faced for some time with two insurgent groups: a small rebel movement based among ethnic Chinese in rural Sarawak, East Malaysia, and a group of 1,200 to 1,400 trained members of the Communist terrorist organization that has grown out of the remnant insurgents of the Communist Party of Malaya under Chin Peng's command.[35] The core of the latter group survived counterinsurgency operations in Malaysia and was able to establish itself in three southern Thai provinces across the Malaysian border. In the absence of effective coordinated drives by Malaysian and Thai forces, the insurgents have been able to hold out. If a secure supply route should become available, and if a sanctuary for them could be built on Thai territory similar to the one Cambodia under Sihanouk provided for the Viet Cong, the scale of insurgency in Malaysia could rise considerably. These are some of the realities confronting the Malaysian government.

Malaysia has been cautious in its commercial dealings with mainland China. Trade is channeled through a state trading organization in what seems to be a deliberate effort to prevent Chinese dominance of these operations. The gestures toward Peking described above, ending with mutual diplomatic recognition in May, 1974, are not intended as an invitation to the Chinese Communists to extend their influence down the Malayan peninsula. Rather they are aimed at placating Peking in the hope that the Chinese Communists will be willing to stop their overt support of local insurgents and to settle for a neutral area in Southeast Asia. The presumed attraction to Peking would be that such a neutral zone could also serve as a southern buffer for Communist China from the Soviet Union and, in the less probable case, from the United States. Toward this end, Malaysia has increased its economic contact with the Soviet Union in recent years, partly as an offset to the potential rise of Peking's influence. The Soviet Union, in turn, has become increasingly active in Malaysia.

Singapore. The somewhat complex picture we have drawn provides an illustration of how a country nonaligned with the United States but basically in sympathy with the West has felt compelled to develop other foreign policy options in the face of the anticipated rise of Soviet and Chinese power, concomitant with an apparent withdrawal of the United States. A similar perception of American policy may be found in Singapore; the proposed solution, however, reflects Singapore's special situation. Singapore shares with Malaysia the concern that a shift in Thailand's posture could increase the chances of revival of insurgency in Malaysia.[36] In particular, Singapore fears that racial conflict between Malays and the ethnic Chinese in Malaysia could become a significant factor in providing the insurgency with young Chinese recruits. In this manner, a Communist-sponsored insurgency could be transformed into a racial war. While the Republic of Singapore has been busy trying to create a new sense of national identity in a multiracial society, it has not had a great deal of time to achieve its objective since separation from the Malaysian Federation in 1965. Singapore's population is nearly two-thirds Chinese, while across the border ethnic Chinese make up a minority group approximating the native Malays in number and considerably exceeding them in terms of economic well-being. This potentially explosive situation has resulted in numerous clashes over the years, including a major riot in May, 1969, and was, in fact, the most important single reason why Singapore was established as a separate state. In Malaysia, according to some students, the traditional compromise formula of power sharing between Malays and Chinese had broken down, and a new modus vivendi must again be found for the two races to live in peace.

Although Singapore and Malaysia were both targets of Sukarno's confrontation during the first half of the 1960s, fear of an anti-Singapore alignment of Malaysia and Indonesia has not disappeared, and racial distrust has continued. Thus, Singapore's concern about a Communist insurgency is expressed in a context of potential racial as well as regional conflict. From the viewpoint of Singapore, a nightmarish but conceivable scenario might be (1) the revival of large-scale Communist insurgency in Malaysia, following a reorientation of Thailand's foreign policy, (2) transformation of the above insurgency into a civil war on racial lines, and (3) internal pressure in Singapore in favor of intervention in Malaysia and the "spilling-over" of the conflict to Singapore, either with or without a Malaysia-Indonesia entente. These are dangers which Singapore seeks to avert. They are not produced by American policy, but their chances of occurrence may be increased if the United States withdraws from Asia.

The effect of American policy shifts is viewed in Singapore in several ways. First, a U.S. withdrawal in Indochina, together with long-term instability in Vietnam, which premature U.S. withdrawal or an unstable cease-fire settlement would induce, could result in the kind of insurgency described above even in the absence of a deliberate American concession of a sphere of influence to Communist China. The Chinese Communists have their own interests in and ambitions for Singapore and Malaysia and may believe that there are opportunities worth exploiting. To offset increased influence from Peking, other balancing forces are required. The Soviet Union is available to offer its services and Japan's interest in Singapore from the point of view of trade, investment, and, above all, secure passage of its oil tankers and other shipping through the Malacca Straits is also strong. Militarily, however, Japan cannot counter the Soviet Union or Communist China. Japan is also economically most vulnerable to external pressure. In the absence of an adequate U.S. military presence, a shadowy tripartite balance of power, supplemented with the presence of other nations, is all that remains. A quadrilateral balance with the active participation of the United States—involving both large American investments and the presence of the Seventh Fleet, albeit at a distance, in both the Pacific and the Indian Oceans—would be ideal from Singapore's point of view. However, the elements of a stable quadrilateral balance are not assured.

Singapore's plans for its own security are worth special attention because they constitute a model for small nations which cannot defend themselves on their own. Three components are involved. First, a domestic arms buildup is being carried out in order to deter aggression by its neighbors, specifically, Malaysia and/or Indonesia. Second, a loose alliance has been formed to bolster its own capability as an additional safeguard against small aggressions. In this case, the loose alliance is the Five-Power Defense Arrangement among Australia, New Zealand, the United Kingdom, (ANZUK), Malaysia, and Singapore for the defense of the last two countries. Both Malaysia and Singapore can also use the same arrangement as a means to encourage cooperation between themselves, because different units of the armed forces of the other three countries are stationed in Malaysia and Singapore in such a manner that their effectiveness is predicated on Malaysian-Singapore cooperation, although the arrangement provides a restraining influence on Malaysia, which has little to fear from Singapore. Finally, the big powers are all invited to acquire a stake in the continued prosperity of Singapore and the maintenance of free passage in the Malacca Straits. Singapore hopes to convince the big powers that freedom of the Malacca Straits for their individual shipping can be best assured only by maintaining the independence and integrity of Singapore. Success of this policy is predicated on several conditions: (1) that all the big powers desire free passage for themselves, (2) that each will not tolerate control of the straits by another big power, and (3) that each is unable to exercise sole control to the exclusion of the others.

Singapore's approach differs from that of Malaysia in that it seeks to establish a realistic balance among the United States, the Soviet Union, the PRC, and Japan, which could eventually lead to effective "neutralization." It does not ask for neutralization in the absence of an effective big-power balance. The present difference in approach may be explained by Malaysia's not being immediately identified in the minds of the big powers with security of free passage in the Malacca Straits. In this respect, the claim by both Malaysia and Indonesia over extended territorial water limits that would put the Straits under their control may have the indirect effect of raising their strategic value to the big powers.

The Philippines. As in Thailand, the reaction in the Philippines to

America's new policy focuses on three issues: reduction of U.S. bases, military assistance, and domestic insurgency. Philippine sentiments toward U.S. bases are mixed. On the one hand, nationalism demands their reduction and ultimate return. On the other, the benefits to the local economy and the international balance of payments are fully recognized. However, because of nationalistic clamor and domestic political considerations, it has sometimes been necessary for the Philippine government to assume a posture contrary to its economic interests. Some U.S. cutting back has already taken place. For instance, the Sangley Point Naval Station was returned to the Philippines in September, 1971, as a result of new base negotiations. With the Vietnamese cease-fire, further base reductions in the Philippines is to be expected. The scale will depend largely upon the level of U.S. naval and air presence to be maintained in Asia in the future.

Officially, like Thailand and Indonesia, the Philippines welcomed the initial announcement of the Nixon Doctrine, with particular reference to the military and economic assistance promised to U.S. allies and other nations willing to defend themselves and whose security was also of vital American concern. Unfortunately, throughout the 1960s, economic growth in the Philippines was among the lowest in Southeast Asia, and little evidence of any rapid change for the better appeared in the early 1970s. The economy appears in chronic need of external support. In another critical sector, the local insurgency front, the combined strength of armed regular and support forces of the original Huk insurgents was estimated to number no more than 900 in late 1969, a sharp decline from the 12,000-man force in the early 1950s.[37] However, while both the bandit-type insurgents and a separate Soviet-oriented group have been on the decline, a third group of Maoist insurgents under the banner of the New People's Army has become an important element in the present decade.[38] Reportedly financed by Peking, this group is allied with student radicals engaged in active urban guerrilla warfare who provide a vehicle of recruitment for the New People's Army. If there is adequate coordination of the urban and rural elements of the insurgency, it is conceivable that the scale of internal conflict could well expand. In addition, Moslem unrest has plagued Mindanao in the South; in this regard, the militant Arab states, such as Libya, pose a potential threat of external involvement.

Because of the insurgency problem, the Philippines is greatly concerned about Peking's support of revolutionary movements in other Asian countries. In this sense, too, Taiwan is to the Philippines like Thailand is to Malaysia, inasmuch as a Taiwan dominated by hostile forces could become a channel for supplies from the Chinese mainland to insurgents in the Philippines. The Philippines also shares a common concern with Malaysia, Thailand, Singapore, and Indonesia: In Philippine eyes, the large local ethnic Chinese community could become a source of internal instability. Up to now, however, this Chinese element has been primarily pro-Taiwan. By maintaining diplomatic relations with the Republic of China, the Philippines may have managed to reduce a potential threat, although Malaysia's recognition of Peking may pave the way for a similar change on the part of the Philippines.

From time to time, the Philippines has chosen to make friendly gestures toward mainland China, as well as the Soviet Union, although no diplomatic or economic relations are maintained with either Communist country as of this writing. These gestures have been multiplied since July, 1971, including a visit by a Philippine senator to Peking and that of Mme. Marcos to Moscow, exchanges of athletic teams with Peking, etc. Immediately following the July, 1971, announcement from Washington, President Marcos called for a summit meeting of Southeast Asian countries to discuss the implications of the Nixon visit. Early in 1972, diplomatic relations were established with Rumania and Yugoslavia. On June 9, 1972, after a meeting of the Philippine National Security Council, Marcos stated, "Now we must renegotiate not only the military bases agreement, but all other agreements with the U.S. We have started a study of the new U.S. policy toward Southeast Asia, including the U.S. congressional policies which give a low priority to the Philippines." [39] Because of historical associations some Filipinos continue to have the sense of a special relationship with the United States. Others are beginning to question whether this sentiment is fully justified or reciprocated. However, there is as yet no clear indication of a reorientation of Philippine policy.

The absence of a direct external threat has contributed to inertia and inaction which characterized the Philippines position in the past. There are those who believe that a considerable American military presence is essential to the maintenance of governmental authority in the Philippines, although even with the American presence one should not be surprised if the scale of insurgency were again to rise. Since 1972, martial law has been invoked by President Marcos. Thus, the same policy pattern has been set as in Thailand (until the fall of Thanom) and South Korea, namely, consolidation of power by the ruling government in the face of a potential increase in internal and external challenges.

Indonesia. Contrary to the perceptions of the Nixon Doctrine described so far, those in Indonesia have stressed its positive aspect. Indonesia regards the Doctrine as an American acknowledgment that a larger role will be given Indonesia in future American foreign policy and defense planning. Indonesia, according to this view, is to become the counterpart of Japan in the southern section of Pacific-Asia. In order to attain this status, Indonesia will have to build up its defense capability and economy. In both these areas Indonesia expects U.S. assistance, and the anticipation has been largely fulfilled thus far. Total "net obligations" for military assistance to Indonesia rose from

$6.2 million in FY 1970 to $18.1 million in FY 1971.[40] The increase was nearly threefold. Corresponding totals for the entire area of Southeast Pacific Asia, excluding Vietnam and Cambodia, rose only from $218.1 million to $270.7 million. (See Table V.4.) The trend continued into FY 1972.

Having emerged from under the shadow of Sukarno, who had brought Indonesia to dire economic straits, the Indonesian government under General Suharto has earnestly begun to rebuild the economy. Unlike most countries in the region, Indonesia even cut back its defense establishment. (See Table V.1.) During 1970–71, Indonesia was successful in curbing inflation, initiating general development, and making further progress in debt settlement. American, European, and Japanese capital is entering the country in large amounts;[41] the petroleum industry, in particular, has made notable progress and has been a principal source of foreign exchange income. This economic revival, fueled by Indonesia's natural wealth, is, however, only one of the advantages the country enjoys.

In addition, having foiled the attempt to establish a "Peking-Djakarta Axis" in 1965, the present leaders of Indonesia are not unduly worried in the short run about any overt move on the part of their potential adversaries on the Chinese mainland. Diplomatic relations between Indonesia and Peking have been in suspension since 1967, while trade relations between Indonesia and Taiwan have grown even after the ouster of the ROC from the United Nations in October, 1971. While Djakarta is not particularly anxious to revive its relationship with Peking, it perceives no immediate threat from the PRC.

The Indonesian army is experienced in guerrilla warfare and has been successful in suppressing insurgency, following the 1965 PKI coup, by practicing its concept of "territorial warfare," which deals with counterinsurgency operation in three stages—intelligence, psychological warfare, and military operations. The army, which sees itself as a mainstay in nation building, is eager to offer other Asian nations the benefit of its counterinsurgency experience. Significantly, Indonesia is almost alone among the Southeast Asian nations in being enthusiastic about the potential of regional defense. It is already cooperating with other Southeast Asian countries in exchange of intelligence on externally supported insurgency and subversion. Some Indonesians are even anxious to expand the functions of ASEAN to include collective defense. In their view, such an arrangement could conceivably embrace South Vietnam, once the Vietnam War is really over and foreign troops are withdrawn. Fundamentally, therefore, Indonesia sees itself in a position of potential leadership in such a regional arrangement by virtue of its large manpower and natural resources. At the same time, despite its emphasis on this possibility of collective defense in the post-Vietnam period, Indonesia continues to espouse nonalignment. The difference in policy between Indonesia and Malaysia is that, while the former considers it possible to develop an independent, nonaligned center of collective power, the latter hopes to find security in neutralization because of its smaller size and inherently lower capabilities. In his call for coordinated regional action at the April, 1972, ASEAN Conference, Adam Malik, the Indonesian foreign minister, stated that the ASEAN countries should reassert their position in the new emerging pattern of power relations, exemplified by the Washington-Peking rapprochement, lest they be affected adversely. "Calculated, well-planned, and coordinated actions" are necessary for this purpose,"[42] said Malik.

A geographical fact to be noted is that, other than the Malacca Straits and short of circumnavigating Australia, passage between the Indian Ocean and the South China Sea can be effected only through the straits of Sunda, Bali, Lombok, and Wetar in the island chain of Indoneisa. This was obviously an important factor in Japan's pre-World War II planning of its "Greater East Asia Co-prosperity Sphere." Indonesia's geography and resources were presumably also prominent in Soviet and Chinese Communist strategic planning before 1965. Between 1955 and 1962, the Soviet Union offered about $2.9 billion of military assistance to the less developed countries. Of this total about one billion went to Indonesia.[43] An additional $200 million of Soviet military aid was granted to Indonesia during the three years up to 1965, when the failure of the PKI coup abruptly changed the character of the Indonesian government. Again, from 1954 to 1970—actually only to 1965, in the case of Indonesia—the Soviet Union gave $272 million of economic aid to Indonesia out of a total of $5.3 billion for the less developed countries of the world. During the same period, Communist countries in Eastern Europe gave Indonesia another $263 million out of their total economic aid of $1.8 billion. Peking, too, offered Indonesia, up to 1965, $105 million out of its total foreign aid of $669 million for the entire 1954—1970 period.[44] There can be no better acknowledgment of the importance both the Soviet Union and Communist China attach to Indonesia than these figures indicate. Probably for this reason, the Soviet Union decided in 1970 to accept the "Paris Formula" for debt settlement which Western creditor countries had previously worked out with Indonesia.[45] The Soviet Union has also resumed trading and discussion of economic aid with Indonesia, but a corresponding resumption of Peking-Djakarta relations has thus far been held back by Indonesia.

The renewed Soviet interest in Indonesia cannot be divorced from Indonesia's claim over the Malacca Straits. Neither Malaysia nor Indonesia is ready to relinquish this claim and agree outright to internationalization, which would adequately serve the interests of the maritime user countries and Singapore. Indonesia, like Malaysia, would like to have it understood that free passage through the Straits must be predicated upon the goodwill of Indonesia.[46]

Australia and New Zealand. Two opposite positions on Australia's security were advanced in a 1968 study[47] on the Nuclear Non-proliferation Treaty and Australian policy. On the one hand, the optimistic view suggested that, mainly because of its geographical position, no potential enemy could mount a successful invasion of Australia. Besides, there was no reason for any country to be hostile toward Australia. On the other, the pessimistic view held that either China or Japan would eventually dominate East Asia and might well regard Australia, if it remained poorly defended, at least as a target of opportunity. If such a threat should materialize, Australia would have to find security either in its own arms or in American power. While this contrast is an obvious oversimplification, it nevertheless is revealing that both Communist China and Japan should be cast in the role of potential enemy. There was no mention of the Soviet Union or, one might add, of Indonesia.

In the long run, Australia cannot but be interested in the policy of Indonesia, its much more populous neighbor immediately to the north. Australia has both security and economic interests in the Malacca Straits. To Australia—and New Zealand—the defense of Malaysia and Singapore constitutes their own forward defense. The enemy could well be an expansionist Indonesia or a potentially threatening China that must be contained. This would seem to be the principal argument supporting their participation in the Korean and Vietnam Wars, and especially for Australia's taking a "big brother's" role in the Five-Power Defense Arrangement.

If the Soviet Union is treated as a Pacific power, it is, of course, farther from Australia than both China and Japan. In the absence of a Soviet navy, Australia might seem well out of harm's way. However, the Soviet Union must now be added to the list of countries of vital concern to Australia's national security. A measure of the maritime progress the Soviet Union has made may be found in the growth of Soviet naval presence in the Indian Ocean.[48] In 1967, Soviet research vessels were first reported in the Indian Ocean. Three Soviet warships made their appearance in 1968; mooring buoys were established in 1969 and seven Soviet ships came to the Indian Ocean in early 1970. During the 1971 war between India and Pakistan, the size of the Soviet force was augmented by a special reinforcement and, for a time, the simultaneous presence of a relief squadron on rotation. A total force of 15–20 vessels was present, including two light cruisers, three or four destroyers, three submarines, and a mine sweeper. This fleet remained even after the American task force, headed by the *Enterprise,* returned to Subic Bay from the Bay of Bengal. Australia can no longer dismiss this Soviet naval presence either from the point of view of defense or from that of domestic politics. Even the Labor government, which has extended recognition to the PRC, will probably be unable to dismiss the implications of the Soviet presence out of hand.

If the Soviet Union was prepared to invest heavily in military aid and economic assistance to Indonesia under Sukarno, whose confrontation with Malaysia and Singapore could not have been staged without Soviet arms, would not the Soviet navy be able to accomplish even more on its own now that it can make its presence felt more directly?

Before Mr. Nixon's Peking visit, Australia and New Zealand had consistently sided with the United States in their China policies. Before the new Labor government, in spite of Australia's competition with Canada as sellers of wheat to Peking, Australia and New Zealand did not rush to recognize Peking after the latter's admission into the United Nations. Also, faced with Soviet naval expansion and the improved Soviet strategic nuclear balance vis-à-vis the United States, the two countries had remained faithful allies under the ANZUS Treaty. Unlike Malaysia and Singapore, where the Soviet Union could be regarded as a countervailing force to be used against China, Australia and New Zealand are faced with an increasing Soviet presence against which Communist China could do little. A cynic might therefore suggest that Australia and New Zealand have no acceptable alternatives particularly at a stage where the Soviet presence does not yet constitute a threat posing an immediate need for desperate measures.

As a source of external support Japan seems to present the only realistic alternative, if there is one. Economically, Japan has already invested heavily in Australia and is one of the latter's largest trade partners. Japanese exports to Australia and New Zealand increased from $168 million in 1960 to $704 million in 1970; Japanese imports from the two countries rose from $374 million in 1960 to $1,664 million in 1970.[49] As Australia's largest customer, Japan was responsible for about one-third of Australia's total exports in 1970. The proportion is rising further. Australia is also a natural source of uranium and many other metals for Japan. However, tendencies of economic nationalism aside, Australia is not fully sanguine about Tokyo's policy once Japan's arms buildup has reached a significant level. One way out of this dilemma would be to have Japan as a member of a multilateral defense arrangement so that restraint on Japanese behavior can be exercised by the other members. This is the same function that the Five-Power Defense Arrangement exercises over Malaysia in its relationship with Singapore; and, on a different level of power, NATO over West Germany. For Australia and New Zealand a similar regional arrangement involving Japan appears to be a viable alternative to a diminished U.S. presence. In the final analysis, there is, of course, still the possibility of developing a nuclear defense capability.

In the light of the preceding discussion it is not surprising that Australians are more than a little curious about the extent to which the United States, under the Nixon Doctrine, will fulfill its treaty commitments, especially if involvement in combat is necessary. To them, appeal to America's national interest as a criterion in fulfilling commitments does not offer sufficiently unambiguous guidance. Only specific actions, such as stepped-up air operations in North Vietnam, the dispatch of the *Enterprise* to the Indian Ocean, and the mining of Haiphong Harbor seem reassuring to Australian defense planners.[50]

CONCLUSION

The preceding discussion has brought out the principal elements in the perceptions of U.S. policy by countries in the region. In the relatively short run, their first concern is with the results of Vietnamization and the rate of reduction of U.S. military presence in Indochina and Thailand. Their second concern focuses on the volume and reliability of the flow of American military assistance to help build up their own capability. In this respect, Thailand and the Philippines are probably more worried than Indonesia. The data in Table V.4 demonstrate American intentions and performance in this respect during Mr. Nixon's first term.

However, for most of the countries under discussion, the really important questions are of a long-term nature. First, neither U.S. policy nor the countries themselves seem to have the proper answer to the following question: Will the resources and stage of economic development of a given country permit an eventual arms buildup to the necessary level for defense. For countries like Thailand and the Philippines, this question boils down to the volume and duration of continued U.S. military assistance. In this connection, one should bear in mind that defense costs have a tendency to grow, partly because of technological changes. Questions about the availability of resources and the proportion which can be allocated to defense arise for those countries that are not recipients of U.S. military grants, i.e., Malaysia and Singapore; they are especially significant for Singapore because of the island republic's very small size. For a country like Indonesia, which has the potential of becoming a significant and economically developed military power, the same question may not be relevant over the very long run. However, it will take a number of years before Indonesia can become an independent power capable of defending itself and rendering aid to others. Besides, even if U.S. military assistance is to continue for a number of years, would the arms buildup in the individual countries be accomplished in time to meet the potentially increasing threats and the changing strategic balances?

Differences in national interest and mutual distrust among countries in the region make collective defense arrangements especially difficult. In addition, existing differences offer certain opportunities for exploitation by external powers. Under these circumstances, collective defense arrangements are unlikely to develop quickly without the galvanizing influence of some big power. From the viewpoint of the smaller nations, the most cogent argument against collective defense is that the summation of weaknesses still results in weakness. This totally futile outlook may be unwarranted, but the difficulty necessarily involved in building collective strength from individual weakness does tend to reduce the chances of success for a joint effort. And without a fully accepted common purpose, all the existing differences tend to be magnified.

What nation can be the galvanizing big power to help structure collective defense in the area? Japan is militarily and psychologically not ready. Japan is also economically too susceptible to external pressure. In addition, many nations still have reservations about the extent and reliability of Japan's benevolence if and when Japan is sufficiently rearmed. Nor should one overlook the fact that, if Japanese trade and investment interests in the area grow further, additional friction may well be generated as a result of the understandable trends toward economic nationalism. If Japan is neither available nor wanted, what other prospects are there?

Certainly, a common perception is a feeling of uncertainty about the long-term availability or willingness of the United States to participate in the defense of individual countries in the area. The degree of U.S. participation opens several questions. First, if Japan will be available as a galvanizing power in a collective security arrangement at some point in the future, would the United States be available to fill this role *ad interim?* Second, would the United States be a long-term participant even after Japan has assumed the functions of the protective big power however improbable such a development might be? Last, will the U.S. defense role in this part of the world be limited to a "blue-water strategy," supported by the air force? Or would the use of U.S. ground forces remain a possibility under certain conditions? In either case, how would the array of U.S. bases in the area be restructured?

This list of questions can be best summarized in one word, uncertainty. In the face of this uncertainty, the different countries in the area have moved in the following directions in varying degrees. First, a few countries have become actively interested in the possibility of a balancing role for the Soviet Union. Second, roughly the same countries have sought accommodation with Peking, albeit with reluctance and caution. Third, most of the countries have moved toward increased regional cooperation on a very long-term, slowly progressing, and non-military basis. Lastly, some leaders in the area have moved toward a different perception of the world scene by supposing that the changing policy of the United States, the Soviet Union, and Communist China are *already* an indication of the disappearance of all principal sources of conflict.

Events in Vietnam and U.S. policies toward Peking and Moscow have been sufficiently ambiguous so that caution and prudence have caused most countries in the region to move relatively slowly. They have explored new options and foreclosed none. They may, however, not be able to do so indefinitely. The policies of other nations may not permit prolonged indecision on the part of the United States, Japan, or the individual smaller nations themselves. Each time an individual nation makes its choice, perhaps prematurely, a degree of freedom is lost for others. Above all, there is Soviet policy to take into account.

NOTES

1. Between 1952 and 1969, a cumulative total of 700 Thai insurgents was reportedly trained in Communist China, 600 in North Vietnam, and 1,000 in Communist-controlled areas of Laos. See Stephen T. Hosmer, "Protracted Warfare in Southeast Asia during the 70's: Some Lessons from the Past Two Decades," paper presented to an Airlie House Conference sponsored by the Institute of International relations, University of South Carolina, 1971.

   A "Free Thai" movement was established in the early 1950s in the Thai Autonomous Region in Yunnan Province of Communist China under Pridi, a former Thai Prime Minister. Radio stations located in the Soviet Union, mainland China, and North Vietnam have been actively beaming broadcasts to Thailand and Malaysia, extolling the successes of local insurgents.

   For an interesting report on antigovernment, anti-U.S. and pro-Maoist programs run by the Barisan Socialis for kindergarten children in Singapore, see the local trade union journal, *Perjuangan,* June 1970.

   For North Vietnamese involvement in Laos, see Paul F. Langer and Joseph J. Zasloff, *North Vietnam and the Pathet Lao: Partners in the Struggle for Laos,* Cambridge, Mass.: Harvard University Press, 1967.
2. The PKI coup at the end of September, 1965, apparently had Peking's support. Its failure, the consequent rise of the rule of the Indonesian Army, and the downfall of Sukarno led to suspension of close ties with both Peking and Moscow.
3. The following approximate geographical distribution of "overseas Chinese" in Southeast Asia may be compared with the total populations of the respective countries:

Million Persons

	I "Overseas Chinese"	II Total Population	III=I/II in %
Thailand	3.5	30.6	11.4
Laos	0.05	3.0	neg.
Cambodia	0.03	6.2	neg.

Continued on page 166

Million Persons

	I "Overseas Chinese"	II Total Population	III=I/II in %
Vietnam (both South and North)	1.1	32.0	3.4
West Malaysia	3.1	8.1	38.3
Sabah	0.1	0.5	20.0
Sarawak	0.3	0.8	37.5
Singapore	1.4	1.9	73.7
Indonesia	3.0	105.0	2.9
Philippines	0.1	32.3	neg.

The above data are cited by Chun-hsi Wu in "Overseas Chinese" in a *Handbook* (Praeger) on the PRC edited by the present author. The same paper also discusses the different concepts used by various authors in defining the term "overseas Chinese." Hence these figures may differ from the estimates of the size of the ethnic Chinese minority by the countries in question.

4. The original membership of SEATO when the pact was signed at Manila on September 8, 1954, included Australia, France, New Zealand, Pakistan, the Philippines, Thailand, the United Kingdom, and the United States. Cambodia, Laos, and South Vietnam are "designated area" under the treaty. Under the 1962 Geneva settlement, Laos was removed from SEATO protection; under Sihanouk, Cambodia renounced aid from SEATO. Both France and Pakistan can no longer be counted as effective members of the alliance.

5. At the fifth meeting of ASEAN foreign ministers in April, 1972, the Singapore Foreign Minister, Mr. Rajaratnam, stated that while ASEAN should remain an organization for economic cooperation, member countries could not isolate their economic efforts from the political issues of war and peace introduced by big powers. "Since relations between the major powers are changing in ways which they themselves may not be sure of," he noted, "there is need for ASEAN foreign ministers to meet to assess not only the intentions of the Great Powers but also to get to know our individual reactions to new developments and rapid changes in our area." Actually, the member countries had been engaged in these discussions; Mr. Rajaratnam's suggestion amounted to making these "extracurricular activities" regular. *Straits Times,* Singapore, April 14, 1972.

6. According to Mr. Nixon, "American withdrawal is the primary goal." *U.S. Foreign Policy in the 1970's,* II, p. 71. In his annual report before the House Armed Services Committee on March 9, 1971, Secretary Laird stated, "Vietnamization has the positive goal of increasing Vietnamese responsibility for *all* aspects of the war and handling of their own

affairs. . . . [Italics added.] Vietnamization . . . is directed toward preparing the South Vietnamese to handle both Viet Cong insurgency and regular North Vietnamese armed forces regardless of the outcome in Paris." *1971 Defense Report*, p. 27.

7. There were many such comments in the U.S. press. For example, in an article in the *New York Times* of May 7, 1972, a correspondent reported from Saigon: "And there is not much that the Americans—with all their air power and frantic effort to replace the tanks and artillery pieces the South Vietnamese have lost—can do about it. Determination is needed desperately now to save South Vietnam, and that seems to be in short supply. It was the unknown factor all along, despite claims by the Nixon Administration that the South Vietnamese could 'hack it,' that Vietnamization was working and that air power could be sufficient to give the Vietnamese the edge over their enemy. Perhaps it would, if the South Vietnamese themselves wanted to resist as much as the enemy wants to attack. And now, many Americans here are concluding, their allies are not game for the fight as they thought." Other similar reports on instances of South Vietnamese losses were all quick in suggesting that Vietnamization had already failed its crucial test. In contrast, quick conclusions based on opposite evidence, such as the South Vietnamese stand at An Loc were never made to suggest that Vietnamization had been successul.

8. See Chapter IV, note 23.

9. The terms contained in Mr. Nixon's television address on May 8, 1972, tied "the complete withdrawal of American forces *from Vietnam*" to "an internationally supervised cease-fire *throughout Indochina*," (together with POW release), the former to follow the latter within four months.

10. While a *pro forma* Soviet statement condemning the United States and demanding an end to bombing and the mining of North Vietnamese waters was being issued, the Soviet Ambassador to Washington accompanied the Soviet Minister of Foreign Trade in a visit to the White House. Other indications were also given by Soviet sources that the planned Moscow summit meeting later in May would not be affected. The official statement from Peking followed essentially the same line and promised "resolute support for the Vietnamese people." But neither Peking nor Moscow threatened countermeasures and no retaliation was made overtly.

11. Agency for International Development, *Summary of Monthly Economic Data for Vietnam*, September-October, 1971.

12. *Ibid.*

13. Hla Myint, *Southeast Asia's Economy in the 1970's*, Manila: Asia Development Bank, November 1970, p. 85.

14. See *Report to the Ambassador from the Director of the U.S. AID Vietnam*, 1970 and 1971.

15. Senator George McGovern promised in his 1972 presidential campaign to withdraw all U.S. forces from Vietnam within 90 days after his inauguration. He would, however, retain a residual force in Thailand until the return of all American POWs held in Vietnam.

16. Cf. Stephen T. Hosmer, *op. cit.*
17. See *United States Security Agreements and Commitments Abroad, Kingdom of Thailand*, Hearings before the Subcommittee on U.S. Security Agreements and Commitments Abroad (the Symington Subcommittee), Senate Committee on Foreign Relations, 91st Congress, 1st session, Part 3, November 10, 11, 12, 13, 14 and 17, 1969. The following observations are based in part upon personal interviews in the winter of 1970-71.
18. During the November, 1969, hearings, Senator Fulbright wanted to have a "cumulative total of what the United States [had] invested in Thailand." The figures supplied were as follows:

U.S. Assistance to, and Military Expenditures in, Thailand, 1949-69

		Million
Economic Assistance		$592.4
Loans (includes $59,300,000 from Eximbank)	$119.4	
Grants (includes $14 million for Peace Corps)	$473.0	
Military assistance (includes MAP* grants, long supply/excess, and other military assistance grants)		743.5
U.S. military expenditures (covers calendar years 1966-69 and includes estimates for calendar years 1963-65)		855.0
Total		2,190.9

*Military Assistance Program

The construction cost of U.S. bases in Thailand was given by Mr. Paul, one of the Subcommittee's roaming investigators, at $700 million. *Op. cit.*, note 18, pp. 748-49.

19. In an interview with the *Bangkok Post* in December, 1970, Dr. Thanat Khoman, the Thai Foreign Minister, was reported to have said, "We want to negotiate [with Peking], to have dialogue." Above reported in the *Straits Times*, December 20, 1970. For a sample of Thai reactions to the news of the planned Nixon trip to Peking, see, e.g., the *Bangkok Post*, July 20 and 26, 1971; also the *Nation*, Bangkok, July 19 and 26, 1971.
20. See the *New York Times*, November 18, 1971.
21. Report by Max Frankel from Bangkok, *New York Times*, November 24, 1971.
22. *Ibid.*
23. *Nation*, November 29, 1971.
24. *Ibid.*
25. *Nation*, November 28, 1971.
26. *Straits Times*, April 14, 1972.
27. Based on James P. Sterba's interview with Lt. Gen. Saiyud Kerdphol, Director of the Command for the Suppression of Communists, *New York Times*, March 27, 1972.

28. Report on Lt. Gen. Saiyud's views in *Nation,* November 13, 1971.
29. Associated Press report, June 3, 1972.
30. See Table V.4.
31. Tun Razak's address at the Indonesian National Defense Institute, as reported in the *Singapore Herald,* Singapore, December 19, 1970.
32. See the *Straits Times.* Kuala Lumpur, in mid- and late July, e.g., July 17, 22, and 27, 1971. Also the Kuala Lumpur Radio broadcasts of this period.
33. Such a reference was made, for instance, by Tun Razak at the Singapore Conference of Commonwealth Prime Ministers in early 1971.
34. Cf. e.g., NCNA, Peking, January 1, 1972.
35. Cf. Stephen T. Hosmer, *op. cit.,* note 1.
36. For a fuller discussion on Singapore and the Malacca Straits see Yuan-li Wu, "Planning Security for a Small Nation: Lessons from Singapore," *Pacific Community,* Vol. 3, No.4, Tokyo, July 1972.
37. Cf. Stephen T. Hosmer, *op. cit.,* note 1.
38. Based on personal interviews in the winter of 1970—71.
39. Associated Press report, Manila, June 10, 1972.
40. See Table V.4.
41. Some of the foreign capital has been channeled through the Inter-Governmental Group on Indonesia (CIGGI) which was formed in 1967 by eleven donor countries plus the IMF, the IBRD, and the Asian Development Bank. See *United States Foreign Policy 1971, A Report of the Secretary of State,* Dept. of State Publication 8634, Washington, D.C., March 1972, p. 85.
42. Cf. *Straits Times,* April 14, 1972.
43. The estimates are from Dept. of State, *Communist States and Developing Countires: Aid and Trade in 1970,* RECS-15, September 22, 1971.
44. *Ibid.*
45. Under the formula agreed to in discussions at Paris, Indonesia's creditor countries would begin to receive interest payments after a certain date. Principal repayment is spread over 30 years, with some partial postponement permitted in the initial years.
46. A Japanese correspondent reported from Djakarta on May 13, 1972, that Malaysia and Indonesia contemplated taking certain measures governing passage through the Malacca Straits. "A) Prior to passage through the straits, all merchant ships and warships should inform Indonesia and Malaysia of their destinations and sailing purposes, and the governments of the two countries will not permit passage through the straits for military purposes; B) submarines are not permitted to sail underwater through the straits but must surface to explain their destination and sailing purpose; C) passage through the straits by U.S. warships destined for the Tonkin Gulf or by Soviet merchant ships carrying war material to North Vietnam will not be considered 'inoffensive navigation' which usually permits ordinary merchant ships to pass through the straits." *Mainichi,* Tokyo, May 14, 1972. According to the Malaysian Prime

Minister, however, innocent passage would be allowed, and Malaysia would take appropriate action only against countries that had committed acts detrimental to Malaysia. He asserted that it was the responsibility of foreign warships to give prior notice when passing through the straits, together with assurance of their peaceful purpose. Kuala Lumpur Radio, May 12, 1972.

47. J.L. Richardson, *Australia and the Non-Proliferation Treaty*, Canberra Papers on Strategy and Defense, No. 3, Canberra: Australian National University Press, 1968.
48. For a more detailed discussion, see Yuan-li Wu, *op. cit.*, note 36.
49. Ministry of Finance, Government of Japan.
50. Based on personal interview.

Chapter VI

The Soviet Union in Pacific-Asia

The preceding two chapters have made it clear that Soviet policy and the potential Soviet role in Pacific-Asia are topics that stir intense interest and speculation. Among the questions asked by various nations the most obvious, of course, is: Will the Soviet Union constitute a threat to our security, given our understanding of other factors, such as future American policy and diminishing U.S. military presence in the area? Second, will it be possible to use the Soviet Union and Communist China as countervailing forces? Third, are there circumstances and specific geographical areas where both Peking and Moscow may feel the need for a buffer, including even the possibility of some American presence, so that the prospective buffer, our own small nation, can hope to survive as an independent entity? Fourth, how strong must we be militarily before we can hope to pursue an independent course in the midst of Soviet-Chinese and perhaps American rivalry? Will our required military capability be attainable, given Soviet and U.S. and even PRC policies? None of these questions can be answered without taking both U.S. and Soviet policies into account.

What the Soviet Union might do in Pacific-Asia is dependent on Soviet preferences, capability, needs, and opportunities. An analysis of these factors should take note of both long-term Soviet policy, independent of developments in the area during 1969–73, and the new requirements and opportunities for the Soviet Union which have emerged during this period, largely in consequence of American policy under the Nixon Doctrine and the adjustments of other nations to it.

THE BREZHNEV DOCTRINE AND COMMUNIST CHINA

Reference was made in Chapter III to the strategic disadvantages the Soviet Union would suffer from having to deal with two potentially hostile fronts at both ends of the vast Soviet territory. In addition, it was pointed out that the large manpower and potential resources of the PRC could in due course pose a real challenge to the Soviet Union, putting the latter in a position somewhat similar to that of Western Europe if deprived of U.S. nuclear protection. The defection of Peking from the Soviet camp replaced a substantial ally and buffer—of the same kind as the Soviet Union's Eastern European satellites—with a hostile power of major proportions. The logical question is what the Soviet Union is prepared to do to prevent such a breach of its security from becoming permanent. Here consideration of the so-called Brezhnev Doctrine becomes relevant.

In an article in the September 26, 1968, issue of *Pravda,* S. Kovalev made the following points in a lengthy discussion on the international duty of socialist countries and their sovereignty. First, the commonwealth of socialist countries derives its well-being from the protection of Soviet armed forces. Second, the interests of the socialist "big family" must take precedence over those of its individual members. Third, the sovereignty of a socialist country is limited and subject to the primacy of the interest of the larger socialist family, headed by the Soviet Union and under its armed protection. Fourth, any departure from this correct approach in handling either internal or international affairs would constitute an activity that can only benefit the imperialists and must, therefore, be stopped. Fifth, all socialist countries have the duty to intervene in order to put an end to such anti-socialist developments; such intervention would indeed be in the interest of the errant member of the socialist commonwealth. Sixth, those socialist countries whose duty requires them to intervene must first use every nonviolent means available to them and have recourse to armed force only as a last resort. These ideas, advanced to justify the armed intervention of the Soviet Union and its allies in Czechoslovakia, were identical to those contained in Brezhnev's address to the Fifth Party Congress in Poland on November 12, 1968.

Under the Brezhnev Doctrine, Mao Tse-tung's anti-Soviet behavior clearly required corrective action. The need for such action became even greater after

July, 1971, and certainly after February, 1972. Two points should be made in this connection, however. First, from the Soviet point of view, corrective action or intervention preferably should not entail violence, or at least large-scale violence. A change in Chinese policy effected through a change in leadership would fall into this category of action. The likelihood of such a change in policy would increase with the removal of Mao. The affair of Lin Piao, who, according to official Chinese Communist sources,[1] attempted to assassinate Mao and died while fleeing the country after the discovery of his plot, seems to be illustrative of such an approach. Peking's version of Lin Piao's plot can be regarded as an indirect attempt to implicate the Soviet Union without actually making an open accusation. Whether the real story was as "simple" and "straightforward" as Peking suggested in July, 1972, has little to do with the fact that some such attempt, whether instigated by Lin himself or not, would be quite plausible. Moreover, it would be logical to assume that Soviet planning for China continues to include this particular option.

Second, since corrective action may in the last resort entail the use of violence, preparatory steps should be taken first. This may explain the large-scale reinforcement of Soviet forces on the China border, especially the major increase in the summer of 1969 and the continued buildup thereafter. Other preparatory measures were being taken behind the borders. According to a *New York Times* report,[2] the Soviet Union installed some special SS11 missiles capable of firing at either intermediate or intercontinental range in the fall of 1969. This development took place together with the construction of more than 90 "mysterious new silos" in an area traditionally used for MRBMs and IRBMs. At the same time, the Soviet Union dismantled the approximately 70 older missiles (SS4s and SS5s), previously deployed in the Far East to cover targets in mainland China and Japan. According to this interpretation, the older missiles that might have been vulnerable to attack by Chinese medium-range bombers, e.g., the TU16s, were replaced by SS11s, which had increased since 1969 to about 970 in number.[3] These SS11s, which can be used at different ranges and are located in the usual IRBM fields, were supplemented by medium-range bombers operating from many new air bases along the Chinese border, as well as large numbers of mobile missiles (the "Scaleboards") deployed on the China front. Soviet forces, therefore, were placed, during 1969, in a position to turn to this option of last resort. They still are in that position.

THE U.S.-SOVIET STRATEGIC ARMS AGREEMENTS AND THEIR IMPLICATIONS FOR COMMUNIST CHINA

One of the benefits of SALT I to the Soviet Union was the acknowledgment of nuclear parity by the United States. The Interim Agreement on

Offensive Missiles, together with the Treaty to Limit ABMs, could be interpreted as the codification of parity in the sense of open recognition by both sides of mutual deterrence through mutual vulnerability. Ironically, while the Soviet Union stressed the concept of "equal security," the agreements really confirmed "equal insecurity," relying upon the sense of vulnerability for the desired restraint on both sides.

There are several implications for Peking insofar as Soviet policy is concerned. First, if the acknowledgment of parity by the United States should have the effect of weakening the credibility of the U.S. nuclear umbrella in the eyes of the European NATO members, European countries may be induced to come to terms with the Soviet Union, either individually or as a group. The trend could be accelerated through Soviet gestures of détente. This potential effect on NATO can be regarded as a long-term Soviet policy without reference to Soviet relations with Communist China. At the same time, if the SALT agreements, augmented by MBFR ("mutual and balanced force reductions"), should, for one reason or another, be conducive to détente in Europe, the Soviet Union would certainly be able to devote more attention, resources, and effort to dealing with mainland China.

Second, under the provisions of the Interim Agreement of Offensive Missiles, the Soviet Union could have either 1,618 or, if it should choose to convert some of these land-based weapons to SLBMs, 1,409 land-based ICBMs, versus 1,054 smaller land-based missiles for the United States. In either case, there would be a substantial Soviet lead in the number of these weapons some of which could be used, if necessary, against China. With recent Soviet advances in MIRV, this possibility has been enhanced. Moreover, under the Treaty to Limit ABMs, the Soviet Union is permitted to provide protection for Moscow and to have another ABM site that could ward off small attacks, such as China might be able to mount. The treaty also precluded the transfer of ABMs by the contracting parties to other states. Thus the Soviet Union was provided with considerable assurance, over the next few years at any rate, that it would have little to fear on this score from Peking and could continue to hold Peking in hostage. In short, the SALT I agreement of May, 1972, preserved Soviet options in dealing with Communist China. On the other hand, if the Chinese nuclear weapons program continues without interruption, sooner or later the present Soviet ABM system will not be able to afford adequate protection. The Soviet Union will either have to allow itself to be deterred and initiate arms control discussions with China or find some other solution.

SOVIET NAVAL PRESENCE IN THE INDIAN AND PACIFIC OCEANS

From the point of view of the Soviet Union, the Asian countries to the south constitute a path of least resistance to its *Drang nach Süden*. One of the more recent historical references to this aspect of traditional Soviet aspirations was contained in the secret protocol to the draft 1940 Four-Power Pact.[4] The fact that most of the countries bordering on the Indian Ocean are developing nations and some gained independence only after World War II presented opportunities for military and economic assistance which the Soviet Union was quick to exploit. The geographical pattern of past Soviet military assistance manifests a very clear emphasis on a more or less continuous belt stretching from West Africa through the Maghreb to the Middle East and South Asia. It requires little imagination to realize that if Soviet influence can be expanded so far to the south, some important advantages would be gained. One is control of Middle East oil, which could seriously affect a major source of energy to Western Europe and Japan.[5] A second advantage would be that access to shore facilities would enable the Soviet Navy to make its presence more keenly felt in the Indian Ocean, a principal area of transit between Europe-Africa and the East. At the same time, more extensive showing of the Soviet flag would help expand Soviet influence in the littoral nations. In addition, the Indian Ocean provides an immense launching pad for SLBMs, which could be aimed at either Soviet or Chinese targets. Thus, there is both a defensive and an offensive Soviet interest in securing the Indian Ocean.[6]

If we bear in mind that the Soviet Black Sea Fleet was able to become a factor in the Eastern Mediterranean during the 1960s, once the Suez Canal is reopened, one result of further expansion of Soviet naval power would be a linking up of the Black Sea Fleet through the Indian Ocean with the Soviet Pacific Fleet.[7]

According to an Australian report cited by Jukes, the number of Soviet ships in the Indian Ocean varied as follows during 1968-1971:

Year	Surface Warships	Submarines	Auxiliaries
1968	6	2	6
1969	7	3	10
1970	10	7	12
1971	10	1	7

The Report of the Joint Committee on Foreign Affairs of the Australian Federal Parliament was issued on December 7, 1971, and might not have all the information for the period of the India-Pakistan War. In terms of ship months, the growth of Soviet naval presence in the Indian Ocean, according to the same source, registered 20 in 1968, 31 in 1969, and 44 in 1970. Again allowing for a possible underestimate of the war period, the preliminary figure for 1971 was put at 42. A sharp increase was registered between 1971 and 1973.

It can of course be argued that the presence of the Soviet Navy in the

Indian Ocean is no more than a natural outcome of the Soviet Union's growth as a world power. As has been mentioned, neither a special Soviet interest in the Indian Ocean nor a Soviet geopolitical design to complete a naval arc from the Crimea to Vladivostok is incompatible with growth of Soviet power. This interpretation of potential Soviet intentions and of Soviet naval deployment is equally significant if we consider the possibility of a Soviet intention to encircle China from the south and from the sea. A naval chain stretching from the Pacific coast of the Soviet Union through the Western Pacific to India would serve such a purpose. In the spring of 1973, the Soviet Union made a special point about its naval vessels sailing through the Taiwan Strait. The significance of this public emphasis was obviously intended for the benefit of the Chinese on both sides of the Strait.

AMERICA'S CHINA POLICY AS PERCEIVED BY THE SOVIET UNION

Prior to Mr. Nixon's visit to Peking, the Soviet Union was highly suspicious that the U.S.-Chinese talks would be directed against its interests.[8] After the meeting, while there were reports that Soviet leaders were more relaxed about the U.S.-Chinese discussions, there were Soviet complaints that the Shanghai Communiqué contained a number of ambiguities. In particular, the Soviet Union believed that the reference in the communiqué to U.S. and Chinese opposition to the seeking of hegemony by any power in Asia was directed at the Soviet Union. Brezhnev himself made public reference on February 26, 1972, to a statement made by President Nixon in a toast in Shanghai, that "our two peoples tonight hold the future of the world in their hands." To the Soviet Union this was a clear reference to U.S.-Chinese discussions and, therefore, to a possible U.S.-Chinese understanding directed against the Soviet Union. This Soviet reaction to the Washington-Peking rapprochement was only natural. It derived from three principal ingredients: Soviet distrust of both Peking and Washington, the tripartite power balance, and the apparent eagerness displayed by both Peking and Washington to talk with each other. Given these three elements it was inconsequential whether or not there was any real intent to "conspire" or to reach secret anti-Soviet arrangements.

In August, 1971, the Soviet Union concluded its Treaty of Friendship with India. This event was followed shortly afterwards by the India-Pakistan War, which led to the partition of Pakistan and the emergence of Bangladesh as an independent state. Mr. Kosygin then met with Sheikh Mujibur Rahman, leader of the new nation, and a joint policy declaration was signed on March 4, 1972.[9] At the time of the war the Soviet ambassador to India reportedly told the Indians that the Soviet Union was ready to intervene against China if the latter were to move against India on the side of Pakistan.[10] The fact that the PRC made no such move was not lost on both combatants. Moscow's agreement with Bangladesh promised Soviet economic and other assistance. The new Pakistani President, Mr. Bhutto, also visited Moscow to obtain Soviet understanding and, presumably, future support in spite of the fact that Pakistan's defeat at the hands of India was a direct consequence of Soviet aid to India. The role the Soviet Union envisaged for itself in relation to both India and Pakistan was an extension of its peacemaking role at Tashkent after the 1965 conflict between India and Pakistan. The series of events in the winter of 1971—72 seems to have been a Soviet response to the Washington-Peking rapprochement, although the Soviet Union did not engage in activities contrary to the direction of its long-term policy. However, events may have advanced Soviet timing because of an impression of greater urgency. For the Soviet Union, the powerlessness of China and the United States' inability to prevent the defeat of Pakistan were clearly demonstrated facts.[11] In addition, the consolidation of Soviet influence in South Asia, including a potentially large foothold in Bangladesh, provided an additional front to China, which was being increasingly encircled by Soviet arms, more so than ever before. China's borders were now surrounded by Soviet power and friends of the U.S.S.R. on all sides except its coastline.

Even the last reservation may soon prove invalid. Apart from the constant presence of the growing Soviet Navy, reverberations in Japan caused by America's new China policy provided the Soviet Union with a new opportunity. Mr. Gromyko's visit to Tokyo in January, 1972, came on the heels of the Nixon-Sato meeting in San Clemente, which failed to produce a genuine understanding that would reestablish policy coordination between the United States and Japan. Since Japan is in search of a new role and may wish to arrive at a delicate balance among the Soviet Union, the PRC, and the United States, the Soviet Union was ready to offer Japan a "Soviet option."[12]

Among the lures the Soviet Union could offer are a degree of accommodation on the territorial issue involving the four islands off Hokkaido, which have been under Soviet occupation since World War II, and prospects of greater trade and investment opportunities.[13] For some time, talks had been held between Japan and the U.S.S.R. on joint projects for the development of Siberian resources, including the opening of a new seaport at Wrangel, east of Nakhodka and facing the Sea of Japan, the supply of Soviet natural gas to Hokkaido by pipeline, development of such resources as timber, copper, coal, and iron ore in Siberia partly for the benefit of Japan, and, above all, the supply of Soviet oil to Japan, involving the proposed construction with Japanese capital of a long-distance pipeline. A cooperative arrangement, under which the Soviet Union would supply Japan with oil, should be considered in conjunction with Soviet plans to take Iraqi oil to supply the Baku refineries and the domestic Soviet market, an arrangement seemingly on its way to completion following the signing of a Soviet-Iraqi treaty of friendship in April, 1972, and the subsequent Iraqi nationalization of Western oil interests. At the September, 1970, meeting of the Japan-U.S.S.R. Economic Committee, the suggestion was made to develop the shipment of container freight on the Trans-Siberian Railway so that the latter might become an economical transport route between Europe and Japan. These and other possibilities would doubtless constitute interesting topics for discussion in conjunction with Soviet-Japanese negotiations on a possible treaty that Mr. Gromyko's visit had in effect opened. Mr. Tanaka's visit to Moscow in 1973 constituted another step in the dialogue. A Japanese loan to the Soviets for the implementation of some of the above-mentioned projects, reported in April, 1974, constituted another.

The great expansion of Soviet influence over Middle Eastern oil resources has already provided the Soviet Union with leverage against Japan. The offer of Soviet oil to Japan as an alternative source of supply may be economically attractive, but it would in no way alleviate Japan's strategic disadvantage. Even if the Soviet Union cannot fully control Japan's oil supply at source, the long sea-lanes from the Persian Gulf to the Japanese islands are especially vulnerable to potential harassment. In addition, Communist China's effort to isolate Taiwan, perhaps unwittingly aided by Japan itself, could conceivably alter the attitude of Taiwan toward the Soviet Union. As mentioned in Chapter IV, Taiwan's strategic position with reference to the lifelines of Japan could become an important point of leverage against Japan, if the island were subject to the influence, if not control, of a big power which would not hesitate to use its military capability.

Not to be overlooked is the provision of the Moscow Treaty to Limit ABMs, which prohibited the transfer of equipment for ABM defense by the contracting parties to other nations. With the added advantage of a possible lead over the United States in offensive nuclear missiles, the Soviet Union may soon find itself in a position to inhibit the development of an independent nuclear capability by Japan. One can envisage a situation in which Japan, having finally decided to go nuclear, is faced with a Soviet demand to cease and desist. In the absence of adequate U.S. support, Japan could find itself seriously constrained in an arms buildup because of Soviet pressure. Peking is not strong enough to be used by Japan as a countervailing force against the Soviet Union, even though its conventional force might serve a similar purpose for the United States, which is itself a foremost nuclear power.

A SOVIET PLAN FOR COLLECTIVE ASIAN SECURITY

The Soviet concept of collective Asian security is predicated on an assumption of U.S. withdrawal from Asia. Shortly before Brezhnev's speech[14] before the International Congress of Communist Parties in June,

1969, an article appeared in *Izvestia*[15] in which its author spoke of a "vacuum that had to be filled." The initial reference was to the British withdrawal from East of Suez. However, the Brezhnev address made it clear that the Soviet Union would like to establish a collective security system in Asia to replace the United States and to contain the PRC. Gromyko[16] and others,[17] both through official media and in visits to Asian countries, have continued to keep the theme alive. Brezhnev's original idea included such countries as India, Pakistan, Afghanistan, Malaysia, and Burma within this potential arrangement. In a broadcast in Japanese on September 10, 1970, Moscow radio suggested that Japanese help and participation would be essential to any Asian collective security scheme if it is to be viable. Total consistency, however, was not observed in policy pronouncements to other audiences. The same radio, in a Chinese-language broadcast on September 18, 1970, said that Chinese leaders should be on guard against resurgent Japanese militarism. The broadcast added that the Soviet Union, far from being hostile to China, had no intention to exclude the PRC from any Asian security pact, nor would such a pact have China as a target. Another statement over the Moscow radio suggested on September 11, 1970, that an Asian security pact should include the Soviet Union, the PRC, India, Pakistan, and other nations on an equal footing, in order to pose an insurmountable obstacle to imperialist expansion.

One could read into this medley of statements and many others that the Soviet concept of an Asian collective security arrangement was little more than a propaganda theme to be exploited as a lure or even, at times, as a red herring. On the other hand, one could take the concept more seriously. In its most expanded form, the Soviet Union appeared to be projecting a future Asian security pact as a replica of the Warsaw Pact. At a less ambitious level, however, an Asian collective security arrangement headed by the Soviet Union could conceivably include India, Pakistan, and a reluctant Japan, as well as some other Asian nations such as Afghanistan, with Peking as its target. Some of the insular Asian states situated on Japan's sea-lanes could be included in order to insure Japanese compliance. Alternatively, if a change in Chinese leadership and/or policy should bring Communist China closer to the Soviet Union, China could be substituted for Japan. These are pure speculations, but they may not be totally alien to Soviet thinking.

While commenting on the India-Pakistan War and its aftermath, *Pravda* noted on February 27, 1972, that events in South Asia had again demonstrated the importance of collective security in the area. Moscow may indeed see the beginning of such an arrangement involving both India and Pakistan. But the specifics are less important than the conceptual framework and the options that the Soviet Union is developing with reference to Japan, South Asia, and other nations in Pacific-Asia.

Among other Asian nations, one would suppose that two major targets of Soviet attention might be Taiwan in Northeast Asia and Indonesia to the south. The importance of both to the Soviet Union has already been discussed. If the Soviet Union intends to form an arc of Soviet presence from India to Japan, Indonesia would be an important supporting link in the chain. Additional links would be the Philippines and Taiwan. Not to be forgotten, however, is the Malay Peninsula on the eastern littoral of the Indian Ocean and the western boundary of the Pacific. In this geopolitical context, Vietnam increases in significance. Even though, as we have argued before, it would be in the Soviet interest to have continued the embroilment and diversion of the United States in Vietnam, many other opportunities may also be developed. From this vantage point, a seemingly more passive Soviet attitude toward Vietnam, especially if such a Soviet position could be used as a bargaining counter in negotiations with the United States, might present advantages to the Soviet Union. This is not to underestimate Soviet apprehension over an imagined U.S.-Chinese conspiracy.

INCREASING SOVIET ECONOMIC TIES WITH PACIFIC-ASIA

Soviet practice in developing closer relations with basically Western-oriented countries has tended to stress, at least initially, economic and trade relations, not to mention "cultural exchange." This has been the case in Latin America, and the same policy seems to have been followed also in Asia. *As of 1970,* prior to the emergence of America's new China policy, however, both the Soviet Union and its Eastern European satellites acounted for only relatively small shares of the external trade of Pacific-Asia. As shown in the following table (VI.1), only West Malaysia (i.e., the peninsular portion of Malaysia, excluding Sarawak and Sabah, or East Malaysia) and Singapore counted the Soviet Union and its Eastern European satellites among their "larger" customers—primarily because of sales of rubber. West Malaysia sold 8.3 percent of its total exports in 1969 to Eastern Europe and 5.9 percent to the Soviet Union. Of Singapore's total exports in 1970, 4.9 percent were sold to Eastern Europe and 3.0 percent to the Soviet Union. Thailand, Indonesia, Australia, New Zealand, and Japan sold 2 percent or less of their exports to Communist Eastern Europe and/or the Soviet Union. Japan purchased 2.5 percent of its total imports in 1970 from the Soviet Union and 3.1 percent from the Soviet Union and its Eastern European satellites as a group. For Thailand, Indonesia, Singapore, West Malaysia, Australia, and New Zealand, Eastern Europe and the Soviet Union supplied only negligible amounts of imports. The preceding pattern showed relatively little change *in 1971.* Japan, Thailand, New Zealand, India, and Pakistan increased their exports to the Soviet Union during 1970–71; Japan and Indonesia increased their imports from the Soviet Union during the same period. However, for the other

Table VI.1 Countries in Pacific-Asia Ranked in Terms of the Percent Shares of Eastern Europe (Including the Soviet Union) and the Soviet Union in Their Total Exports and Imports in 1970*

	Exports to		Imports from	
	Eastern Europe	Soviet Union	Eastern Europe	Soviet Union
West Malaysia (1969)[x]	8.3	5.9	Japan[xx] 3.1	2.5
Singapore	4.9	3.0[xx]	Thailand 1.4	0.8
Indonesia[x]	...	1.9	Indonesia (1969)[x] 0.9	0.5
Japan[xx]	2.3	1.8	Singapore 0.9	0.4
Australia	2.3	1.5	West Malaysia 0.7	0.3
New Zealand	2.2	1.5	Australia 0.7	0.1
Thailand[x]	0.4	0.1	New Zealand 0.4	0.2

SOURCE: *Battle Act Reports*, Department of State, 1968 and 1971. For the original data, see Appendix.
x—Decline in absolute and relative share since 1966.
xx—Decline in relative share since 1966.
*In comparison with South Asia:

| India | 20.2 | 13.4 | India (1969) 19.5 | 12.9 |
| Pakistan | 11.8 | 4.3 | Pakistan 7.3 | 2.5[xx] |

countries, trade with the Soviet Union either declined or showed little change. It would, therefore, take considerable expansion of Soviet trade and other economic relations with these Asian countries before the Soviet Union could acquire a significant economic leverage in furtherance of its political and strategic aims.

However, there are exceptions, and several points should be borne in mind lest we come to definite conclusions too hastily. First, as of 1970, the Soviet Union was responsible for 13.4 percent of India's total exports; if we include with the Soviet figure exports to the Eastern European satellite countries from India, the proportion would rise to 20.2 percent. Similarly, imports from the Soviet Union and from Communist European countries were responsible for 19.5 percent of India's total imports in 1969. Even in the case of Pakistan, whose relations with the Soviet Union were not the most cordial, 11.8 percent of Pakistan's exports and 7.3 percent of its imports in 1970 were accounted for by the Soviet Union and its Eastern European satellites. Although the Soviet share per se was only 4.3 percent of Pakistan's exports and 2.5 percent of its imports, the important point is that Soviet economic ties with Asian countries, partly via the other members of the Warsaw Pact, could very well assume significant proportions as the example of India has demonstrated.

Second, the increase for the Soviet Union and its European satellites in imports from the same Pacific-Asian countries was much more impressive both absolutely and in relative shares than was the case in their exports to Pacific-Asia in general. The principal exceptions were Japan, primarily because of the phenomenal growth of its foreign trade during this period, and Indonesia, as a result of political shifts after the abortive Communist coup in 1965.

Lastly, because of the lag in the reporting of trade statistics, data on developments in 1972 and later are not readily available. It was during this period, however, that substantial efforts were exerted by Soviet and Eastern European countries to expand their trade in Pacific-Asia. Moreover, with the exception of Japan—and Singapore in the case of its imports—trade with Peking was small during this period. The Chinese too did not begin their latest trade effort in Southeast Asia until after 1971. In the absence of up-to-date statistics, therefore, the exact trade situation in Southeast Asia regarding both Peking and Moscow is not yet clear.

INTENTION OR CAPABILITY?

One can either reach dire conclusions on the basis of the expansion of Soviet influence discussed in this chapter or dismiss these developments as unimportant by choosing the appropriate assumptions about Soviet intentions. If one concludes that the Soviet Union aims at attaining global primacy and will exploit every available opportunity, pessimistic conclusions are in order. On the other hand, if the Soviet Union merely aims at securing certain better defensive positions with no intention whatsoever of exploiting them, now or in the foreseeable future, the mere improvement of its ability to exploit opportunities will not necessarily pose a serious threat. To debate Soviet intentions at this point would be a futile and fruitless exercise, since there is an unbridgeable gap between those who rely on past experience and those who either dismiss the relevance of history or base their prognostications on its assumed discontinuity. One cannot deny, however, that the Soviet Union has increased its options during 1969–1974.

NOTES

1. See Chapter III above.
2. Report by William Beecher, *New York Times*, March 3, 1972.
3. *Ibid.*
4. Cf. T. B. Millar, "Geopolitics and the Military Strategic Potential," a paper presented at an Indian Ocean conference, Center for Strategic and International Studies, Georgetown University, March, 1971.
5. For a fuller discussion of the strategic significance of raw material supply see the author's *Raw Material Supply in a Multipolar World, 1973.*
6. For a discussion of this subject and speculation on possible Soviet interest in the denuclearization of the Indian Ocean, see Geoffrey Jukes, "Indian Ocean in Soviet Naval Policy," *Adelphi Papers*, No. 87, International Institute for Strategic Studies, London, May 1972.
7. For data on Soviet fleet strength in the Indian Ocean, see the *New York Times*, January 16 and March 20, 1972. Cf. also Yuan-li Wu, *op. cit.*, and Geoffrey Jukes, *op. cit.*
8. Cf. *New York Times*, February 18, 1972.
9. *New York Times*, March 4, 1972.
10. *New York Times*, January 11, 1972.
11. There were reports at the time that but for U.S. diplomatic pressure, West Pakistan itself might have suffered far more severely at India's hands.
12. See note 5.
13. See Saburo Okita, "Japan-U.S.S.R. Economic Relations, Present and Future," *Nihon Keizai No Vision* (Future Vision for the Japanese Economy), April, 1968, Tokyo, Diamond Publishing Co., 1968.
14. See *Pravda*, June 8, 1969.
15. *Izvestia*, May 29, 1969.
16. Cf. *Pravda*, July 11, 1969.
17. Cf. Kirill Mazurov, Soviet First Deputy Prime Minister, in *Pravda*, August 16, 1970.

APPENDIX: Foreign Trade Statistics of Selected Countries in Pacific-Asia and South Asia

Value: millions of dollars Index: 1966=100
Exports to
(1) the U.S.S.R., (2) All Eastern Europe (Including the U.S.S.R.),
(3) Communist China, (4) All Countries

From:		1966	1967	1968	1969	1970	1971
Cambodia	(1)	.5	.7	....	....	....	....
	(2)	5.4	5.2	....	....	....	....
	(3)	5.7	6.6	....	....	....	....
	(4)	67.3	83.0	66.5	78.0	....	....
	(1)						
	(2)	Index omitted for lack of more recent data.					
	(3)						
	(4)						
Thailand	(1)	*	1.1	.2	.1	.8	6.0
	(2)	5.8	2.3	3.0	4.1	2.6	8.1
	(3)	....	*	....	*	....	....
	(4)	604.4	681.1	653.5	706.8	710.3	830.9
	(1)	....	....	....	....	....	....
	(2)	100.	39.	51.	70.	44.	139.
	(3)	....	....	....	....	....	....
	(4)	100.	112.	108.	116.	117.	137.
Malaysia	(1)	95.8	64.0	66.0	78.4	69.4	49.8
	(2)	114.1	76.2	87.8	110.2	91.8	68.0
	(3)	21.2	6.4	23.9	44.6	21.6	17.4
	(4)	1019.1	1003.3	1050.9	1326.9	1369.6	1276.6
	(1)	100.	67.	69.	82.	72.	52.
	(2)	100.	67.	77.	96.	80.	60.
	(3)	100.	30.	113.	210.	102.	82.
	(4)	100.	98.	103.	130.	134.	125.
Singapore	(1)	36.1	29.4	36.3	42.2	46.5	37.8
	(2)	49.4	42.3	49.9	71.6	76.0	78.6

Appendix—Continued

From:		1966	1967	1968	1969	1970	1971
Singapore	(3)	44.8	31.3	26.5	57.1	22.7	15.2
(Continued)	(4)	1102.2	1140.0	1271.1	1548.8	1553.7	1754.8
	(1)	100.	81.	101.	117.	129.	105.
	(2)	100.	86.	101.	145.	154.	159.
	(3)	100.	70.	59.	127.	51.	34.
	(4)	100.	103.	115.	141.	141.	159.
Indonesia	(1)	25.9	15.0	17.0	10.8	19.5	8.7
	(2)	39.7	23.7	18.2	12.9	19.5	8.7
	(3)	9.5	.7	*	....	....	....
	(4)	678.6	658.0	762.0	845.0	1009.3	1246.9
	(1)	100.	58.	66.	42.	75.	33.
	(2)	100.	60.	46.	32.	49.	22.
	(3)	100.	7.	....	....	....	....
	(4)	100.	97.	102.	125.	149.	184.
Australia	(1)	33.0	20.4	38.9	45.1	72.1	69.1
	(2)	69.0	62.6	78.9	78.4	111.7	118.9
	(3)	83.5	191.2	89.3	119.0	129.3	27.2
	(4)	3080.8	3295.1	3403.1	4045.0	4786.1	5234.7
	(1)	100.	62.	118.	137.	218.	209.
	(2)	100.	91.	114.	114.	162.	172.
	(3)	100.	229.	107.	142.	154.	33.
	(4)	100.	107.	110.	131.	155.	170.
New Zealand	(1)	14.5	5.4	10.9	14.4	18.4	27.4
	(2)	21.3	11.9	15.8	20.2	27.0	36.9
	(3)	7.1	10.6	5.8	4.6	4.4	0.9
	(4)	1061.4	978.7	989.4	1182.0	1200.7	1369.1
	(1)	100.	37.	75.	99.	127.	189.
	(2)	100.	56.	74.	95.	129.	173
	(3)	100.	149.	82.	65.	62.	13.
	(4)	100.	92.	93.	111.	113.	129.

Appendix—Continued

From:		1966	1967	1968	1969	1970	1971
Japan	(1)	214.0	157.7	179.0	268.3	341.0	377.9
	(2)	273.2	228.5	232.7	341.9	447.6	537.7
	(3)	315.2	288.3	325.5	390.8	568.9	378.7
	(4)	9777.2	10,442.4	12,972.7	15,991.3	19,319.2	24,018.1
	(1)	100.	74.	84.	125.	159.	177.
	(2)	100.	84.	85.	125.	164.	197.
	(3)	100.	91.	103.	124.	180.	184.
	(4)	100.	107.	133.	164.	198.	246.
India	(1)	182.4	181.0	185.4	221.4	271.4	287.4
	(2)	295.1	301.0	319.0	351.5	410.2	433.9
	(3)	....	*	*	....	....	....
	(4)	1605.8	1613.6	1753.0	1833.7	2025.9	2107.4
	(1)	100.	99.	102.	121.	149.	158.
	(2)	100.	102.	108.	119.	139.	147.
	(3)	....	....	....	....	....	....
	(4)	100.	100.	109.	114.	126.	131.
Pakistan	(1)	26.8	25.4	14.0	22.9	31.1	36.5
	(2)	47.2	49.8	50.4	70.0	85.6	87.0
	(3)	30.2	34.7	25.5	28.9	39.3	30.2
	(4)	600.8	593.6	720.2	681.5	723.3	666.0
	(1)	100.	95.	52.	85.	116.	136.
	(2)	100.	106.	107.	148.	181.	184.
	(3)	100.	115.	84.	96.	130.	100.
	(4)	100.	99.	120.	113.	120.	111.

SOURCE: *Battle Act Reports,* Department of State, 1968, 1971, and 1972.
*Negligible.

Appendix—Continued
Imports from
(1) the U.S.S.R., (2) All Eastern Europe (Including the U.S.S.R.), (3) Communist China, (4) All Countries

To:		1966	1967	1968	1969	1970	1971
Cambodia	(1)	3.3	1.5	....	....	....	....
	(2)	11.3	3.9	....	....	....	....
	(3)	17.8	8.7	....	....	....	....
	(4)	111.1	96.1	....	122.0	....	....
	(1)	....	....	....	....	....	....
	(2)	....	....	....	....	....	....
	(3)	100.0	49.0	....	....	....	....
	(4)	....	....	....	....	....	....
Thailand	(1)	2.8	3.8	3.6	2.6	10.5	3.8
	(2)	9.7	13.1	12.7	9.4	18.1	10.8
	(3)	*	*	*	....	*	....
	(4)	1218.7	1066.8	1146.7	1230.2	1298.6	1288.3
	(1)	100.	133.	126.	91.	367.	136.
	(2)	100.	135.	130.	96.	186.	111.
	(3)	....	....	....	....	....	....
	(4)	100.	87.	94.	101.	106.	106.
Malaysia	(1)	1.7	1.9	2.4	3.1	3.3	3.1
	(2)	4.1	5.4	6.5	6.7	7.1	6.9
	(3)	56.6	62.9	57.3	57.1	53.9	44.7
	(4)	860.1	838.9	908.3	915.6	1111.5	1111.5
	(1)	100.	112.	141.	182.	194.	182.
	(2)	100.	132.	159.	163.	173.	170.
	(3)	100.	111.	101.	101.	95.	79.
	(4)	100.	98.	106.	106.	117.	117.
Singapore	(1)	3.1	6.6	9.4	11.6	10.6	10.5
	(2)	6.3	11.9	17.6	23.0	22.6	18.5
	(3)	88.8	124.7	150.3	136.7	125.9	132.9
	(4)	1328.3	1436.5	1660.9	2039.8	2461.3	2827.6
	(1)	100.	213.	303.	374.	342.	339.
	(2)	100.	189.	279.	365.	359.	293.
	(3)	100.	140.	169.	154.	142.	150.
	(4)	100.	108.	125.	154.	185.	213.

Appendix—Continued

To:		1966	1967	1968	1969	1970	1971
Indonesia	(1)	32.	4.7	5.9	5.	5.1	13.5
	(2)	66.	15.4	15.0	9.	15.1	13.5
	(3)	46.	54.2	....	39.	30.0	....
	(4)	583.	649.0	831.0	961.	893.3	1173.7
	(1)	100.	15.	16.	16.	16.	42.
	(2)	100.	23.	23.	14.	23.	20.
	(3)	100.	118.	....	85.	65.	....
	(4)	100.	111.	143.	165.	153.	201.
Australia	(1)	1.5	2.1	2.1	2.7	3.6	2.2
	(2)	17.4	17.3	21.9	22.4	29.8	23.8
	(3)	25.4	27.8	30.5	34.7	35.5	40.9
	(4)	3196.8	3456.0	3857.7	4004.2	4543.0	4693.2
	(1)	100.	140.	140.	180.	240.	147.
	(2)	100.	99.	126.	129.	171.	137.
	(3)	100.	109.	120.	137.	140.	161.
	(4)	100.	108.	121.	125.	142.	147.
New Zealand	(1)	0.4	0.4	0.6	1.1	1.9	0.6
	(2)	3.1	3.4	2.8	4.7	5.1	3.7
	(3)	4.1	4.1	4.6	5.6	5.0	5.6
	(4)	997.9	889.8	834.0	1002.5	1162.9	1250.6
	(1)	100.	100.	150.	275.	475.	150.
	(2)	100.	110.	90.	152.	165.	119.
	(3)	100.	100.	112.	137.	122.	137.
	(4)	100.	89.	84.	100.	117.	125.
Japan	(1)	300.4	454.0	463.5	461.6	481.1	496.3
	(2)	349.0	562.0	572.4	574.9	592.4	579.4
	(3)	306.3	269.5	224.2	234.6	253.8	323.4
	(4)	9523.5	11,664.0	12,988.3	15,024.7	18,882.7	19,721.3
	(1)	100.	151.	154.	154.	160.	165.
	(2)	100.	161.	164.	165.	170.	166.

Appendix—Continued

To:		1966	1967	1968	1969	1970	1971
Japan	(3)	100.	88.	73.	77.	83.	106.
(Continued)	(4)	100.	122.	136.	158.	192.	207.
India	(1)	150.7	132.9	196.0	284.4	167.5	108.8
	(2)	281.2	259.2	333.9	429.9	316.8	251.8
	(3)	*	*	....	....	....	....
	(4)	2750.1	2691.7	2627.9	2209.3	2124.8	2176.7
	(1)	100.	88.	130.	189.	111.	72.
	(2)	100.	92.	119.	153.	113.	90.
	(3)	....	....	....	....	....	....
	(4)	100.	98.	96.	80.	77.	79.
Pakistan	(1)	27.6	26.0	35.9	30.0	29.2	23.9
	(2)	47.9	58.9	84.7	89.5	83.9	78.5
	(3)	28.5	33.7	29.6	26.4	27.8	35.0
	(4)	899.7	1101.1	995.9	1010.7	1150.6	925.9
	(1)	100.	94.	130.	109	106.	86.
	(2)	100.	123.	177.	187.	175.	164.
	(3)	100.	118.	104.	93.	98.	123.
	(4)	100.	122.	111.	112.	128.	103.

SOURCE: *Battle Act Reports,* Department of State, 1968, 1971, and 1972.
*Negligible.

Chapter VII

Conditions for Security in Pacific-Asia and U.S. Strategic Interests

AN AMERICAN-PREFERRED SCENARIO

An outline of a new balance of power in Pacific-Asia consistent with U.S. hopes was suggested in Chapter II. This "American-preferred scenario" which is, it should be said, nothing more than a model designed for purposes of discussion, is predicated on a reduction of American military presence in the post-Vietnam period as the result of successful Vietnamization. (It is obviously not a statement of U.S. policy.) The model assumes that the reduction and redeployment of U.S. military presence would dovetail with other international developments under compatible circumstances. These developments and conditions may be summarized as follows.

First, there should be an increase in the military strength of Japan, so that the security of that country can be safeguarded with reduced American presence. Furthermore, the arms buildup of Japan should be of such a nature and magnitude that it would not alarm the Southeast Asian countries and Australasia, causing some of these countries to turn toward Peking and/or Moscow as sources of countervailing power. Conversely, the Japanese arms buildup should not be so deficient as to make Japan an unworthy and undependable partner in a regional collective security arrangement involving some or all of the same countries. Certain relationships require special provisions. For example, it is necessary that Japan see its self-interest in such a way as to provide help to the continued growth and stability of South Korea, at least in economic terms. By the same token, Japan should not, in its haste to come to terms with the PRC, adopt policies toward Taiwan which might cause the latter either (1) to fall under the influence of mainland China or (2) to become, in desperation, vulnerable to approaches from the Soviet Union. Either development would expose Japan's lifelines to a serious threat close to its home waters. Finally, Japan should steer a middle-of-the-road course toward both the Soviet Union and the PRC while following a consistent policy of close cooperation with the United States, including unrestricted use of facilities needed in a Far Eastern emergency.

Second, the same U.S.-preferred scenario is predicated on an assumption that South Korea and Taiwan will both continue policies keeping them free from Soviet or PRC influence. South Korea must be able to build up its armed strength and its economy so that it can (1) withstand pressure from the North and (2), having attained this position, be able to reach a modus vivendi with the North. If this can be accomplished, the Korean Peninsula could then become a buffer zone safeguarding the security of Japan from the north and west. For Taiwan, a position of stability can be obtained only if, as a result of economic growth during a period when mainland China is in no position to carry out any physical threat, its population decides to remain an independent entity. This will require that its present de facto independence be converted into a de jure independence at some opportune moment in the not too distant future. By relinquishing its competitive claim to the mainland as long as the latter is under effective Communist control, Taiwan might hope to obtain Communist Chinese acquiescence, if not consent. A practical arrangement, if not a formal settlement, would then be possible following patterns worked out by other nations divided after World War II. Another condition concomitant with economic growth, which is predicated on maintenance of freedom of the seas, is the further strengthening of Taiwan's defense, so that any attempt by mainland China to resort to a military solution will encounter a very high and perhaps incalculable cost.

Third, the American-preferred scenario requires that the Southeast Asian nations strive to enhance their economic development in order to carry a heavier defense burden. Another condition is a maximal effort to achieve political and social stability so as to minimize discontent and prospects for future insurgencies. Finally, these nations should be willing to work together for collective defense, invite the cooperation of an appropriately armed Japan and resist the blandishments and temptations of both Peking and Moscow.

Australia, which conceivably could become a nuclear power, should have a defense policy of a type that can be coordinated with the U.S. nuclear posture in a relationship resembling that of Japan.

As for the Soviet Union and Communist China, the American-preferred scenario incorporates an assumption that the two Communist powers will continue to be antagonists and act as rivals, thus offsetting each other's influence in Pacific-Asia. This means that neither will want the other to control the Korean Peninsula and that neither will be able to gain a dominating position in Japan or Taiwan. It means that neither will be able to break down the barrier of nationalism in the Southeast Asian countries or to exploit intraregional differences to expand its own influence. The stress on continued rivalry and distrust implies no expectation of open military conflict leading to a decisive Soviet victory (since a PRC victory is not conceivable in the circumstances) or a change in Chinese policy and/or leadership making China either ineffectual or subservient to Soviet pressure. These conditions, if fulfilled, will rule out both the PRC and the Soviet Union as sources of effective threat to other powers in the region, permitting the latter to find security in spite of a reduced American military presence.

CONDITIONS THAT MIGHT LEAD TO A SOVIET-PREFERRED SCENARIO

In the last two chapters we have already examined actual and possible developments in Pacific-Asian countries which derive in part from response to U.S. policy as they perceive it. In the case of Japan, one concern of students of Japanese affairs is the possibility that it may feel compelled to develop an independent nuclear capability. A consequence of such a development might be an adverse reaction in other Asian nations, driving them, perhaps, to closer relations with either the Soviet Union or Communist China because of their distrust of Japan. The cumulative effects of such a process are not fully clear, but a common apprehension exists beyond doubt.

Another possibility is that Japan may be unwilling or unable to develop its armed strength. Preservation of the nuclear option, combined with postponement of a decision actually to go nuclear in the hope that such a decision would not be necessary, characterized the policy of the Sato government. In the post-Sato period and with a new and fervent desire for normalization of relations with Peking, the long-term rate of Japan's rearmament may be slowed. If this happens and if the Soviet Union (or the PRC) should reach a position where it can demand that Japan halt future nuclear plans, Japan may find itself no longer in a position to exercise its present option. If, under these hypothetical conditions, Japan should come to believe that U.S. nuclear and conventional forces are inadequate to protect it, seeking an accommodation with the Soviet Union or China could become the only viable alternative.

From still another angle of approach, given Sino-Soviet rivalry and a Soviet policy of forestalling any future Sino-Japanese alliance, the Soviet Union will unquestionably wish to exert strong leverage against Japan. In the post-1973 energy crisis period, given Japan's painful experience, Moscow is in a better position today to accomplish this objective than is Peking. In these circumstances, Japanese inability to steer an independent course because of military weakness and economic vulnerability, together with diminishing confidence in the U.S. alliance, may ultimately force Japan into an alignment with the Soviet Union. Japanese policy could contribute to such a development by overestimating (1) America's desire to withdraw from Asia and (2) both Peking's staying power and the U.S. estimate of China's power. Another factor that could lead to the same result is the Japanese desire to appear to be following a China policy independent of that of the United States, a posture that could confuse other nations and be misinterpreted by some. Still another source of potential misunderstanding between Japan and the United States lies in the economic field. Protectionism and economic rivalry can undermine political relations and lead to shows of independence which may eventually become conflicting and mutually incompatible policies.

The dangers to the independence of Taiwan and South Korea arising from changes in Japanese policy and their misunderstanding by other countries have already been pointed out. Because of the public discussion on normalization of relations with Peking, the impact on Taiwan has received more attention, but Korea's situation is not substantially different. Neither South Korea nor Taiwan appears to be convinced, in spite of repeated U.S. assurances, that the United States would use adequate force to protect their independence if required, although they see their own interests as tied closely to their historical U.S. alignments.

In Southeast Asia, as we have pointed out, there are different types of risks. One is that some nations will be unable to develop their economy, bear the necessary defense burden, and create a general political and social environment unfavorable to insurgency. Another is the specific possibility, related to the proposed settlement in Vietnam, that some Southeast Asian nations will regard U.S. policy toward China as an actual concession to Peking and a plan of withdrawal from Asia. Some countries may, therefore, accept Soviet influence with more enthusiasm than they might in other circumstances. Others, again, may attempt to counter Soviet influence with Chinese connections but fail to manage the delicate balance. Some may distrust Japan to the point of being unwilling to work together with Japan in a collective defense arrangement. Given its own domestic political and constitutional considerations, lack of welcome on the part of other nations may in turn discourage Japan and preclude the emergence of an effective collective defense arrangement. And, since it is fair to assume that both Soviet and

Chinese offers will be made more attractive as time passes, it is not impossible for the Southeast Asian nations to become aligned with Moscow and/or Peking in some unpredictable manner.

Given the Soviet drive to extend its influence in both the Indian Ocean and the Western Pacific, one may expect not only a revival of the ideas of a Soviet-sponsored Asian security arrangement, but even its partial implementation. The future course of events could be altered by a limited alignment involving, for instance, the Soviet Union, India, and Pakistan. A Soviet-Japanese pact would totally upset the power balance in the Western Pacific. A submissive China or a softening of the hostile relationship between the two Communist countries would reinforce a Soviet-Japanese alignment.

Obviously, it is unlikely that all the developments unfavorable from an American point of view will come to pass, just as it is improbable that the American-preferred scenario can be realized in its entirety. There are always random developments and surprises due to political, economic, technical, and even personnel changes that none can foresee. While it is impossible to develop a "surprise-free" scenario, a point already conceded in relation to our attempts to construct one suited to American objectives, it is possible and useful to attempt corresponding constructions for the other powers concerned. A Soviet-preferred scenario would have some of the following characteristics.

It would include (1) a change in leadership in China so that a fairly effective Chinese authority might work in concert with the Soviet Union or, at least, not offset Soviet efforts; (2) a Japan aligned with the Soviet Union; (3) a Taiwan and a Korea dominated by Soviet influence as a result of the first two circumstances; (4) a Malay Peninsula in which there is greater Soviet influence as a result of the failure of the balance of power policy; (5) an Indonesia caught by these developments before its own economic growth and defense buildup can reach appropriate levels; (6) an Australia that finds itself a lonely outpost facting potential threats from both the Indian Ocean and the Pacific; and (7) a Philippines torn by insurgency although, perhaps, the only remaining bridgehead for American influence because of its long historical ties with the United States. We have left out the Indochina states and Thailand because the above conditions would necessarily sever their alignment with the United States. This Soviet-preferred scenario would involve not only the withdrawal of the United States from mainland Asia, but its virtual exclusion from the Western Pacific. Given this scenario, an American economic presence would not be tolerated except on Soviet terms.

A PRC-PREFERRED SCENARIO

A PRC-preferred scenario would not exactly parallel that of the Soviet Union. Peking cannot expect to exercise the influence the Soviet Union might otherwise wield to serve its own interests unless they happen to coincide with

Soviet interests. The most Peking can hope for would be a China-dominated "Greater East Asian Co-prosperity Sphere" which would include alignment with Japan under Chinese primacy and a sphere of influence extending from Indochina through the Malay Peninsula to Indonesia, including, perhaps, the Philippines. It is doubtful that China could bring Australia into its sphere on these terms. A relatively more feasible PRC-preferred scenario would include (1) an alignment with Japan in which China would be the dominant partner; (2) control over Taiwan achieved through successful isolation of the island; (3) a buffer zone on the Korean Peninsula, where the coexistence of North and South Korea would serve to keep Soviet influence at bay; and (4) a Chinese Communist-dominated Indochina and Thailand. This would be a short-term PRC-preferred scenario. The extension of its influence down the Malay Peninsula to Indonesia, a Chinese dream before 1965, would be reserved for a slightly more distant future. This scenario differs from the American-preferred one in a number of respects, but the most important differences consist of the role of Japan, the fate of Taiwan, and the future of Indochina and Thailand. Since any Chinese attempt to create such a favorable situation for themselves will be met with Soviet countermoves, as experience in recent years has shown, Soviet and Chinese interaction is more likely to lead to a position favorable to the Soviet Union. To offset this tactical imbalance, Peking will have to try to divert Soviet interest elsewhere, e.g., the Middle East or Western Europe, or alternatively seek more American support. The October, 1973, war in the Middle East and its aftermath could provide such an opportunity. Seeking American support, however, could frustrate Peking's desires concerning Taiwan and Japan unless it is successful in bringing about the isolation and fall of Taiwan through divided counsels between Washington and Tokyo, supplemented by internal weakness in Taiwan. When all factors are taken into consideration, the chance of realization of the Chinese-preferred scenario is significantly smaller than that of the other two, because it would require both the United States and the Soviet Union to make serious mistakes at the same time.

U.S. POLICY AS AN ACTIVE INFLUENCE IN SHAPING THE STRATEGIC ENVIRONMENT IN THE WESTERN PACIFIC

The preceding discussion has pointed to the major risks facing U.S. policy in Pacific-Asia. Apart from precipitate withdrawals, the principal risks consist of the misperception of U.S. policy by other countries, especially Japan, and the absence of faith in U.S. avowals that it will fulfill its treaty commitments. Our analysis has tried to show how some of these misperceptions have come about and how the same failure to understand U.S. policy is shared by segments of American opinion itself, which adds to the confusion.

Not all the factors that will affect future developments in Pacific-Asia are susceptible to U.S. control. However, U.S. policy can still influence the perception and response of others, and U.S. policy, of course, is the primary determinant of American capability in the region. In this connection let us consider some important aspects of U.S. policy as determinants of the future strategic context in Pacific-Asia.

U.S. CREDIBILITY AND CONFIDENCE BUILDING

First, renewed confidence among U.S. allies and a display of U.S. resolve probably constitute the most urgently required stabilizers. In trying to influence the perceptions of both allies and potential adversaries, it is important to note that the amount of resolve and capability required to reassure an ally who thinks in terms of defense is essentially different from that required to deter a potential aggressor, especially if the latter is a conservative planner. An ally requires a greater display of resolve and capability than is needed to create uncertainty in the mind of the aggressor and deter him from actual attack. Similarly, one must not confuse capability to fight a war in aid of an ally with deterrent capability in the eyes of either an adversary or an ally. The more confident an ally is in his own capability and in the capability and resolve of the United States, the lower will be the required level of U.S. presence on the spot. The same applies to the perception of the adversary. All this implies that both the safe level of U.S. force reduction and the geographical aspect of deployment of a smaller force in Pacific-Asia are functions of confidence. When allied confidence is low, a greater presence and more forward defense will be required. The contrary is true when confidence is high or is building. If this reasoning is correct, what is needed is not to slow down the pace of reductions in order to avoid undermining confidence. When confidence is fully reestablished, force reductions required for budgetary or other reasons will be safe and feasible.

THE CONCEPT OF "TOTAL FORCE"

The concept of total force planning in collective defense, which involves using all available U.S. and allied resources to develop integrated foreign and defense policies, is compatible with American policy as outlined in President Nixon's Foreign Policy Reports. It could have the psychological effect of offering U.S. allies the needed reassurance of long-term U.S. interest in their welfare and security. *Integrated* total force planning between the United States and its allies would confirm that the United States is prepared to accept real interdependence in collective defense of the Western Pacific. The *psychological impact* in defense and foreign policy planning and its effect on U.S. credibility, allied confidence, and deterrence of potential adversaries, as well as the requisite level of American forward presence, must be fully appreciated and utilized.

ALLOCATION OF DEFENSE FUNCTIONS

One way to enhance allied confidence is to increase the defense capability of the country in question. Within a given budget, capability can be increased only through the more effective use of available resources. One approach to employing U.S. and allied resources in total force planning is to allocate to each member of the partnership those defense functions that it can perform with relatively higher efficiency. For instance, the United States may be entrusted with defense functions requiring more advanced technology, while an ally in Pacific-Asia is responsible for operations utilizing cheaper local resources. This approach could result in the employment of less U.S. manpower and more local manpower with resultant savings because of differences in manpower costs and relative productivity. It would not, however, call for a general substitution of Asian for U.S. manpower.

Such an allocation of defense functions between the United States and its allies would have to take into account special local conditions and resource availability. Again, there is no prima facie preference for any particular service or its components as the appropriate U.S. or allied contribution. It is conceivable for certain functions to be performed by a U.S. naval force in one case, while other functions may be performed by the U.S. Army in another case. The appropriate resource for a particular defense function may be of U.S. or allied origin and may be supplied from any one of the services depending upon the special conditions of the individual case. On the whole, though, relative accessibility of resources and related advantage make it probable that more allied manpower and less U.S. ground forces will be involved.

A RESOURCE POOL OR FUND

This approach to defense planning preferably should be carried out on a multilateral basis. However, existing bilateral arrangements between the United States and several countries in Pacific-Asia can provide a beginning. Wherever possible, there should be a move in the direction of multilateral planning in order to increase the amount of the total resources available and to make effective use of a larger pool of resources. A logical subordinate concept is to view total resources derived from the United States and other nations devoted to collective defense in Pacific-Asia as a resource "fund." The fund can be enlarged through contributions to it by different nations. These contributions can be in different forms. One can, for example, envision financial contributions by Japan which would not violate its present constitutional strictures. Such a fund would be a variant form of "burden-sharing" used in financing the infrastructure of NATO and other joint activities of the Atlantic Alliance. It would not be a great departure from accepted practice. A good specific example for such joint planning may be the institution of multinational patrol of the sea lanes in the Indian and Pacific Oceans, an idea at one time advanced by Prime Minister Lee Kuan Yew of Singapore.[1]

CHOICES IN FORWARD DEFENSE

As mentioned earlier, given a high level of allied confidence in U.S. capability and resolve and a similar expectation on the part of potential adversaries, one could deploy all U.S. forces at home and still exert the necessary deterrent effect in a forward area thousands of miles away. In reality, these conditions do not now exist. After several years of readjustment under the Nixon Doctrine, the forward areas outside Indochina particularly requiring psychological bolstering are Korea, Thailand, and Taiwan. Improvement in allied confidence in South Korea and Taiwan would have an indirect beneficial effect on Japan. The importance of maintaining a forward presence in Thailand needs little explanation if the settlement of the Vietnam War is not to end in the fall of South Vietnam under renewed Communist military pressure.

If we disregard South Vietnam, where the final settlement will more probably be influenced by U.S. domestic political considerations than by other security issues in Pacific-Asia, the United States is faced with several alternatives in the choice of forward defenses. First, it could choose to retain the present forward defense perimeter and maintain U.S. ground and air units in both Korea and Thailand. Second, it could choose to exclude either Korea or Thailand or both from this line. Third, it could add the Taiwan Strait to Korea and/or Thailand in the area excluded from the forward perimeter. Fourth, it could even exclude Japan over and above Korea, Thailand, and the Taiwan Strait. Alternative four amounts to the removal of all U.S. ground and air presence from the Western Pacific. The third alternative would be tantamount to the fourth, since its long-term effect on Japan will be the same. The choice between the first and second alternatives would be influenced by budgetary considerations and the attitude of Congress and by the ability of the United States to work out a cooperative arrangement with Japan and the two allies in question. U.S. budgetary considerations will, of course, reflect the current American scale of priorities. Putting aside this issue for the moment, a cooperative arrangement involving Japan, Korea, and Thailand would have to be predicated upon Japanese willingness to contribute to the defense of the two countries in question and to adopt a China policy in line with that of the United States. In regard to South Korea, a continued U.S. presence during the period of modernization of the Korean forces and an increase in Japanese assistance in order to develop a stronger Korean economy seem essential. The same is true in regard to Thailand. An example of the kind of major economic assistance project which might be examined is the construction of the Kra Canal, which has been often proposed. A new link between the Indian and Pacific Oceans with both Japanese and Thai interest and presence could introduce another barrier to the extension of Chinese as well as Soviet influence down the Malay Peninsula.

A JOINT U.S. RESERVE FORCE FOR PACIFIC-ASIA

Partial force reductions would become more feasible under the first alternative. They should, however, be preceded by the creation of a joint reserve with existing forces which would be stationed in Korea and Thailand and could help reverse the psychological impact. Rotation of reserve units carried out between the two countries would demonstrate the immediate availability within the region of larger forces than those stationed in either country alone. This flexibility in deployment would make it possible to cut back on the aggregate size of forces stationed in forward areas. It would also be important that any downward trend be interrupted by occasional upward shifts. This would be necessary to create the impression that the size of forces stationed in a particular country at any time is a technical matter of deployment rather than an indication of diminishing U.S. willingness to fulfill commitments.

THE BASING STRUCTURE

Depending upon the forward defense line chosen, the number and nature of old bases to be retained and of new bases to be created will depend on the allocation of defense functions between U.S. and allied forces and the provision for their support. Allowance should also be made for an expansion of forces in an emergency and the need for specific U.S. support functions. Some points to be considered are the function of the bases as a deterrent to a potential adversary, the need to minimize their vulnerability to light attack, and their location in areas away from concentrations of allied civilian population. Finally, the usefulness of each individual base should be considered as part of an integral structure in which the individual components support one another. (For instance, air bases in Korea, Japan, Taiwan, and the Philippines together constitute an integrated air defense system.) Following the close of the Vietnam War, a consolidation of bases will be called for. However, the preservation of minimal facilities in each allied country will be necessary in order to retain options for the future and to bolster confidence. Apparent redundancy may be necessary. Plans to use bases in Japan in a crisis might fail because access might, in fact, be denied following changes in Japanese policy and attitude. Consolidation of bases simply to avoid redundancy may have to be postponed until the right psychological moment. All matters considered, there is a distinct advantage in having island bases close to the shore lines of allied countries since they can be augmented by artificial "floating bases" when the need arises.

MILITARY ASSISTANCE

A method of increasing the capability of "total force" is to develop equipment adapted to local requirements. This frequently means equipment with not only a lower production cost but also lower maintenance and repair costs. Too often in the past, a disproportionate share of U.S. military assistance has been expended on maintenance and operating costs of U.S. equipment in allied hands. In FY 1970, for instance, 67.5 percent of the total obligational authority for military assistance went for noninvestment purposes, leaving only a third of the total for acquisition of new equipment. Under these conditions, an ostensibly large military assistance program may not be able to produce the rapid force buildup one would otherwise expect.[2] This is an area in which joint U.S. and allied efforts in R&D could lead to an increase in productivity and savings in both initial and current cost. Where the unit cost of new equipment is high, loss per unit during operations may become too heavy a burden on the country in question. The October, 1973, Middle East War and its impact on Israel offer a good example. Knowledge on the part of an adversary that such heavy losses could be easily incurred would lower the effectiveness of the deterrent posture.

U.S. military assistance can also be made more effective if multinational pooling can be developed in repair and maintenance, as well as in the use of common equipment. Common equipment supplied by the United States to more than one recipient can in many instances be repaired and maintained in facilities jointly used by more than one nation. While the primary purposes may be the avoidance of duplication and an increase in productivity, appropriate facilities of this kind could contribute to the development of multinational defense cooperation within the region. Prodding by the United States may be necessary in order to overcome the natural desire of each recipient nation to have its own facilities for all its equipment.

Above all, however, the effectiveness of military assistance is predicated upon sound long-term planning. If military assistance continues to be used as a weapon in domestic party politics in the United States, neither funding nor the delivery schedule can be relied upon. Long-term planning must then give way to short-term makeshifts, by far the least satisfactory and economical way to make effective use of limited defense resources. The net result is often exasperation which seems designed to create a negative psychological impact on both recipient and donor.

REDUCING THE LOCAL DEFENSE BURDEN

A word should be said on ways in which an augmented defense burden in the Pacific-Asian countries might be minimized. One method is to combine the military duties of local forces with part-time or full-time civilian work. A second is the creation of large trained reserves, which are required to take refresher courses periodically and are subject to immediate call-up in a crisis. Still another is to use the period of military service to train members of the armed forces in technical skills which will increase their productivity when they return to civilian life. Lastly, special units of armed forces may be used in civic action projects, such as the employment of the engineer corps in road construction, port development, etc. None of these ideas is new, but they deserve more careful consideration and wider adoption.[3] Incidentally, almost all these methods have been common practice in the Chinese Communist armed forces and have resulted in a considerable saving of PRC's defense burden.

THE ROLE OF TACTICAL NUCLEAR AND OTHER SOPHISTICATED WEAPONS

Finally, the United States must consider the hypothetical situation in which a reduced American conventional presence will be unable to provide adequate aid to an area faced with conventional aggression. For many years, NATO has grappled with the problem of determining the threshold of nuclear escalation. The same problem must now be faced in Asia. If the continuous development of nuclear weapons by Peking is not interrupted by either internal political dissension or by Soviet intervention, a point will eventually be reached when the Chinese nuclear force is large enough to provide a shield for conventional aggression. If a U.S. ally cannot resist this aggression by conventional means, even with American aid, would the United States be prepared to use more powerful weapons, including tactical nuclear weapons? What would be the principles governing such use? How would such a decision be made? Some U.S. allies, including Japan, are distrustful of U.S. readiness to provide nuclear support if they are faced with defeat in a conventional aggression. If they can, they will, therefore, try to develop their own nuclear weapons. If they cannot be dissuaded from this course of development, what would be the proper U.S. policy?

For the Soviet Union an appropriate policy in such a situation may be an attempt to stop this development by direct intervention, although failure to follow this same policy a decade ago in the case of Communist China has reduced the credibility of future Soviet threats against a would-be nuclear aspirant, such as Japan. The ABM treaty of 1972 prohibits the transfer of ABM equipment to other nations, and the non-proliferation treaty has a similar provision for nuclear weapons and means for their manufacture. Neither treaty offers guidance on what the United States should do as a matter of policy if an ally should decide that its national interest demands the development of its own nuclear force. Would it not be better to move toward a multinational defense arrangement before these difficult issues have to be resolved or before other nations feel compelled to adopt their own policies, which might prove to be detrimental to the American-preferred scenario? Furthermore, should not other sophisticated non-nuclear weapons for defense be developed and made available to allies? Above all, if such non-nuclear options do exist, knowledge about their availability must be shared with allies.

PRUDENCE AND IMAGINATION IN PLANNING

The above discussion has focused on ways in which U.S. defense policy might be used to influence events in Pacific-Asia so as to increase the probability of favorable developments. Of course, not all these policies will be adopted; if they were, they would not necessarily work out in a fully satisfactory manner. In addition, there are uncontrollable events, including technological surprises. Even the best plan may go wrong. The prudent policy-maker cannot, therefore, afford to ignore the possibility that his own assumptions about circumstances favorable to his plans may not be realized. In order to minimize untoward consequences, he must preserve viable alternatives.

On the other hand, the imaginative policy-maker cannot afford not to take certain risks. In addition, he should be prepared to recognize favorable opportunities he had no reason to expect in his original planning and seize upon them when they occur. Ability to respond to unexpected events is essential to the process of policy formulation.

Thus, *alternative plans must be available both to meet contingencies,* i.e., when the assumptions of one's initial plans are not realized in an adverse manner, *and to exploit opportunities,* i.e., when one's initial assumptions are changed favorably. In order to preserve such flexibility in Pacific-Asia, there are several basic requirements. One is to provide for the possibility of a rapprochement between Moscow and Peking and the "normalization" of Sino-Soviet relations. Those who might dismiss this possibility should ask themselves if they foresaw in the early 1950s the intensity reached by Sino-Soviet quarrels in the 1960s. If not, their assumption that this falling out, complete as it may seem, cannot be patched up in the 1970s is open to doubt. Another possibility to be prepared for is a shift in Chinese leadership and a dramatic about-turn of Chinese policy, although several different kinds of shifts are possible. Still another necessary condition for preserving several options is that Japan will find it always in its interest to maintain economic and military cooperation with the United States. This will require making the security of the sea lanes and the assured supply of imports to Japan a function of the goodwill of the United States and its allies. Lastly, it is important not to miss any opportunity which might lead to closer regional cooperation.

One cannot go beyond generalizations in this volume, but the principles are clear. They are to engage in both contingency and opportunity planning, to increase available options, and not to throw away alternatives gratuitously. One must be prepared for situations where one's assumptions are wrong.

We cannot assume that other nations will always see U.S. policy as we would like it to be seen. Our adversaries may not understand the "rules of the game" and exercise suitable restraint. Our faithful ally may not always remain faithful because U.S. policy has been misunderstood. Yet, even as we make mistakes, so will our adversaries. In the real world, we must not only plan under uncertainty, but we must also allow for imperfect planning by ourselves and all other policy-makers. In order to achieve the necessary degree of flexibility in policy-making in a democracy, our own policy makers must above all convince their fellow citizens (1) that the risks inherent in their policies are justified by the potential rewards of success and (2) that there is a need for preserving and enlarging policy options without which risk-taking must be strictly limited in view of the severe penalties of failure.

THE DANGER OF UNRESTRAINED NATIONALISM

In conclusion, it should be noted that a policy based on national self-interest alone may eventually be self-defeating. A country can safeguard its national interest in a narrow sense as long as other nations believe it is in their interest to adopt compatible policies. Such judgments, however, normally hinge on relative strength. If the first nation has unchallengeable power and is prepared to pay the cost of remaining in that position, its policies are unlikely to be challenged. If that nation is no longer willing to pay this cost, its policies will not remain unchallenged. However, even if that nation is prepared to pay the cost, it may prove unable to retain a position of superiority because of the emergence of other competing centers of power and new technologies. Once its unchallenged superiority has disappeared, that nation cannot assume that other nations will always adopt policies compatible with its own. Once we abandon the assumption of other nations' compatible policies, the outcome of a policy based entirely on national interest can no longer be certain.

In Pacific-Asia, the ultimate outcome of U.S. policy is faced with other nations' policies that may be incompatible on two grounds. One is economic nationalism, which could lead to a conflict of national interests. Another is the natural instinct of survival that may prompt other nations to seek accommodation with powers potentially hostile to the United States. Thus, while nationalism is useful as an ally when it is directed against a common enemy, it may become a potentially destabilizing force no less threatening and destructive than one's original adversaries. Encouragement of nationalism as a means of increasing security for the smaller nations needs to be balanced by a simultaneous effort to create a sense of community among all the free nations of Pacific-Asia and of the world. This is an effort which must be made and one in which the United States must join and lead.

NOTES
1. Prime Minister Lee's proposal, made in Tokyo in 1973, could well become a catalyst in the formation of a future Pacific-Indian Ocean Defense Agreement, a concept previously advanced by Frank N. Trager. See Trager, "What is Security in Southeast Asia," *Air University Review*, Maxwell Air Force Base, Alabama, 20 (November-December 1968).
2. See comment by General Robert Warren, *Foreign Assistance and Related Agencies Appropriations for 1970*, Hearings before a Subcommittee of the House Committee on Appropriations, 91st Congress, First Session, (1969), p. 700.
3. These suggestions have been advanced for Vietnam in the postwar period. See Hla Myint, *Southeast Asia's Economy in the 1970's, Overall Report*, Manila: The Asian Development Bank, November 1970, pp. 96—97.

Index

Alignment
  Indonesian, attitudes toward, 159–160
  patterns of, 130–133
    comparisons of, 138
  See also Realignment
Alliance, patterns of, 139
Americans, attitude toward national defense policy, 2
Anti-ballistic missiles, deployment of, by United States and Soviet Union, 6
Anti-Ballistic Missile Treaty, implications of, 27
ANZUK, 156
ANZUS treaty, 138, 162
ASEAN, 150, 159, 160
Atlantic Alliance, 198
  Nixon Doctrine and, perception of, 163
  security of
    Japan and, 162
    threat to, by Soviet Union, 161, 162
  views on, 161

Balance of power
  between Communist China and Soviet Union, 57, 58
  conditions and assumptions for, 50–51, 58–59
  Nixon Doctrine and, 12
  in Pacific-Asia
    risks in, 194–195
    scenario for
      American preferred, 191–193
      Communist China preferred, 195–196
      Soviet Union preferred, 193–195
  Sino-Soviet dispute and, 48–50, 51

Bangladesh, agreement with Soviet Union, 176–177
Brezhnev Doctrine, Communist China and, 172–173
Budget, federal, outlay of, by function, 37t

China, *See* Peking; People's Republic of China; Republic of China
Chinese, in Pacific-Asian countries
 ethnic group of, 138
 distribution of, 165t–166t
Chou En-lai, 60, 66, 100–101
 meeting with Kissinger, 62
 See also Nixon–Chou Joint Communiqué
Collective defense
 attitudes toward, 163–164
 Indonesian, 159
 plans for
  Soviet Union, 178–180
  United States, 197
Communist countries, "international duties" of, 172
Credibility, United States, building of, 197

Defense
 basing structure in, United States role in, 200
 burden of, reduction in, 201–202
 forward defense, choices in, 199–200
 functions, allocation of, 198
 Japanese, budget for, 45
 military assistance, United States role in, 201
 of Pacific-Asian countries
  alternatives in, 142–144
  expenditures in, 139t, 140
  United States action in, 90–91
 planning
  resource pool, 198–199
  by United States, 12–14, 203–204
 policy, United States, 89
  adjustment of, events related to, 3–4, 5, 6
  attitudes toward, 2
  perceptions of
   by Japanese, 108–109, 111–112
   by Pacific-Asian countries, 164–165
 reserve forces in, 200
 United States
  budget of, decline in, during Nixon Administration, 36–37, 38, 40–41
  outlay for, 38t, 39t
 See also Collective defense; International defense; specific country

Economic growth, comparison of, 139t
Economic policy, United States, announcement of, 96
Energy crisis, effects of, on Japan, 101–104
European Defense Improvement Program, 33
Exports, from Pacific-Asia
 to Soviet Union and Eastern Europe, 181t
 statistics on, 184t–186t

Five Power Defense Arrangements, 156
Ford Administration, 15
Foreign aid, decrease in, during Nixon Administration, factors in, 41–43
Foreign policy, United States, 89
 adjustment of
  indications of, 4–5
  Nixon Doctrine and
   elements in, 7–9
   emphasis in, 9–11

China-Washington, 57
clarification of, events related to, 11–12
process of, adjustments in, 2–3
shift in, events related to, 3
Fukuda, Takeo, 99

Ho Chi Minh, 74

Imports, to Pacific-Asia, from Soviet Union and Eastern Europe, 181t
  statistics on, 187t–189t
Indian Ocean, Soviet navy in, 174–176
India-Pakistan War, 90, 160, 161
  Soviet Union role in, 176–177
  United States response to, 5
Indonesia
  army of, 159
  collective defense, attitude toward, 159
  economic aid to, by communist countries, 160
  economic status of, 158–159
  Nixon Doctrine and, perceptions of, 158
  nonalignment and, attitudes toward, 161
Interim Agreement of Offensive Missiles, provisions of, 174
International defense, Japanese role in, 45–46
  effect of United States on, 46–48

Japan
  arms buildup of, scenario for
    Soviet Union, 193–194
    United States, 191–192
  collective defense and, attitudes toward, 164
  -Communist China relations, normalization of, 100–101
  defense of
    alternatives in, 105–106
    modification of, 106
    buildup in, 105–112
    role of South Korea in, 104–105
    threats to, 92
    by United States
      agreement of, Japanese perception of, 108–109, 111–112
      counter-balance strategy in, 107–108
      Nixon Doctrine and, response to, 93–96
  economic relations of, with Australia and New Zealand, 162
  effect of energy crisis on, 101–104
  emerging power of, 44–48
  imports to, dependence in, 97–98
  militarism of
    data on, 122t
    fear of, 142
  nuclear weapons and, development of
    attitudes toward, 107, 110–111, 127t
    capacity in, 109–110
    Soviet Union restraint of, 178
  Peking policy toward, 78–79
  role in balance of power, 51
  -Soviet Union meetings, agreements from, 177–178
  Taiwan and
    issue of, perception of, 96–100
    relations with, 99
  United States and
    forces in, decline in, 3
    policy of, perception of, 96

Kao Kang, 66
Kissinger, Henry A.
  meetings with Chou En-lai, 62
  visit to Peking, 5
Korea
  Peking policy toward, 80

Korea (*Continued*)
  response to Nixon Doctrine, 92
  United States forces in, reduction in, 3
  See also North Korea; South Korea

Laird, Melvin R., defense planning and, 12, 13–14
Lin Piao, 67

Malaysia
  alliance with United States, factors in, 142
  insurgent groups in, 154
  neutralization in Southeast Asia, interpretation of, 152
  recognition of Peking, 154
  threats to, by Communist China, 152, 154
Mao Tse-tung, 74
Marshall Plan, philosophy of, 146
Military
  of non-communist countries, strength of, comparison of, 140t–141t
  of United States, transfers to Pacific-Asia, 153t

Nationalism, unrestrained, danger of, 204–205
Neutralization, of Southeast Asia
  Malaysian interpretation of, 152
  plans in, 156
  Thai response to, 150–151
New Zealand, security of
  Japan and, 162
  threats to, Soviet Union and, 165
Nixon Administration, 60
  effects of, on United States posture in Pacific Asia, 3–7
Nixon-Chou Joint Communiqué, 61, 62, 74

United States declarations in, 5
Nixon Doctrine
  analysis of, basic questions in, 19–20
  application of, 3
  assessment of, 14–16
  characteristics of, 2
  evolution of, 9–11
  implementation of, 89
  inception of, 7–9
  influence of, on Japanese defense buildup, 105–112
  Japan and
    response to normalization of relations with Communist China, 100–101
    Taiwan and, 96–100
    security of, 93–96
  limitations of, 1
  negotiations under, with Peking and Moscow, 11–12
  perception of, by South Korea, 112–114
  response to, by Northeast Asian countries, 91–92
  See also Policy, United States
Nixon, Richard M., 1, 3, 60
  visit to Peking, 4, 5, 61, 63, 162
    announcement of, events following, 66–69
  response to
    by Japan, 96
    by Soviet Union, 176
    by Thailand, 150
  results of, 5, 12
Nixon-Sato Joint Communiqué, 91
Non-communist countries, military strength of, comparisons of, 140t–141t
North Korea
  defense of, statistics on, 127t–128t
  -Peking relations, 74, 76
North Vietnam

-Peking relations, 74, 75, 76
United States bombing of, 4
Nuclear Non-proliferation Treaty, 161
Nuclear weapons
  in Communist China, 64–65
  development of, 202
  Japanese attitude toward, 107, 127t
  regarding capability in, 109–110

Okinawa, reversion to Japan, 3, 47, 107

Pacific-Asia, American policy in, interpretation of, 149–162
Pacific-Asian countries
  comparisons of
    economic growth and expenditures, 139t, 140
    regarding peace and war, 135–136
    defense of, alternatives in, 142–144
    economic ties with Soviet Union, increase in, 181, 182
    military transfers to, by United States, 153t
  Nixon Doctrine and
    perception of, 163
    concerns in, 163
    response to, comparisons in, regarding peace and war
      alliance and alignment patterns, 138
      Chinese ethnic factors, 138
      geographical influences, 136–137
      mutual distrust, 137
    overseas Chinese in, distribution of, 165t–166t
  See also specific country
Pakistan. See India-Pakistan War
Peking
  admission to United Nations, 5, 96
  -Moscow negotiations, 11–12
  placation of socialist neighbors, methods in, 73–78
  policy of
    toward Japan, 78–79
    toward Korea, 80
    toward Taiwan, 79
    toward United States
      Doctrine of Revolutionary Diplomacy, 69–72
      rapprochement with, 57–63, 70, 71–72
  United States and
    negotiations, style of, 80–84
    threat to, 72–73
  See also People's Republic of China; Republic of China
Peng Teh-huai, 66
People's Republic of China (PRC)
  Brezhnev Doctrine and, 172–173
  change in Politburo membership, 68
  internal disunity in, 68–69
  events related to, 66–68
  -Japanese relations, normalization of, 100–101
  military strength of, 123t–124t
  negotiations with United States, 57
    methods in, 57–58
  nuclear weapon program of, 64–65, 66
  recognition of, by Malaysia, 154
  -Soviet Union
    balance of power between, 57, 58
    effect of dispute on, 4, 48–50, 51
    negotiations, 90
    relations, United States view on, 193
    strategic arms agreement and, implications in, 173–174
    threat of, 143
  -United States policy, Soviet view of, 176–179
  See also Peking; Republic of China
Philippines, 163

Philippines (*Continued*)
American policy and, response to, issues in, 157, 158
-communist country relations, 158
insurgency problem in, 157–158
Policy, United States
influence on strategic environment, 196–205
Nixon Doctrine and, execution of, 2–3
perception of, 90
Japanese, 96
response to, by Northeast Asian countries, 91–92
See also Defense; Economic policy; Foreign policy

Realignment, dynamics of, 89–91
Republic of China (ROC)
-Japan relations, 99
military strength of, 123t–124t
new cabinet of, 122
options of, 120–121
factors in, 122
negotiation with Communist China, 121
recognition of Taipei, attitudes toward, 121
response to Nixon Doctrine, 92
security of, 93
stability of, attainment of, United States view on, 192
threat to, perception of, 118–119
political, 119–120
withdrawal from United Nations, 5
Republic of Korea. *See* South Korea
Rogers, William P., 5, 99, 145

Sato, Eisaku, 3, 47, 91, 96, 99
Schlesinger, Arthur, 31, 32
SEATO treaty, 138

Singapore
American policy and, conception of shifts in, 155–156
situations in, 154–155
communist insurgence in, 155
neutralization, 156
security of, plans in, 156
Southeast Asia. *See* Pacific-Asia
South Korea
arms buildup of, United States view for, 192
defense of, statistics on, 127t–128t
military assistance to, by United States, 128t
modernization of forces, options in, 114
contacts with non-hostile nations, 114–117
negotiations with North Korea, 114–116
regional defense cooperation, 117–118
Nixon Doctrine and, perception of, 112–114
role in Japanese security, 104–105
security of, 93
South Vietnam. *See* Vietnam
Soviet Union
agreement with Bangladesh, 176–177
-Communist China
balance of power between, 57, 58
Brezhnev Doctrine and, 172–173
negotiations, 90
under Nixon Doctrine, 11–12
economic aid to Indonesia, 160
forces of
conventional
vs. NATO, 28–34
restraint of, sources for, 44
on Sino-Soviet border, buildup of, 63–64
goals of, 182–183

-Japan meetings, agreements from, 177–178
naval force of, 161–162
  expansion of, 34–36
  in Indian and Pacific Oceans, 174–176
Pacific-Asia and
  economic ties with, increase in, 180, 182
  potential role in, 171–172
  plan for collective Asian security, 178–180
role in India-Pakistan War, 176–177
strategic power of, vs. United States, 20–29
threat of, 143
  on China border, 61–62
  factors in, 66
  Peking response to, 62, 63
  to Pacific-Asian countries, geographical influences on, 136–137
Strategic arms
  balance of
    between United States and Soviet Union, 22t–23t
    contrasts in, 26–27
    levels of damage in, 24
    quality assessment in, 27–28
    shift in, 20
    factors in, 25–26, 27
    parity in, 20, 24
    potential situations from, 28–29
    statistics on, 22t–23t
  limitations of, by United States and Soviet Union, negotiations on, 6
  agreements in, 6–7
Strategic Arms Limitations Talks (SALT), 24, 25, 111
  aspects of, 20
  continuation of, 106
  effect of, 174
  implications of, for Communist China, 173–174
  policing of, costs in, 29

Taiwan
  issue of, Japanese perception of, 97–100
  Peking policy toward, 79
Tanaka, Kakuel
  visit to Moscow, 105
  visit to Peking, 100
Thailand, 163
  defense forces of
    expansion of, 151–152
    United States grants for, 152
  institution of martial law in, 150
  Nixon Doctrine and, perception of, 149–150

Union of Soviet Socialist Republics. *See* Soviet Union
"United Front" policy, 69
United Nations, admission of Peking, 96
United States
  -China policy, Soviet Union view of, 176–179
  dollar, devaluation of, results of, 6, 33

Vietnam
  disengagement from, 3
  United States and
    policy in, interpretation of, 144–146
    withdrawal from, 14
  See also North Vietnam
Vietnamization, 163
  interpretation of, by United States, 145
  long-term, economic factors in, 146–149

Vietnamization (*Continued*)
  significance of, 144
  success of, variables in, 144–145
Vietnam War, 46
  impact of, 43–44
  United States defense posture during, 1–2
Warsaw Pact, conventional forces of, vs. NATO, 31t–32t
Weapons, non-nuclear vs. nuclear, 202–203
  See also Nuclear weapons

1311